EMERGENT U.S. LITERATURE

MW00353172

Emergent U.S. Literatures

From Multiculturalism to Cosmopolitanism in the Late Twentieth Century

Cyrus R. K. Patell

NEW YORK UNIVERSITY PRESS
New York and London

NEW YORK UNIVERSITY PRESS
New York and London
www.nyupress.org

References to Internet websites (URLs) were accurate at the time of writing.
Neither the author nor New York University Press is responsible for URLs that
may have expired or changed since the manuscript was prepared.

LIBRARY OF CONGRESS CATALOGING-IN-PUBLICATION DATA
Patell, Cyrus R. K.
Emergent U.S. literatures : from multiculturalism to cosmopolitanism in the late twentieth
century / Cyrus Patell.
pages cm
Includes bibliographical references and index.
ISBN 978-1-4798-9372-0 (hardback) -- ISBN 978-1-4798-7338-8 (pb)
1. American literature--Minority authors--History and criticism. 2. American literature--
20th century--History and criticism. 3. Multiculturalism in literature. 4. Cosmopolitanism
in literature. I. Title.
PS153.M56P38 2014
810.9'920693--dc23
2014020830

New York University Press books

Manufactured in the United States of America

10 9 8 7 6 5 4 3 2 1

Also available as an ebook

CONTENTS

ACKNOWLEDGMENTS

This book has its origins in my contribution to the *Cambridge History of American Literature, Volume Eight: Prose, 1940–1990*, which was edited by Sacvan Bercovitch and published in 1999. I am grateful to Saki for his years of mentoring and friendship, and particularly for inviting me to participate in the *Cambridge History* project, first as the Associate Editor for volumes one and two, then as a contributor to volume seven. For that, and for countless other moments of scholarly inspiration, I will always be in his debt.

My interest in the dynamics of emergent literatures began to take shape during my tenure as President's Postdoctoral Fellow at the University of California at Berkeley from 1991 to 1993. I am grateful both to the UC President's Office and to the Department of English at Berkeley for providing me with the resources necessary to begin the research published here. I am also grateful for grants from New York University's Research Challenge Fund and the Stein Fund of the NYU English Department.

I am deeply grateful to Eric Zinner, my editor at New York University Press, for believing that my account of late twentieth-century emergent U.S. literatures could emerge from the cocoon of the *Cambridge History* transformed into something that could take flight on its own and for sticking with the project through three rounds of revision. I also owe a debt of gratitude to Amritjit Singh and three additional, anonymous readers who critiqued the manuscript for NYU Press at different stages. The suggestions made by Eric and the readers enabled me to improve the book and sharpen its argument in ways that I could not have foreseen.

I owe thanks to three research assistants, Amanda Rowell, Lindsay Reckson, and Allison Green, who spent time helping me to refine different aspects of the project. Over the years, colleagues and friends generously took time out to read portions of the manuscript and offered suggestions that have proved to be invaluable. I want to cite, particularly, Nancy Bentley, Kyung-Sook Boo, Andrew Brown, T. Susan Chang, Una Chaudhuri, Elizabeth Fowler, Julie Greenblatt, Josephine Hendin, Suzanne Keen, Ellyn Lem, Shireen Patell, Ray Ryan, Anne Sanow, Karen Skinazi, Werner Sollors, and Blakey Vermeule.

Two of my colleagues in the NYU English Department have been particularly inspirational—Philip Brian Harper and Bryan Waterman—and I thank them for the collegiality, brilliant ideas, and good cheer that they have shared with me over the years.

At NYU Abu Dhabi, my colleagues and students have helped me to understand cosmopolitanism—and its crucial importance for the future of our global civilization—in ways that I could not have imagined when New York was the primary point of reference for my professional life. I am particularly grateful for the friendship of Shamoon Zamir, who has helped me to rekindle my love of classic literature of all kinds.

I am fortunate to have had inspirational teachers at every stage of my life. I thank Mary Evelyn Bruce, Thomas Squire, Jane Mallison, Gregory Lombardo, Gilbert Smith, Donald Hull, John V. Kelleher, Warner Berthoff, Saki Bercovitch, Leo Marx, Werner Sollors, and Philip Fisher for schooling me in the joys of learning and scholarship.

Special thanks are due to my friends Rosa Choi and Wasel Safwan Choi, who exemplify the kind of boundary-crossing I describe in my first chapter. I'm glad to have a painting by Wasel on the front cover of the book.

Completing this project would not have been possible without the love and guidance of my wife and colleague, Deborah Lindsay Williams, my *sine qua non*. She has read drafts of this manuscript more times than either of us can count. Without her belief in its importance, I surely would not have had the fortitude to put it through all those rounds of revision.

I dedicated my contribution to the *Cambridge History of American Literature* to my late grandmother Francisca D. Raña, who emigrated to the United States from the Philippines in 1971 and who became an American citizen twenty-five years later at the age of ninety-two. She lived for just over a century, and I was privileged to be able to celebrate her hundredth birthday with her.

I dedicate the present book to my parents and to my children. My late mother, Estrella Patell, and my father, Rusi Patell, instilled in me the importance of education at an early age and sacrificed much to provide me with the best education imaginable. I can think of no greater legacy to pass on to my sons, Liam and Caleb, than the love of learning that was my parents' enduring gift to me.

Introduction

Theorizing the Emergent

When I was growing up, strangers would ask me, "Where are you from?" and I'd say, "New York" or "the Upper West Side." They'd look vaguely disappointed: "No, I meant what's your background." I wasn't really being disingenuous, though I was well aware what the first question really meant. It's just that I never particularly identified with either of my parents' cultural traditions. My father is a Parsee, born in Karachi, when Karachi was a part of India, and my late mother was a Filipino. They had met at the International House at Columbia University, my father coming from Pakistan to study mathematical statistics, my mother from the Philippines to study literature and drama. We spoke English at home, and my parents had gradually lost their fluency in their mother tongues (Gujarati and Tagalog, respectively). What I identified with was being *mixed* and being able to slip from one cultural context to another. To my Parsee relatives, I looked Filipino; to my Filipino relatives, I looked "bumbai"; and to my classmates—well, on the rare occasions when someone wanted to launch a racial slur, the result was usually a lame attempt to insult me as if I were Puerto Rican.

We weren't particularly religious at home, though we did celebrate Christmas and made it a point to attend the Christmas Eve services at Riverside Church in New York, a few blocks up the street from where we lived. My mother sometimes liked to attend Easter services there as well. It was always assumed that I would become a Zoroastrian like my father. As my mother explained it, that way I could keep my options open. I could convert to Christianity but not to Zoroastrianism later, because Zoroastrianism didn't accept converts. But, when the time came during third grade for my *navjote* ceremony to be performed, we couldn't find a priest. We kept hearing excuses along the lines of, "I would do it, but my mother-in-law is very old-fashioned." The problem was that my mother was a Christian—oddly enough a Protestant, unlike most Filipinos, because my grandmother had converted to a Pentecostal sect before my mother's birth. Eventually, we managed to secure the services of a priest from Mumbai who was traveling in the United States and spending some time in New York. Four years later, we had to go to London to have my sister's ceremony done.

It was an early lesson in the dynamics of culture, though it would take me years to recognize it: my parents' marriage was an emblem of cosmopolitan cultural mixing, while the priests' belief in the importance of cultural purity served as an emblem of all the forces that are arrayed against cosmopolitanism. I suppose, therefore, that it's somewhat predictable that in recent years I have chosen to work on what I call "emergent literatures"—literatures that express marginalized cultural identities—and found myself increasingly interested in theories of cosmopolitanism.

*   *   *

This book was almost called *U. S. Multicultural Literatures*, a title that one of the press reviewers suggested in lieu of the one I had proposed. The people in charge of marketing at NYU Press apparently concurred, because they wanted the book to be a candidate for classroom adoption, and they did not believe that enough teachers and students around the country would recognize the term *emergent*. "Multiculturalism," however, is a term that would be familiar to our target audience. The problem with the title *U. S. Multicultural Literatures*, however, is twofold. For one thing, the book does not include accounts of African American literature or women's literature, two mainstays of current multicultural curricula. Instead, the book presents a comparative overview of the histories of the literatures produced by Asian Americans, gay and lesbian Americans, Hispanic Americans, and Native Americans during the second half of the twentieth century and the beginning of the twenty-first.[1] These are literatures that were generally included in late-twentieth-century conceptions of multiculturalism, but had less standing than either African American or U.S. women's literatures. They were, if you will, the minority literatures within "U.S. minority literature."[2] Suggestive rather than exhaustive, this book presents ways of mapping the overlapping concerns of the foundational texts and authors of these literatures during the late twentieth century, by which I mean the period that spans roughly 1968 to 2001.[3] My goal is to give readers a sense of how these foundational texts work as aesthetic objects (rather than merely as sociological documents) crafted in dialogue with the canonical tradition of so-called "American Literature," as it existed in the late twentieth century, as well as in dialogue with each other. Occasionally, I will dwell on particular texts that strike me as signal achievements, in order to convey a sense of their distinctive flavor. The book will, I hope, serve as a resource for readers and teachers who wish to put together reading lists that explore traditions of U.S. literature with which they are not yet familiar.

A second way in which the title *U. S. Multicultural Literatures* would have been misleading is that it would have suggested that I support the idea of "multicultural literatures" as a conceptual category. In fact, what I will present is a critique of "multicultural literatures" as they are commonly understood today. What I will argue is that the literatures I discuss are more powerfully and completely understood if they are seen as "emergent literatures" rather than "multicultural literatures."

A *literature*, in the sense that I am using it here, is an institution of culture. It is a form of expression produced by some group that has cohered (or that can be seen to cohere) around a cultural identity based on nation, race, ethnicity, class, religion, gender, sexuality, or any of a number of other categories.. A group of writings becomes a literature when those who produce it (the writers) or those who consume it (a group that includes readers, critics, teachers, and publishers) regard it as such. Thus, for example, Asian American writers in the early twentieth century were considered exotic anomalies and "Asian American Literature" as a category did not exist until the early 1970s.

An *emergent literature* is a literature that exists within a certain relation to established literary forms. My conception of the *emergent* is founded on Raymond Williams's analysis of the dynamics of modern culture—an analysis that served, I believe, as the implicit foundation for minority discourse theory in the 1990s.[4] Williams characterizes culture as a constant struggle for dominance in which a hegemonic mainstream seeks to defuse the challenges posed to it by both *residual* and *emergent* cultural forms. According to Williams, residual culture consists of those practices that are based on the "residue of . . . some previous social and cultural institution or formation," but continue to play a role in the present, while emergent culture serves as the site or set of sites where "new meanings and values, new practices, new relationships and kinds of relationships are continually being created." Both residual and emergent cultural forms can only be recognized and indeed conceived in relation to the dominant: each represents a form of negotiation between the margin and the center over the right to control meanings, values, and practices.[5]

When I discuss Williams's model of culture with students, I always stress that this description does not mean that residual cultures should be considered "unimportant" or "minor." On the contrary, they are major parts of any cultural formation. One example that I frequently offer to students comes from Ralph Waldo Emerson's journal of 1840:

> In all my lectures, I have taught one doctrine, namely, the infinitude of the private man. This, the people accept readily enough, & even with loud commendation, as long as I call the lecture, Art; or Politics; or Literature; or the Household; but the moment I call it Religion—they are shocked, though it be only the application of the same truth which they receive everywhere else, to a new class of facts.[6]

Emerson is living in post-Enlightenment, post-Jacksonian market society, when the influence of the old republican biblical culture presumably has fallen away. Promulgating his doctrine of "the infinitude of the private man" in his lectures on various subjects, he finds resistance only when he begins to talk about religion. It may no longer be at the center of the dominant ideological consensus, but the old-time religion is still powerful: Emerson has to take it into account, as he tries to push the envelope of cultural forms. Residual culture is still powerful culture.

Emergent cultures are powerful, too, but on the other end of the spectrum. Either way, as Williams observes, "since we are always considering relations within a cultural process, definitions of the emergent, as of the residual, can be made only in relation to a full sense of the dominant."[7] In other words, it makes no sense to think of the emergent apart from the dominant: the very definition, or self-definition, of the emergent depends on the existence of a dominant culture. The idea of the *emergent* thus offers a way of conceptualizing the projects of the literatures produced by Asian Americans, gay and lesbian Americans, Hispanic Americans, and Native Americans after 1968. Inspired by a dominant "American" literary tradition that seems to exclude them and their writings, these writers find themselves with one foot inside and one foot outside of the U.S. literary mainstream.

An *emergent literature* is therefore the literary expression of a cultural group that defines itself either as an alternative to or in direct opposition to a dominant mainstream. What makes the literature emergent is the fact that it portrays beliefs and practices that are taken to be "new" by the dominant culture, though in some cases they may in fact be thousands of years old. At the same time, it is crucial to emphasize that an emergent literature is the expression of a *cultural identity*: avant-garde literatures are also literatures that identify themselves with the "new," but an avant-garde literature that is not the expression of a cultural identity, that orients itself, for example, around a set of formal practices or a philosophical stance, is not what I am describing as an "emergent literature." Indeed, as we will see, at various moments in their histories, many U.S. emergent literatures have adopted formally conservative modes of expression.

The strategies that emergent writers adopt depend on the kind of relationship that they wish their writing to have with regard to what the reader-response theorist Hans Robert Jauss calls the "horizon of expectations." This horizon is created both by social practice—what Jauss describes as "the milieu, views and ideology of [the] audience"—and by literary tradition. Jauss argues that

> A literary work, even when it appears to be new, does not present itself as something absolutely new in an informational vacuum, but predisposes its audience to a very specific kind of reception by announcements,

> overt and covert signals, familiar characteristics, or implicit allusions.
> It awakens memories of that which was already read, brings the reader
> to a specific emotional attitude, and with its beginning arouses expecta-
> tions for the "middle and end," which can then be maintained intact or
> altered, reoriented, or even fulfilled ironically in the course of the read-
> ing according to specific rules of the genre or type of text. . . . The new
> text evokes for the reader (listener) the horizon of expectations and rules
> familiar from earlier texts, which are then varied, corrected, altered, or
> even just reproduced.[8]

This model suggests that the meaning of a literary text is a function not
only of its author's intention in writing it but also of the milieu into
which it is received, which includes its reader's social, cultural, historical, aesthetic, and personal contexts. Meaning, in other words, is a
negotiation between writer and reader through the medium of the text.

When Herman Melville's novel *Moby-Dick* was published in 1851,
readers couldn't really make heads or tails of it. It wasn't what they
expected a novel to be. In fact, at the turn of the century, it was classified in many prominent libraries as a treatise on cetology.[9] *Moby-
Dick* challenged the familiar rules, but American readers were not
yet equipped to understand or appreciate that challenge. Simplifying
greatly, we might say that despite the radicalism of *Moby-Dick*, the horizon of expectations of its potential audience remained unchanged.

On the other hand, the disparity between the horizon of expectations
and the new work that questions it can result in a "change of horizons,"
according to Jauss, by "[negating] familiar experiences or by raising
newly articulated experiences to the level of consciousness."[10] In the case
of *Moby-Dick*, this change of horizons came about in the mid-twentieth
century, when a group of scholars led by F. O. Mathiessen proclaimed
the existence of a mid-nineteenth century tradition called the American Renaissance and set *Moby-Dick* at its center.[11] Critics and readers
were ready to appreciate the white whale: it was literary real estate just
waiting to be developed. Now many people think of *Moby-Dick* as the
Great American Novel. It has become a "classic," which Mark Twain
once described as "a book which people praise and don't read."[12] The
changing status of *Moby-Dick* over time is an example of "a second kind
of horizonal change" that can occur when a literary text is deemed to be

a classic and thus becomes incorporated into a new horizon of expectations that conceals what was once regarded as its subversiveness. What was once a challenge to a literary tradition becomes the exemplar of that literary tradition. In other words, we tend to think of a classic as a text that is embedded in traditions and conventions, and we forget that many texts now considered classics were written in order to question and challenge the traditions and conventions of their times.

Another example of these shifting horizons can be found in the history of Harriet Beecher Stowe's best-selling novel about American slavery, *Uncle Tom's Cabin*, published at roughly the same time as *Moby-Dick*. Stowe's novel was once thought to be radical, even to be a text that may actually have started a war. Unlike *Moby-Dick*, *Uncle Tom's Cabin* did not challenge the prevailing horizon of expectations for a novel in formal terms. Knowing that she was dramatizing a subject—anti-slavery—that was often considered unpalatable by the audience she wished to reach, Stowe sugar-coated her subject through the use of sentimental and Christian doctrine. As one Stowe scholar puts it, "Sometimes critics have assumed that it was the subject of antislavery which made *Uncle Tom's Cabin* a powerful novel. It is perhaps more exactly true to say the opposite—that because *Uncle Tom's Cabin* was a powerful novel, antislavery became a powerful cause."[13] By the beginning of the twentieth century, however, *Uncle Tom's Cabin* was generally regarded, at best, as just another piece of sentimental fiction, at worst as an example of American racist logic. By the 1970s, it had become something else: a touchstone of American feminist criticism.[14] It becomes the job of the student of literature to regain the original horizon of questioning and subversiveness once again.

Sometimes, however, the second round of questioning occurs as the result of the emergence of a new text that refers back to the classic and recasts it in a different light. For example, the works of certain postmodern writers like Gabriel García Márquez, Carlos Fuentes, or Milan Kundera have enabled us to see works like Cervantes's *Don Quixote* (1605–1615), Sterne's *Tristram Shandy* (1759–1767), or Diderot's *Jacques le Fataliste* (1796) with fresh eyes. In the early part of the twentieth century, emergent ethnic writers frequently adopted strategies akin to Stowe's, choosing familiar literary styles such as a realism that could enable readers to concentrate on *what* they were writing rather than *how* they were writing it. Readers came to assume that ethnic writing was about realistic representation rather than formal experimentation. By the late twentieth century, however, emergent writers like N. Scott Momaday or Maxine Hong Kingston could make use of more adventurous narrative strategies because, in the aftermath of modernism, mainstream audiences had become accustomed to formal experimentation in literary novels. Emergent writers weren't the only ones to benefit from the canonization of modernist practice: *Moby-Dick* finally found an audience in the mid-twentieth century because it was seen to be a modernist novel *avant la lettre*.

As a category, the *emergent* is useful to the literary historian because it offers a dynamic model of the interactions of literary cultures, a model that focuses our attention on the fact that literatures are not simply sets of texts but rather institutions of culture with normative practices that evolve over time. Thus, the negotiations that take place between marginalized U.S. literatures and whatever canon of literature occupies the center always involve not only questions of literary influence among writers, but also other factors that previous literary historians might have considered to be extrinsic to literary studies. Such factors include the design of school curricula, the creation of departments and programs in colleges and universities, the practices of publishers, the editing of anthologies, and the awarding of literary prizes.[15] These factors help to shape the horizon of expectations to which writers look as they produce texts, and when writers think of themselves as participating in something called a "literature," they are often thinking about the ways in which their writing fits into institutional structures that are governed by such factors as sales expectations, syllabi, anthologies, and prizes. The genre of the Native American novel, for example, was brought into being by N. Scott Momaday's winning the Pulitzer Prize in 1968. The novelist James Welch describes Momaday's award as a crucial turning point for Native authors: "suddenly people started to notice Indian literature, [and] the way kind of opened for Indians; . . . younger people who didn't think they had much of a chance as a writer, suddenly realized, well, an Indian can write."[16] Early Chicano novelists essentially looked around and thought to themselves, "Nobody's giving us any prizes, so we'll make up one of our own, and we'll make up an anthology of our own too." The writer Tomás Rivera once remarked to the critic Juan Bruce-Novoa that the Chicanos were the first people to have an anthology before they had a literature.[17] Moreover, as the critic Héctor Calderón has noted, the history of twentieth-century Chicano literature is marked by the fact that "almost all Chicana and Chicano writers of fiction have earned advanced degrees in the United States." Although Chicano literature "may inform the dominant culture with an alternative view of the world filtered through myth and oral storytelling or offer an oppositional political perspective," Calderón argues that "this is done . . . from within educational institutions. We must realize," he writes, "how institutionally Western" Chicano literature is.[18]

As a result of both their training and their teaching, these authors find themselves deeply influenced by canonical traditions of U.S., English, and European literature, and the literature that they produce is necessarily *hybrid* in the sense that Mikhail Bakhtin used the term. Bakhtin describes *hybridization* as "a mixture of two social languages within the limits of a single utterance, an encounter, within the arena of an utterance, between two different linguistic consciousnesses, separated from one another by an epoch, by social differentiation or by some other factor."[19] Thus, for example, the protagonist of Maxine Hong Kingston's novel *Tripmaster Monkey: His Fake Book* (1987) is named Wittman Ah Sing, a reference to the great poet of individualism. The reference is not only being made by "Kingston": it is also being made by the character's parents, who know exactly what they're doing in naming him. Momaday cites as influences not only the different Native American traditions to which he belongs, but also Dickinson, Melville, and Faulkner.[20] Without these writers, his novel—and thus the tradition of the Native American novel that it engendered—would not have been possible.

The idea that a literature is an institution of culture is a crucial part of the conception of the emergent in which this book is grounded. When I use the terms *emergent writer* or *emergent text*, they should be understood as shorthand for the more cumbersome "writer or text belonging to a literature identified as emergent." In other words, I mean for *emergent* to be understood as a description of *literatures*—bodies of texts—rather than as a description of individual writers or individual texts. Each of these literatures in turn will replicate the dynamics of dominant, residual, and emergent. The power of Williams's model of culture as the dynamic interplay of the forms is that it works at every level of culture. So, for example, if both Asian American literature and Hispanic American literature are "emergent" in their negotiations with the canonical tradition of U.S. literature that emerges after World War II, there are within these two literatures, as we will see, dominant discourses associated with masculinity against which emergent discourses associated with feminism or queerness position themselves. My argument that Jewish American literature and African American literature should not be regarded as emergent literatures in the period from 1968 to the beginning of the twenty-first century is an argument about the institutional standing of these literatures. It does not mean that a reader will not detect aspects that seem emergent within the writing, say, of Toni Morrison or Colson Whitehead. Indeed an awareness of the dynamics of dominant, residual, and emergent might enhance a reading of novels such as Morrison's *Paradise* (1997) or Whitehead's *The Intuitionist* (1999), and it might even serve as a productive way of understanding Whitehead's writing as a response to Morrison's dominance within the field of African American literature. My point, however, is that the literature with which both Morrison and Whitehead are primarily associated—African American literature—is no longer emergent during the period that is the subject of this book.

The emergent model thus helps us to gain a more subtle understanding of the ways in which texts and authors interact with one another and the ways in which bodies of literature are produced. The model encourages us to investigate the ways in which U.S. culture's reception of previous texts by emergent authors influences the production and reception of future texts from emergent literary cultures. So, for example, it enables us to understand a moment, early in *Tripmaster Monkey*, when we find Wittman beginning his literary career by imitating the poetry of LeRoi Jones (Amiri Baraka). Wittman writes poetry that sounds very "black." For Wittman, blackness is a cultural template that signifies radicalism: revolutionary poetry, he believes, should sound like Jones's poetry. *Tripmaster Monkey* is in part about how Wittman learns to leave the template behind and create something new.[21]

In addition to helping us to conceptualize the strategies used by these literatures to gain audiences during the mid-twentieth century, the emergent model also gives us a way of understanding developmental inequalities among the literatures that are produced by different cultural traditions. It helps to explain, for example, why in the mid-1980s a progressive approach to American prose fiction after 1940 would immediately identify the contributions of African American writers and women writers, but neglect Native American, Asian American, Hispanic American, and gay and lesbian writers.[22] In *The Disuniting of America*, a critique of multiculturalism first published in 1991, Arthur Schlesinger, Jr., argues that "twelve percent of Americans are black" and the "pressure to correct injustices of past scholarship comes mostly on their behalf." This assertion became the foundation for Nathan Glazer's argument in *We Are All Multiculturalists Now* (1997) that African Americans played a decisive role in the victory of multiculturalism during the so-called "culture wars" of the 1980s: "blacks are the storm troops in the battles over multiculturalism. . . . [T]heir claim that they must play a larger role in the teaching of American literature and history, indeed should serve to reshape these subjects, has a far greater authority and weight than that of any other group." As a result, Glazer suggests, "we all now accept a greater degree of attention to minorities and women and their role in American history and social studies and literature classes in schools." And, although Glazer regards the presence of women's studies within multiculturalism as counterintuitive, he makes the historical argument that at the moment that women's studies came to prominence as a field of scholarly inquiry, "both women's studies and the new ethnic and racial studies could trace a common history, arising in the same decades, drawing on similar resentments, and a common new awareness of inequality." Indeed, Glazer argues, the field of women's studies has become "so large a part" of multiculturalism "that it often outweighs the rest."[23]

The concept of the *emergent*, however, draws our attention to those groups that have played a less prominent role in the rise of multiculturalism. If multiculturalism often boils down, as Glazer suggests, to the "universalistic demand" that "all groups should be recognized," he notes that some groups "have fallen below the horizon of attention."[24] The concept of the *emergent* refocuses our attention on precisely those groups that struggled for notice even as African American studies and women's studies established themselves as legitimate academic fields. It enables us to identify a set of literatures that are fighting for canonical

notice even as they are engaged in critique of the prevailing conceptions of what constitutes "American Literature."

The *emergent* thus gives us a model with which to discuss the relationship between mainstream U.S. culture and those practices that it
deems "deviant." It points us to the structural similarities between U.S.
ethnic writing and the writing of gay and lesbian Americans. The experience of being in the closet—an abiding subject for gay and lesbian
writing—is akin to the feeling of being caught between cultures that
ethnic Americans undergo when they are encouraged to dehyphenate
themselves. Mainstream U.S. culture fosters an oppositional relationship with gay culture by luring gay men and women into mimicking
its thinking by what Paul Monette calls "halving the world into us and
them," even as it attempts to keep gay culture divided by making it difficult for gay men and women to acknowledge one another openly.[25]

The idea of the *emergent* also focuses attention on a change in attitude that occurred in the aftermath of the civil rights movement. No
longer is "assimilation" the abiding goal of those who write from the
cultural margins. "America was multiethnic from the start," writes
Schlesinger in *The Disuniting of America,* and he argues that

> the United States had a brilliant solution for the inherent fragility, the
> inherent combustibility, of a multiethnic society: the creation of a brand-
> new national identity by individuals who, in forsaking old loyalties and
> joining to make new lives, melted away ethnic differences—a national
> identity that absorbs and transcends the diverse ethnicities that come to
> our shore, ethnicities that enrich and reshape the common culture in the
> very act of entering into it.

Schlesinger cites Hector St. John de Crèvecoeur's remark in *Letters
from an American Farmer* (1782) that "the American is a new man,
who acts upon new principles. . . . *Here individuals of all nations are
melted into a new race of men*"—an early formulation of the idea of
the melting pot. Schlesinger laments the loss of the melting pot ideal,
even as he recognizes that "the United States [never] fulfilled Crèvecoeur's standard. . . . For a long time the Anglo-Americans dominated
American culture and politics and excluded those who arrived after
them. . . . We must face the shameful fact: historically America has been

a racist nation."[26] Glazer notes that "assimilation today is not a popular term. . . . The 'melting pot' is no longer a uniformly praised metaphor for American society, as it once was. It suggests too much a forced conformity and reminds people today not of the welcome in American society to so many groups and races but rather of American society's demands on those it allows to enter."[27] Rather than a cultural stew whose flavor is constantly changing as immigrants add new ingredients to the mix, the melting pot became a metaphor for homogenization.

In 1915, Theodore Roosevelt gave a speech in which he debunked the idea of the "hyphenated American":

> There is no room in this country for hyphenated Americanism. When I refer to hyphenated Americans, I do not refer to naturalized Americans. Some of the very best Americans I have ever known were naturalized Americans, Americans born abroad. But a hyphenated American is not an American at all. This is just as true of the man who puts "native" before the hyphen as of the man who puts German or Irish or English or French before the hyphen. Americanism is a matter of the spirit and of the soul. Our allegiance must be purely to the United States. We must unsparingly condemn any man who holds any other allegiance. But if he is heartily and singly loyal to this Republic, then no matter where he was born, he is just as good an American as any one else.[28]

Roosevelt was speaking after the outbreak of war in Europe in 1914, and his concern was with those American citizens who might "vote as a German-American, an Irish-American, or an English-American"— who might vote, in other words, in a way that puts the interests of some other nation ahead of those of the United States.[29] Many Americans neglected or refused to make Roosevelt's distinction between the "naturalized American" and the "hyphenated American," assuming that it was impossible for any immigrants to become truly naturalized.

Ethnic writers of the early part of the twentieth century often sought to understand and represent the ways in which they and those like them were portrayed as different, incomprehensible, inscrutable, and uncivilized—in short, portrayed as "others" who could not be assimilated. They sought a solution to what I call *the impasse of hyphenation*, the idea that the American who belongs to a minority group is caught between two incompatible identities, the minority (Jewish, Italian, Irish, Black, Asian, Hispanic, Native, etc.) and the majority ("American"). The writer Frank Chin called this, in the Asian American context, the "dual personality," as if somehow all Asian Americans were split down the middle and made schizophrenic by U.S. culture.[30] Identity thus becomes a matter of either/or: either "American" or whatever it is that precedes the hyphen.

Emergent writers think of themselves differently. They realize that they are writing from the margins of U.S. culture, but feel themselves to be sufficiently empowered to offer a challenge to the center. Their goal is not to enter the mainstream but to divert and transform it: they seek to add their own distinctiveness to the stew of U.S. culture in such a way that the flavor of the stew is altered. For example, like earlier Asian American writing, such as Sui Sin Far's story "The Wisdom of the New" (1912) or John Okada's novel *No-No Boy* (1957), Kingston's novel *Trip-master Monkey* registers the pain of being caught between two cultures. But Wittman Ah Sing is not interested in kowtowing to mainstream attitudes about either identity or art. Instead, he wants to define an identity for himself that can truly be called "Chinese American," an identity in which the "Chinese" is no longer marginalized by the "American." No longer would the phrase "Chinese American" be some kind of oxymoron: it would simply be another way of talking about the "American." The idea of the *emergent* highlights the fact that U.S. ethnic writing has become less interested in strategies of assimilation than in strategies of negotiation, which offer a solution to the impasse of hyphenation: they embrace the idea of hybridity, dramatizing the idea that all American identities are hybrid—and always have been.

With its emphasis on practices that are produced by cultural groups, the idea of the *emergent* helps us to gain insight into one subject of these negotiations between margin and center, namely the relationship between the universal and the particular in U.S. writing. Emergent ethnic writers no longer accept without question the universalizing logic of individualism that lies at the heart of U.S. liberal culture. This logic is based upon what political theorists call *ontological individualism*, the belief that the individual has an *a priori* and primary reality and that society is a derived, second-order construct. From Ralph Waldo Emerson in the nineteenth century to John Rawls in the twentieth, U.S.

theorists of individualism have typically sought to shift the ground of inquiry from culture and society to the individual, translating moments of social choice into moments of individual choice. This strategy is a literal application of the motto *e pluribus unum*—"from many, one"—which expresses the idea that the United States is nation formed through the union of many individuals. In the hands of thinkers like Emerson and Rawls, the customary sense of this motto is reversed: they move from the many to the one, to the single individual, paring away differences in order to reach a common denominator that will allow them to make claims about all individuals.[31]

Thus Emerson writes about "the soul" in essays like "The American Scholar" (1837) or "Self-Reliance" (1841), and once he has established that every person has a fundamental equality in the soul, he begins to make universalist generalizations about all human beings. Emerson, in other words, doesn't ignore social questions, but rather he recasts them as questions of individual choice, using the soul as his point of entry. Likewise Rawls reinvents contract theory to create what he calls "the original position of equality," a thought experiment in which each participant knows that he or she will live in a society in which there are going to be inequalities—of class, race, gender, talent, intelligence, hair color, wealth—but is unaware of how he or she will be marked by those inequalities. From behind what Rawls refers to as "the veil of ignorance," the Rawlsian individual thus argues with others about how to construct the best society, without knowing what attributes he or she will have once that society comes into being. The original position, however, is in fact a rigged game, because Rawls believes that in the end an individual would choose only one kind of society: namely, a society in which the lot of the least well-off is maximized. Confronted with the possibility that he or she might end up at the very bottom of society, each individual would choose to create a society in which that bottom is not as bad as it would be in other societies. One might choose, for example, a non-slave state instead of a slave state, because the person who is worst-off in a non-slave state would still not be a slave. For Rawls, the original position is ultimately reducible to one set of arguments: he believes that every single individual, if he or she were rational, would choose in the same way. That is his way of shifting the ground to the individual.[32]

Aware that mainstream U.S. culture has a large stake in preserving both the logic of either/or and the logic of universalist individualism, emergent ethnic and gay writers promote something else: a *cosmopolitan* perspective that is conceived in contradistinction not primarily to nationalism, as in earlier theories of cosmopolitanism, but in contradistinction to the idea of universalism. In *Postethnic America: Beyond Multiculturalism* (1995), David Hollinger "distinguish[es] between a universalist will to find common ground from a cosmopolitan will to engage human diversity." According to Hollinger,

> Cosmopolitanism shares with all varieties of universalism a profound suspicion of enclosures, but cosmopolitanism is defined by an additional element not essential to universalism itself: recognition, acceptance, and eager exploration of diversity. Cosmopolitanism urges each individual and collective unit to absorb as much varied experience as it can, while retaining its capacity to advance its aims effectively. For cosmopolitans, the diversity of humankind is a fact; for universalists, it is a potential problem.[33]

I'd go further: cosmopolitanism conceives of difference, not as a problem to be solved (as it is for Emerson or Rawls), but rather as an opportunity to be embraced.

Multiculturalism, of course, is a response to universalism that ostensibly privileges the claims of difference over those of universalism. If multiculturalism responds, as Glazer suggests, to the "universalistic demand" that "all groups should be recognized," it does so by stressing toleration and pluralism. Hollinger argues that, as institutionalized in the United States, multiculturalism promotes the goal of cultural diversity by advocating a pluralism that "respects inherited boundaries and locates individuals within one or another of a series of ethno-racial groups to be protected and preserved." According to Hollinger, this kind of pluralism "differs from cosmopolitanism in the degree to which it endows with privilege particular groups, especially the communities that are well established at whatever time the ideal of pluralism is invoked."[34] In other words, the logic of contemporary multiculturalism goes something like this: I like my culture (because it's mine), but I respect yours. I want you to respect mine. I prefer mine (because it's mine), and I imagine that you prefer yours (because it's yours). I really can't comment on your culture, because I don't belong to it. I cherish my long-standing practices and values, and out of respect I'll refrain from commenting on your long-standing practices and values. If I happen to find some of your long-standing practices and values distasteful or even repugnant—well, we'll just agree to disagree. Even if, for example, one of those practices is slavery.

You would be hard pressed to find a multiculturalist who would actually suggest that slavery might be tolerated in certain cultural contexts, but such a position is simply the logical endpoint of the idea that we cannot make moral judgments about other cultures' practices without engaging in cultural imperialism and domination. As a result, multiculturalists are often skittish about making judgments across cultural boundaries. Hollinger describes contemporary multiculturalism as a "bargain" in which different cultural groups agree: "You keep the acids of your modernity out of my culture, and I'll keep the acids of mine away from yours."[35]

Emergent writers realize that such a bargain is not only undesirable but also untenable. Contemporary emergent writing sets itself against the idea of cultural purity that lies behind contemporary U.S. multiculturalism and identity politics. Emergent writing demonstrates the power of what the philosopher Kwame Anthony Appiah calls "cosmopolitan contamination." Cultures, in Appiah's account, never tend toward purity: they tend toward change, toward mixing and miscegenation, toward an "endless process of imitation and revision."[36] To keep a culture "pure" requires the vigilant policing often associated with fundamentalist regimes or xenophobic political parties. Like Williams's account of the interaction of dominant, residual, and emergent cultures, Appiah's description of culture is about "conversation across boundaries." Such conversations, Appiah writes, "can be delightful, or just vexing: what they mainly are, though, is inevitable."[37]

Studying emergent literatures inevitably leads one to study the dynamics of cosmopolitanism. Like cosmopolitan theorists, emergent writers are committed to difficult conversations in which fundamental values are subject to examination and questioning. In a variety of ways, sometimes through style or form, sometimes through subject, emergent literatures bring us face-to-face with difference and then even closer—perhaps we might say, mind-to-mind. They ask us to think, "What if?"—to engage in thought experiments in which we experience difference. In this way, emergent literatures promote a cosmopolitan perspective. And they suggest, perhaps, that in this respect the idea of the *emergent* is ultimately most useful as a heuristic tool through which to understand the cosmopolitan dynamics of the literary impulse itself.

1

From Marginal to Emergent

Wittman Ah Sing, the protagonist of Maxine Hong Kingston's novel *Tripmaster Monkey: His Fake Book* (1989), has a problem. Named for the great poet of American individualism and steeped in American cultural history, Wittman wants to be a latter-day Jack Kerouac, but to his chagrin, he comes to realize that the real Kerouac would never have seen him as a protégé. To Kerouac, Wittman could only have been another Victor Wong, preserved for posterity in Kerouac's novel *Big Sur* (1962) as "little Chinese buddy Arthur Ma."[1] Wittman wants to be an American Artist—he wants to carve a place for himself in American cultural history—but finds that first he must disengage himself from the subordinate place that American culture has made for him on the basis of his ethnicity.

Wittman's manic narrative registers the pain of being caught between two cultures, of being increasingly drawn away from the Chinese culture of his ancestors, which he admires, by the dominant, mainstream culture of Whitman, Kerouac, Marilyn Monroe, and UC Berkeley, which he also admires. Wittman wants to define an identity for himself that can truly be called "Chinese American," but to do so he must prevent his Chinese inheritance from being transformed into a safely exotic form of cultural residue: he must prevent the "Chinese" from being marginalized by the "American." Wittman's goal is to create a form of public art that can redefine what it means to be "Chinese

American"—redefine it for himself, his community, and the larger culture of which both he and his community are a part. In the course of the novel, Wittman discovers that his cultural identity is necessarily hybrid, and he suspects that every American identity is, in fact, necessarily hybrid, though mainstream U.S. culture has worked hard to deny that fact. *Tripmaster Monkey* thus dramatizes the predicament faced by all U.S. late-twentieth-century minority cultures, whether oriented around ethnicity or around sexuality: how to transform themselves from marginal cultures into emergent cultures capable of challenging and reforming the mainstream.

This transformation depends in large on a shift in perspective. Part of what it means to be emergent is to associate yourself with the idea of the new. Remember that Raymond Williams, in his original theorization of the idea of the emergent, identifies it as the site or set of sites where "new meanings and values new practices, new relationships and kinds of relationships are continually being created."[2] This newness, however, is a matter of perspective: what is new is what looks new from the vantage point of the dominant. So it should not surprise us to discover that some cultural forms that we might designate as emergent are, in fact, hundreds, perhaps even thousands, of years old. For example, elements of homosexual experience played an important role in the cultures of classical Greece and Rome and of medieval Islam,[3] but gay and lesbian culture remains in an emergent and oppositional position in the United States today, as the continuing resistance in many parts of the country to the idea of "gay marriage" demonstrates.[4] "The project of our enemies is to keep us from falling in love," writes Paul Monette in his memoir, *Becoming a Man: Half a Life Story* (1992): "It has always been thus, the history written by straight boys who render us invisible, as if we were never there. . . . If you isolate us long enough and keep us ignorant of each other, the solitary confinement will extinguish any hope we have of finding our other half."[5] We find a similar assault upon a minority's sense of community in a moment from Leslie Marmon Silko's *Ceremony* (1977) when the narrator describes the character Auntie's worldview: "An old sensitivity had descended in her, surviving thousands of years from the oldest times, when the people shared a single clan name and they told each other who they were; they recounted actions and words each of their clan had taken, and would take; from before they were born and long after they died, the people shared the same consciousness." But Auntie feels that Christianity has "separated the people from themselves; it tried to crush the single clan name, encouraging each person to stand alone, because Jesus Christ would save only the individual soul."[6] The holistic communitarianism that Auntie longs for is ancient, but in Silko's novel it becomes an alternative that can be transformed into a site of new resistance.

The potential for resistance is a crucial component of the emergent: according to Williams, a truly emergent culture must be "substantially alternative or oppositional" to the dominant, and it is an article of faith among minority discourse theorists that opposition to the dominant culture is an experience that all U.S minority cultures share. As Abdul JanMohammed and David Lloyd put it in the introduction to *The Nature and Context of Minority Discourse* (1990), "Cultures designated as minorities have certain shared experiences by virtue of their similar antagonistic relationship to the dominant culture."[7] Drawing on the work of the postcolonial theorist Frantz Fanon, JanMohammed and Lloyd argue "that minority discourse is, in the first instance, the product of damage—damage more or less systematically inflicted on cultures produced as minorities by the dominant culture. The destruction involved is manifold, bearing down on variant modes of social formation, dismantling previously functional economic systems, and deracinating whole populations at best or decimating them at worst." [8] Minority discourse theory in the United States has been greatly influenced not only by the work of Williams but also by postcolonial theory, which has offered insights into the ways in which dominant cultures colonize the subjectivities of those whose cultures they marginalize, whether those subjectivities belong to subjugated native peoples, to immigrant populations, or to ethnic, racial, religious, sexual, or other minorities. What emergent writers in the United States share with native intellectuals in colonial and postcolonial contexts is the common project of decolonizing themselves.

When Silko's character Auntie thinks about the cultural damage suffered by Native American cultures in the aftermath of European colonization, she thinks first of the linguistic damage that has occurred: "the fifth world had become entangled with European names: the names of the rivers, the hills, the names of the animals and plants—all of creation

suddenly had two names: an Indian name and a white name". The influential Kenyan dramatist, novelist, and critic Ngugi wa Thiong'o offers
a similar insight in *Decolonising the Mind* (1986) when he writes, "The
bullet was the means of physical subjugation. Language was the means
of spiritual subjugation." The imposition of English on the peoples
of Kenya was a powerful way for the British to take cultural control,
which, Ngugi argues, was a crucial part of the process of colonization:

> Colonialism imposed its control of the social production of wealth
> through military conquest and subsequent political dictatorship. But
> its most important area of domination was the mental universe of the
> colonised, the control, through culture, of how people perceived them-
> selves and their relationship to the world. Economic and political control
> can never be complete or effective without mental control. To control a
> people's culture is to control their tools of self-definition in relationship
> to others.

Ngugi dropped his given name—"James"—in 1972 as a way of resisting
Christianity's linguistic colonization of his people, and he would eventually renounce English as a language for African literary production,
turning instead to his native Gikuyu. "We as African writers have always
complained about the neo-colonial economic and political relationship
to Euro America," Ngugi writes and then asks: "But by our continuing
to write in foreign languages, paying homage to them, are we not on the
cultural level continuing that neo-colonial slavish and cringing spirit?
What is the difference between a politician who says Africa cannot do
without imperialism and the writer who says Africa cannot do without
European languages?"[9]

In the United States, the process that Ngugi describes occurs not
simply through imposition of English as the national language, but also
through the powerful mythologies generated by U.S. popular culture.
Recalling the powerful force exerted by Hollywood during her childhood in the Philippines, the Filipino American writer Jessica Hagedorn
reflects:

> Even though we also studied Tagalog, one of our native languages . . . and
> read some of the native literature . . . it was pretty clear to most of us

growing up in the fifties and early sixties that what was really important, what was inevitably preferred, was the aping of our mythologized
Hollywood universe. The colonization of our imagination was relentless
and hard to shake off. Everywhere we turned, the images held up did not
match our own. In order to be acknowledged, we had to strive to be as
American as possible.[10]

Named for a derogatory stereotype of Filipinos, Hagedorn's novel *Dogeaters* (1990) depicts the culture of the Philippines as the quintessential
damaged culture, transformed by its encounter with America into an
empty simulacrum that eschews its native forms in order to model itself
on the sham culture depicted in Hollywood movies. The novel begins
in "the air-conditioned darkness of the Avenue Theater, . . . Manila's
'Foremost! First-Run! English Movies Only!' theater," where one of the
novel's central characters, a young girl named Rio Gonzaga, sits with
her "blond" "mestiza" cousin, Pucha, the two of them "enthralled" as
they watch Jane Wyman, Rock Hudson, and Gloria Talbott in *All That
Heaven Allows*: "we gasp at Gloria's cool indifference, the offhand way
she treats her grieving mother. Her casual arrogance seems inherently
American, modern, and enviable."[11] Written in a present-tense pastiche
of first-person narrative, third-person narrative, fictional newspaper
accounts, to which are added quotations from the Associated Press, a
poem by José Rizal, a speech by William McKinley, and Jean Mallat's
ethnographic study *The Philippines* (1856), *Dogeaters* depicts a thinly
veiled version of the corrupt regime presided over by Ferdinand and
Imelda Marcos from 1965 to 1986. Casual arrogance marks the novel's
depiction of the repressive social apparatus: the military regime led by
General Nicasio Ledesma is ruthless, brutal, and efficient in its use of
torture, rape, and murder to eliminate the enemies of the President and
the First Lady. But even more powerful in ensuring the regime's dominance is the culture's ideological apparatus, which operates through
religion, education, and (perhaps most powerfully) popular culture.

Dogeaters permits us to enter the thoughts of characters from the
full spectrum of social classes: from Madame First Lady to the theater
cashier, Trinidad Gamboa, from Severo Alacran, the richest man in the
Philippines, to the junkie mulatto deejay, Joey Sands. Linked together
through a series of violent events that culminate in an assassination,

these characters are even more tightly bound together by their common fascination with the movies. "What would life be without movies?" the First Lady asks an American journalist off the record: "Unendurable, *di ba*? We Filipinos, we know how to endure, and we embrace the movies. With movies, everything is okay *lang*. It is one of our few earthly rewards."[12] Linking its characters together through violence and pop culture, the novel suggests that violence and pop culture are themselves inextricably linked. The entire country is addicted to the radio soap opera *Love Letters,* and Rio tells us in the novel's first chapter that "without fail, someone dies on *Love Letters.* There's always a lesson to be learned, and it's always a painful one. Just like our Tagalog movies."[13] The connection is vividly dramatized in the novel's most chilling scene, a gang rape carried out by military officers and a presidential aide while *Love Letters* plays in the background.

Dogeaters vividly explores the effects of American cultural colonization abroad, but emergent writers frequently dramatize the fact that American culture colonizes at home as well. Within its own boundaries a dominant culture seeks to colonize the imaginations of those whom it has marginalized. Mainstream U.S. culture teaches gays and lesbians that they are perverts and deviants; it constructs "Americanness" and "homosexuality" as opposites; it encourages gays and lesbians to remain closeted, to assimilate quietly—"don't ask, don't tell." In *Becoming a Man,* Monette describes the experience of being made to feel like an enemy of the culture, a spy in one's native land:

> I speak for no one else here, if only because I don't want to saddle the women and men of my tribe with the lead weight of my self-hatred, the particular doorless room of my internal exile. Yet I've come to learn that all our stories add up to the same imprisonment. The self-delusion of uniqueness. The festering pretense that we are the same as they are. The gutting of all our passions till we are a bunch of eunuchs, our zones of pleasure in enemy hands. Most of all, the ventriloquism, the learning how to pass for straight. Such obedient slaves we make, with such very tidy rooms.

Mainstream U.S. culture fosters an oppositional relationship with gay culture by luring gay men and women into mimicking its thinking by "halving the world into *us* and *them*," even as it attempts to keep gay culture divided by making it difficult for gay men and women to acknowledge one another openly.[14]

The experience of being in the closet is akin to the experience of cultural hybridity—the feeling of being caught between cultures—that ethnic Americans undergo when they are taught to deny the parts of themselves that lie outside of mainstream U.S. culture. Tayo, the protagonist of Silko's *Ceremony*, remembers what he was told at the V. A. hospital: "the white doctors had yelled at him—that he had to think only of himself, and not about the others, that he would never get well as long as he used words like 'we' and 'us.'" Like many late-twentieth-century Native American writers, Silko conceives of Native American culture and history as primarily communitarian in nature and therefore set against the grain of the American national culture's celebration of individualism. So Tayo thinks to himself that he has "known the answer all along, even while the white doctors were telling him he could get well and he was trying to believe them: medicine didn't work that way, because the world didn't work that way." Kingston's Wittman Ah Sing finds himself in an analogous position in *Tripmaster Monkey*, sitting in the unemployment office watching "a cartoon about going for a job interview" that gives him hints about "good grooming," which turn out to include the following pieces of advice: "COME ALONE to the interview. DO NOT take friends or relatives with you." Wittman immediately realizes the nature of the message implicit in these dicta: "An X through my people. Adios, mis amigos. . . . An American stands alone. Alienated, tribeless, individual. To be a successful American, leave your tribe, your caravan, your gang, your partner, your village cousins, your refugee family that you're making the money for, leave them behind. Do not bring back-up."[15]

What Monette, Silko, and Kingston are confronting here is the logic of ontological individualism that has been so dominant within U.S. culture. As I argued in the first chapter, American theorists of individualism from Ralph Waldo Emerson to John Rawls have typically sought to shift the ground of inquiry from culture and society to the individual, thereby translating moments of social choice into moments of individual choice. And one of the most powerful claims that U.S. culture makes about individuals is that sexuality, ethnicity, and cultural hybridity are contingent, incidental, and ultimately irrelevant aspects of individual identity.

Richard Rodriguez's controversial autobiography, *Hunger of Memory* (1982), makes a powerful case for the applicability of this model of identity-formation to individuals designated as minorities by mainstream U.S. culture. Arguing that class is the true dividing line in U.S. culture, Rodriguez argues that middle-class Americans of all races and ethnicities who are in a position to think like individualists should do so. His opposition to both bilingual education and affirmative action (which have made him unpopular among Chicano activists) is based on the belief that such remedies are unnecessary for middle-class individuals who have the opportunity to participate in America's culture of individualism.

The benefits—and the potential losses—that result from this stance can be seen most poignantly in Rodriguez's rendering of what is the classic situation for the ethnic minority subject: being forced to choose between the culture of his parents and the dominant culture that surrounds him. Having summoned the courage to raise his hand and speak up in class, Rodriguez tells us that "at last, at seven years old, I came to believe what had been technically true since my birth: I was an American citizen." This gain, however, entails a loss: "the special feeling of closeness at home was diminished" by "the dramatic Americanization" that he and his siblings underwent: "gone was the desperate, urgent, intense feeling of being at home; rare was the experience of feeling individualized by family intimates. We remained a loving family but we were greatly changed. No longer so close; no longer bound tight by the pleasing and troubling knowledge of our public separateness."[16] For Rodriguez, the loss is completely offset by the gain. It is never, for him, really a question of choosing between two equally viable cultural groups. There is only one group—the dominant group—and it is one to which he does not belong. In other words, Rodriguez presents himself from the outset as "tribeless," and he conceives of emergence not as a struggle between cultures, but as a process of personal metamorphosis. It is in this shifting of the ground of analysis from the group to the individual that *Hunger of Memory* proves itself to be a classic account of American self-making, a contribution to the Emersonian and Rawlsian traditions of American liberalism.

The last pieces of advice that the cartoon offers to Wittman Ah Sing deal with the question of language: "SPEAK clearly and answer questions honestly. BE business-like and brief." The cartoon exhorts its audience to present a public self that is likely to succeed in mainstream culture, and it is the development of this public self that Rodriguez charts in his autobiography. In arguing against bilingual education, Rodriguez writes: "Today I hear bilingual educators say that children lose a degree of 'individuality' by becoming assimilated into public society. . . . But the bilingualists simplistically scorn the value and necessity of assimilation. They do not seem to realize that there are *two* ways a person is individualized. So they do not realize that while one suffers a diminished sense of *private* individuality by becoming assimilated into public society, such assimilation makes possible the achievement of *public individuality*." The achievement of this public individuality has a price: "it would never again be easy," Rodriguez tells us, "for me to hear intimate family voices." But it is a price that Rodriguez is willing to pay, though he nonetheless tries to minimize its cost, naturalizing this split between private and public individuality by ascribing it to the "inevitable pain" of growing up: "The day I raised my hand in class and spoke loudly to an entire roomful of faces, my childhood started to end." Childhood is indeed full of pain, and children often find themselves at odds with their families, but what is different about the particular pain that Rodriguez describes is that it is the product of the dominant culture's attempt (in Wittman Ah Sing's phrase) to put an X through his people. Almost in passing, Rodriguez tells us that "the bilingualists insist that a student should be reminded of his difference from others in mass society, his heritage." But "heritage" is a subject upon which Rodriguez chooses not to dwell, setting it aside without further comment. The price for the achievement of his public individuality, then, is alienation from family, ancestors, and heritage. What Rodriguez fails to points out is that it is only members of minority cultures who must pay this particular price.[17]

In seeking to portray class as the primary determinant factor in American life, Rodriguez must deny his identity as an ethnic hybrid (and, though this is not made explicit in the text, his identity as a gay man). He is thus forced to inflict damage not only upon himself—by sacrificing his "private individuality"—but also upon his family. In a later essay he describes the beginning of his Americanization as his "emergence as a brat" and admits that he "determined to learn English, initially, as a way of hurting [his parents]."[18] Rodriguez's autobiographical writings provide a case study in the ways that America's minority cultures internalize the damage inflicted upon them by mainstream culture. There is a tension in Rodriguez's text between the argument he is making—about the primacy of class over ethnicity as a determinant of identity—and the ethnically inflected episodes that he uses to illustrate that argument.

Hunger of Memory is indeed an emergent text: it transforms American liberalism because it asserts the right of a person of color to participate in the American liberal tradition, a right recognized in theory but not yet fully realized in practice. Paradoxically, however, the text can assert this right only by denying the relevance of its author's racial, ethnic, and sexual identity. In other words, the text is forced to abjure the very qualities that make it emergent. Because Rodriguez's aim is not to transform mainstream U.S. culture but rather to detail a strategy for becoming part of it, he seeks to naturalize what other authors might represent as a process of cultural damage. Rodriguez chose to describe the hardships he has undergone as fundamentally similar to the hardships that any American faces when trying to achieve a public voice. But his text leaves us with the uncomfortable feeling that what it is recording—almost despite itself—is the damage specifically inflicted upon minorities by mainstream U.S. culture.

To put Rodriguez's rhetorical strategies in perspective, we might compare *Hunger of Memory* to another text that portrays the inevitability of Americanization, John Okada's novel *No-No Boy* (1957). The novel's protagonist, Ichiro, has suffered the humiliation of being interned in a camp with other Japanese Americans and decides, when he is later drafted, not to serve in the American army.[19] Ichiro has chosen to side with his non-assimilationist mother, and he goes to prison for it. Returning home to Seattle after the war, Ichiro thinks to himself what he is unable to say to his mother, that there was a time when "we were Japanese with Japanese feelings and Japanese pride and Japanese thoughts because it was all right then to be Japanese and feel and think all the things that Japanese do even if we lived in America." But then

> there came a time when I was only half Japanese because one is not born
> in America and raised in America and taught in America and one does

not speak and swear and drink and smoke and play and fight and see and hear in America among Americans in American streets and houses without becoming American and loving it. But I did not love enough, for you were still half my mother and I was thereby still half Japanese and when the war came and they told me to fight for America, I was not strong enough to fight you and I was not strong enough to fight the bitterness which made the half of me which was you bigger than the half of me which was America and really the whole of me that I could not see or feel.[20]

This passage, taken from a long interior monologue in the middle of the novel's first chapter, embodies the novel's recognition of the extent to which Japanese Americans suffer from the idea of the "dual personality," the idea that the "Asian" and the "American" are incompatible selves at war with one another within the Asian American individual. Trapped within a logic of either/or, Okada's protagonist believes that he must choose either to be Japanese or to be American. What *No-No Boy* explores is the deep regret that Ichiro feels after his release, the sense that he has made a mistake, that he has chosen wrongly. And he comes to believe that he has chosen foolishly because what appeared to be a choice was, in fact, never really a choice. *No-No Boy* portrays resistance to assimilation as futile, but it differs from *Hunger of Memory* because it openly explores the pain of cultural hybridity, which it can only understand as a state of violence. *No-No Boy* anticipates a narrative strategy that has proven to be central to the project of producing emergent literature in late-twentieth-century America.

This strategy is to understand hybridity as a crucial fact about identity and to depict the ontology of hybridity as an ontology of violence. Writers as disparate as N. Scott Momaday, Leslie Marmon Silko, Oscar Zeta Acosta, Jessica Hagedorn, Maxine Hong Kingston, and Paul Monette depict characters who have internalized the dominant culture's understanding of hybridity as a state of violence and self-division. For example, the mixed-blood war veteran, Abel, in Momaday's *House Made of Dawn* (1968) experiences his mixed blood as a clash between contradictory frames of reference, a clash that fractures his consciousness, leading him to treat wartime combat as if it were ritual, and ritual as if it were actual combat. The vicious schoolyard beating of a "meek, nervous kid" by a group of "Irish toughs" is an unforgettable incident that occurs early in Monette's memoir *Becoming a Man*; later, when threatened by a "football jock" two years older than he, Monette describes himself as "a prisoner who spills all the secrets as soon as he sees the torture room, before the first whip is cracked." Being in the closet is for Monette an experience of pain: "When you finally come out, there's a pain that stops, and you know it will never hurt like that again, no matter how much you lose or how bad you die." Worst of all, he finds that being in the closet has made him internalize the hatred directed toward him: "it makes me sick to hate the way my enemies hate."[21]

"Decolonization," wrote the seminal postcolonial critic Frantz Fanon, "is always a violent phenomenon." Gay and lesbian texts share with texts of ethnic emergence a preoccupation with the violence of living on the margins of U.S. culture. In fact, many gay and lesbian activists believe that gay studies, queer theory, and the gay rights movement should pattern themselves on "the ethnic model" in order to gain political power. The problem with this strategy, as Dana Takagi points out in her contribution to the anthology *Asian American Sexualities: Dimensions of the Gay & Lesbian Experience* (1996), is "the relative invisibility of sexual identity compared with racial identity. While both can be said to be socially constructed, the former are performed, acted out, and produced often in individual routines, whereas the latter tends to be more obviously 'written' on the body and negotiated by political groups." This caveat—about the extent to which identities like "Asian American" or "gay and lesbian" can be considered performative—is an important one. But it applies to bodies and not texts, to authors rather than their work. For all texts are "performed, acted out, and produced . . . in individual routines": all of them represent a decision either to "pass" as mainstream or to present themselves as "emergent." In this sense, both ethnic and gay writers share the dilemma that addles Kingston's poet-protagonist at the end of the first chapter of *Tripmaster Monkey*: "Does he announce now that the author is— Chinese? Or, rather, Chinese-American? And be forced into autobiographical confession. Stop the music—I have to butt in and introduce myself and my race." Whether the question is race, ethnicity, or sexuality—and we could perhaps argue for the inclusion of gender and class as well—the dilemma is that of the marginalized author who would be emergent.[22]

Kingston's novel suggests that the dilemma of whether or not to introduce one's race was not something that Herman Melville faced: "'Call me Ishmael.' See? You pictured a white guy, didn't you?" Some queer theorists might beg to differ, however, arguing that texts like "Benito Cereno" (1855) and "Billy Budd" (1924) bear the signs of struggle evident when a gay writer chooses to pass for straight: one of the major subjects in Melville studies during the 1990s has been the question of whether the author was, in fact, either gay or bisexual. Melville, it seems, may have been closer to the margins of U.S. culture than the canonical tradition would have us believe.[23]

For gay and lesbian writers, being emergent entails both establishing the literary right to explore the dynamics of gay life—in particular the dynamics of gay eroticism—and "outing" those gay authors who have been assimilated into the mainstream literary canon with no acknowledgment of the impact that their sexualities may have had upon their literary art. Part of the project of American queer theory in the 1980s and 1990s has been to locate the closets within the texts of writers like Melville, Henry James, and Willa Cather, to understand what Eve Kosofsky Sedgwick has called "the epistemology of the closet."[24] Judith Fetterley, for example, argues that the power of Cather's *My Ántonia* is "connected with its contradictions" and that "these contradictions are intimately connected to Cather's lesbianism." Unable to write freely about lesbian desire, Cather finds a "solution to the inherent contradiction between American and lesbian" by conflating the two and portraying the land both as female and as an object of desire: according to Fetterley, "in the land, Cather successfully imagined herself; in the land, she imagined a woman who could be safely eroticized and safely loved."[25] Such rereadings of canonical authors have a double effect: first, they demonstrate the existence of a longstanding tradition of gay and lesbian writing upon which openly gay writers can now draw; second, they demonstrate the extent to which mainstream U.S. culture has been shaped by gay sensibility. It is no accident, such critics argue, that America's bard, Walt Whitman, was a homosexual: who better to embody the ideology of individualism than a gay man cut off from the rest of his "tribe" (to use Paul Monette's word)?[26]

Whether Whitman looms as a force of liberation or constraint depends, however, upon an author's subject position. To Paul Monette, who uses one of Whitman's *Calamus* poems ("I Hear It Was Charged against Me") as the epigraph for *Becoming a Man*, he is a forefather to be cherished and emulated. For Maxine Hong Kingston, however, Whitman represents the canonical American tradition—so full of the writings of white men—that places the emergent ethnic writer into an oppositional position. Whitman is a figure with whom to struggle and contend and, if possible, one to appropriate, too.

For many emergent ethnic writers in the United States, another strategy for resistance has been to draw on non-Anglo-American and non-European mythological beliefs and stories. Native American authors draw upon what remains of their tribal cultures, in part because tribal ways represent an integral part of their personal identities, but also because their depictions of tribal cultures help to preserve those cultures, not simply in memory but as living cultures. The novelist N. Scott Momaday's Kiowa name is "Tsoai-talee," which means "Rock-tree Boy," a reference to Momaday's being taken as an infant to Tsoai, a place sacred to the Kiowas that appears on U.S. maps as "Devil's Tower, Wyoming." The name connects Momaday to a Kiowa legend that his great-grandmother told him and that he tells this way in his memoir, *The Names* (1976):

Eight children were there at play, seven sisters and their brother. Suddenly the boy was struck dumb; he trembled and began to run upon his hands and feet. His fingers became claws, and his body was covered with fur. There was a bear where the boy had been. The sisters were terrified; they ran, and the bear after them. They came to the stump of a great tree, and the tree spoke to them. It bade them climb upon it, and as they did so it began to rise into the air. The bear came to kill them, but they were just beyond its reach. It reared against the tree and scored the bark all around with its claws. The seven sisters were borne into the sky, and they became the stars of the Big Dipper.[27]

Momaday tells interviewers that he imagines himself to be the reincarnation of that boy and uses storytelling to enable himself to explore what it means to live under the sway of a legend: "All things can be accepted, if not understood, if you put them into a story. It is exactly what the Kiowas did when they encountered that mysterious rock formation. They incorporated it into their experience by telling a story about it. And that is what I feel that I must do about the boy bear."[28] Momaday's writing re-enacts the story-making that loomed so large in the lives of his ancestors; its very existence represents a way of resisting both the cultural eradication pursued by the U.S. government in the nineteenth century and the cultural mummification wrought by those whose images of the Native American remain rooted in nineteenth-century stereotypes.

Other emergent ethnic writers give prominence within their fictions to figures or places that embody the ideas of subversion and resistance. One such figure is the trickster, who appears throughout Native American tribal mythologies in such manifestations as Coyote, Crow, Jay, Hare, Loon, Raven, Spider, Wolverine, and Old Man. Sometimes a heroic, even god-like figure, the trickster can also be a liar and a cheater, a fool and a bungler, but he is almost always connected to the telling of stories. In *Love Medicine* (1984; expanded edition, 1993) and *The Bingo Palace* (1994), Louise Erdrich draws on Chippewa tales of the trickster Nanabozho to create figures of both comedy and subversion in Gerry Nanapush, a member of the radical American Indian Movement, who has a knack for escaping from prison by squeezing into unimaginably small spaces, and his son, Lipsha Morissey, who embarks on a vision-quest for three days and ends up having visions of American fast food. Maxine Hong Kingston sets a trickster figure at the heart of *Tripmaster Monkey*: alluding to Wu-Cheng-en's sixteenth-century Chinese folk novel *Hsi Yu Chi* (translated into English as *The Journey to the West*), Wittman Ah Sing calls himself "the present-day U.S.A. incarnation of the King of the Monkeys." Wu-Cheng-en's Monkey King, Sun Wu Kong, is a master of transformation, undergoing seventy-two of them in the course of his story, and Wittman seeks to revolutionize American literature by tapping into Sun Wu Kong's transformative powers, particularly those that arise from his ability to tell tales. The Native American writer Gerald Vizenor (Chippewa) draws attention to the parallels between the Native American and Chinese trickster traditions in his novel *Griever: An American Monkey King in China* (1987), whose protagonist, Griever de Hocus, a visiting professor at

Zhou Enlai University in Tianjin, is described as a "mixedblood tribal trickster, a close relative to the oldmind monkeys."[29] Elsewhere, Vizenor has argued that the trickster is a natural resource for both Native American tribal narratives and for postmodernism because he is the embodiment of deconstructive strategies—"chance and freedom in a comic sign"—and thus disrupts and resists institutionally sanctioned ways of reading.[30]

For Chicano writers, the most potent deployment of mythical belief has been the collective re-imagining of Aztlán, the Chicano homeland. In the Nahuatl language of ancient Mexico, "Aztlán" means "the lands to the north," and Chicanos use it today to refer to what is now the Southwestern United States. "The ancestors of the Aztecs named their homeland Aztlán," writes the novelist Rudolfo Anaya, "and legend placed it north of Mexico. Aztlán was the place of origin, the sipapu, the Eden of those tribes. There they came to a new relationship with their god of war, Huitzilopochtli, and he promised to lead them in their migration out of Aztlán."[31] That migration southward led to the establishment of the new Aztec nation of Tenochtitlán, which would eventually be conquered by Cortés in 1521. For all of its bloodthirstiness, the Spanish conquest of Mexico ironically resulted in a true melting pot, a nation less obsessed than its northern neighbor with ideas of blood purity, and thus most Mexicans and Chicanos are products of the fusion of both Native American and Spanish bloodlines and cultures.

It is no accident that the rebirth of interest in Aztlán occurred in tandem with the rise of the Chicano Movement during the 1960s, a time when, according to Anaya, the "absorption of the Chicano into the mainstream American culture was occurring so quickly that unless we re-established the covenants of our ancestors our culture was threatened with extinction."[32] Seeking Chicano origins in Aztlán was a way of emphasizing the Native American roots of Chicano identity and thus of de-emphasizing its roots in the Spanish conquistadors, the first invaders and occupiers of America and forerunners in that sense of the U.S. government. "The naming of Aztlán," writes Anaya, "was a spontaneous act which took place throughout the Southwest" and was codified at the Chicano Youth Conference held in Denver, Colorado, in March 1969. The document adopted at the conference—"El Plan Espiritual de Aztlána"—concluded with this declaration:

Brotherhood unites us and love for our brothers makes us a people whose time has come and who struggle against the foreigner "Gabacho," who exploits our riches and destroys our culture. With our hurt in our hands and our hands in the soil, We Declare the Independence of our Mestizo Nation. We are a Bronze People with a Bronze Culture. Before the world, before all of North America, before all our brothers in the Bronze Continent, We are a Nation, We are a Union of free pueblos, We are Aztlán.[33]

The modern invocation of the myth of Aztlán represents the conscious deployment of an ancient myth of origin for the purpose of political and cultural resistance. In 1972, the radical dramatist Luis Valdez co-edited an activist anthology of Mexican American literature entitled *Aztlán*; Anaya entitled his second novel *Heart of Aztlán* (1976) and pushed the mythopoetic techniques used in his prize-winning debut, *Bless Me, Ultima* (1972), even further: in *Heart of Aztlán*, myth becomes not just a way of interpreting the world but a way of revolutionizing it.

Emergent ethnic writers, however, often find themselves forced to do violence not only to the tradition of canonical American texts but also to the literary, mythological, and cultural traditions that have given them the opportunity to be "emergent" in the first place. Thus, for example, Frank Chin accuses Kingston of attacking Chinese civilization by rewriting some of its fairy tales and myths.[34] The novelist and critic Paula Gunn Allen (Laguna) accuses Leslie Marmon Silko (Laguna) of violating Native American religious and ethical traditions by transcribing and interpolating into her written texts stories that are meant to be spoken—and spoken only within a clan for specific purposes.[35]

Writers like Kingston and Silko, however, take a dynamic view of traditional myth, believing it to be not a static relic of the past but an ongoing process in the present. So Kingston declares, in a personal statement included in a volume of essays about her first book, *The Woman Warrior: Memoirs of a Girlhood Among Ghosts* (1976): "Sinologists have criticized me for not knowing myths and for distorting them; pirates correct my myths, revising them to make them conform to some traditional Chinese version. They don't understand that myths have to change, be useful or be forgotten. Like the people who carry them across oceans, the myths become American. The myths I write are new, American."[36] Silko provides a similar answer to critics like Allen, an answer embodied in the character of Betonie, the medicine man in *Ceremony*, who includes newspapers and telephone books among his implements of magic. Betonie says: "The people nowadays have an idea about the ceremonies. They think the ceremonies must be performed exactly as they have always been done. . . . They think that if a singer tampers with any part of the ritual, great harm can be done, great power unleashed." Yet, he continues, "At one time the ceremonies as they had been performed were enough for the way the world was then. But after the white people came, elements in this world began to shift; and it became necessary to create new ceremonies. I have made changes in the rituals. The people mistrust this greatly, but only this growth keeps the ceremonies strong."[37]

Drawing from both the center and the margins of American literary culture, however, does not guarantee that these writers will be able to appeal to either constituency. Mid-twentieth-century ethnic writers like Jade Snow Wong, Monica Sone, and José Antonio Villarreal solved the problem of audience by writing in a realist style addressed primarily toward a white readership—a solution that comes to seem less appealing as emergent literatures gain the self-confidence that comes with literary recognition. "I am really a megalomaniac," says Maxine Hong Kingston, "because I write for everybody living today and people in the future; that's my audience, for generations." Her audience, she claims, includes "everyone"—not only Chinese Americans, but also her "old English professors of the new criticism school in Berkeley," as well as "those who are not English majors and don't play literary games." Aware that her writing "deals with a culture that has not adequately been portrayed before," Kingston reveals that she consciously "work[s] on intelligibility and accessibility" when revising her manuscripts. Yet in an essay entitled "Cultural Mis-Readings by American Reviewers," written after the publication of *The Woman Warrior*, Kingston registers the artistic problems involved in bringing these different audiences together. Many of her reviewers, she laments, "praise[d] the wrong things": unfamiliar with many of the historical, cultural, and social contexts that inform *The Woman Warrior*, many reviewers "measur[ed] the book . . . against the stereotype of the exotic, inscrutable, mysterious oriental." To Kingston, such responses demonstrate the failure of her text: "the critics who said how the book was good because it was, or was not, like the oriental fantasy in their heads might as well have said how weak it was, since it in fact did not break through that fantasy."[38]

What must the emergent ethnic writer do to break through the stereotypical assumptions of Eurocentric readers? Kingston claims that the process of heightening "intelligibility and accessibility" does *not* include "slow[ing] down to give boring exposition, which is information that is available in encyclopedias, history books, sociology, anthropology, mythology." After all, she claims, "I am not writing history or sociology but a 'memoir' like Proust. . . . Some readers will have to do some background reading." Yet her second volume, *China Men* (1980), makes a greater attempt to educate her non-Chinese and non-Chinese American readers, because, as she told an interviewer, the reviews of *The Woman Warrior* "made it clear that people didn't know the history—or that they thought I didn't. While I was writing *China Men*, I just couldn't take that tension any more." In her second book, Kingston shifts the balance between myth and history: the mythical imagination of *The Woman Warrior* is tempered in *China Men* by the desire to heighten the historical texture of the narrative. Most telling of all is the decision to include a brief interchapter entitled "The Laws," in which she lists and comments wryly upon pieces of legislation that have affected Chinese Americans, beginning with the Burlingame Treaty of 1868. "The Laws" is not sociology, and it is not boring, but its inclusion does register Kingston's frustration with readers who have not done their background reading and who are content to read her texts from the vantage point of Orientalism. What "The Laws" is designed to demonstrate is that Kingston's characters cannot be safely exiled to the exotic realms of myth; they exist in history—in U.S. history—and they have been the victims of nationally sanctioned injustice.[39]

Kingston's dilemma is familiar to writers and critics of emergent writing, who often claim that their work has a special relation to history. One prominent Chicano critic contends, for example, that history is "the decisive determinant of the form and content of [Chicano] literature" and therefore "cannot be conceived as . . . mere 'background' or 'context'"; it is, instead, "the subtext that we must recover" if we wish to understand Chicano writing.[40] For many literary scholars, in the aftermath of Marxist criticism and the New Historicism, this description of the interconnection between history and literature applies not only to Chicano writing or even to emergent writing more generally, but rather to *all* writing: for the historicist critic, history is the subtext that we must recover if we wish to understand *any* literary text fully. Rather than possessing a special relationship to history, the emergent text simply reminds us forcefully of what is true of every text: that that texts are marked by the historical context—or, rather, by the multiple, intersecting historical contexts—from within which they arise.

It should come as no surprise that the claims made by minority discourse theorists about emergent fiction came to seem banal to historicists in the late 1990s, because emergent ethnic writing (and the criticism that it fostered) played a crucial role in the much-discussed "turn to history" that took place in American literary and cultural studies in the early 1980s. Scholars of ethnic writing have long recognized that the formalism that characterized New Criticism, structuralism, and deconstruction implicitly depends upon the existence of a particular Eurocentric interpretive community. The close reading skills taught at most American high schools and universities prove inadequate to the challenges posed by emergent literature; they do not, for example, help a reader to do more than scratch the surface of a text like N. Scott Momaday's *The Way to Rainy Mountain* (1969), which the Native American novelist and essayist Michael Dorris describes as "a classic of traditional Kiowa literature." Although the text is written in English, Dorris contends that "it cannot be understood without major reference to its tribal symbol system. It may misleadingly appear, like much oral literature when written down, simple and straightforward and the non-Kiowa reader who approaches the work in isolation will likely miss much of its depth and hence most of its beauty and significance."[41] In short, emergent ethnic writing teaches us about the inseparability of text and cultural context, and the contribution of minority discourse theory to late twentieth-century historicism is one of the ways in which Wittman Ah Sing has forced us to reread Walt Whitman, to recall that as a gay man writing about sexuality Whitman was—and, in this respect, still is—an emergent writer.[42]

Part of the project of emergent writing in the United States is to create what Dorris calls "self-history"—history written from within particular communities whose stories are either excluded or distorted by the "standard history" of the nation. American history, as commonly construed, is the history of a nation; self-history is the history of a particular people, a history that typically stretches much further back in time than the founding of the United States and often originates in territories that lie outside of its boundaries. Gay history, a field that came into being only after 1969, started out from the vantage point of self-history: as Paul Monette suggests, mainstream history has always been "written by straight boys who render us invisible, as if we were never there." One of the field's founding texts was a collection of primary documents entitled *Gay American History* (1976), edited by Jonathan Katz, whose qualifications for the undertaking were the result not of a doctorate in history but rather of years spent as a gay activist. The current task of gay history is to lift into visibility the homosexual elements of all cultures—ancient and modern—that have hitherto been hidden from view by standard history.[43]

Ethnic self-history, however, must distinguish itself not only from standard history, but also from the academic sub-discipline known as "ethnohistory," which often provides a wealth of information about ethnic communities but cannot substitute for ethnic self-history because it tends to represent an outsider's point of view. Ethnohistory is generally written from without: according to the anthropologist Harold Hickerson, ethnohistory "consists of the use of primary documents— library and archival materials—to gain knowledge of a given culture as it existed in the past, and how it has changed. . . . In its broadest sense, ethnohistory employs a number of research techniques to see in what way the present-day culture is similar or dissimilar to ancestral cultures; to what degree, in other words, the culture has changed, and what the distinctive historical factors were in determining such change."[44] It is a telling fact about the practice of ethnohistory that the discipline arose in the early 1950s as a result of Congress's passage of the Indian Claims Commission Act in 1946, which gave Native Americans the right to claim redress for losses of land incurred as the result of the U.S. government's violation of laws, treaties, or "standards of fair and honorable dealings." To carry out its mandate, the commission enlisted anthropologists to use historical sources in order to determine whether certain Native American tribes had occupied particular territories, whether they had received fair value for those lands upon removal, and whether those now claiming redress were their rightful descendants. The journal *Ethnohistory* was founded in 1954, primarily to serve scholars engaged in the study of relations between white and Native American cultures.[45]

For many emergent ethnic writers, both "American history" and ethnohistory are things that they learn in school; ethnic self-history is what they learn at home or in the streets of their neighborhoods. Paula Gunn Allen contrasts the education that she received in school (where she was "treated to bloody tales" of "savage Indians" killing "hapless priests and missionaries" and taught "that Indians were people who had benefited mightily from the advanced knowledge and superior morality of the Anglo-Europeans") with the understanding "derived" from her "daily experience of Indian life" and from the teachings of her "mother and the other Indian people who raised" her.[46] The narrator of Fae Myenne Ng's *Bone* (1993) reflects, "We know so little of the old country. We repeat the names of grandfathers and uncles, but they have always been strangers to us. Family exists only because somebody has a story, and knowing the story connects us to a history."[47] Ethnic self-history, in other words, is intimately connected to personal narrative, and as a result, autobiography and autobiographical fiction have played a formative role in U.S. emergent literatures.[48]

Some ethnic autobiographies, like Rodriguez's *Hunger of Memory*, Jade Snow Wong's *Fifth Chinese Daughter* (1945), or Monica Sone's *Nisei Daughter* (1953), devote themselves to charting a process of assimilation into the mainstream of American life. They adopt the individualistic perspective traditionally associated with the Western tradition of autobiography that dates back at least to Rousseau's *Confessions* (1782, and possibly to Augustine's from the fourth century CE), charting individual development as a process of conversion that leads to a sense of self-autonomy. They belong in a history of American emergent literatures because, despite their assimilative stances, they dramatize and document the damage inflicted upon minority cultures in the United States by the mainstream. In contrast, autobiographies like *The Woman Warrior*, Ernesto Galarza's *Barrio Boy* (1971), or *America Is in the Heart* (1946) by the Filipino immigrant Carlos Bulosan describe development in collective rather than individualistic terms; they set themselves against the grain of Western autobiography. Although Bulosan concludes his text with what seems to be a ringing affirmation of the American dream, expressing his "desire to know America, and to become a part of her great tradition, and to contribute something toward her final fulfillment," his conception of that "fulfillment" has little to do with the laissez-faire individualism typically associated with the American Dream. What Bulosan seeks is "the enlargement of the American Dream,"[49] and what his autobiography charts is the development of feelings of communal solidarity. Late in the autobiography, Bulosan recalls attending a meeting in Los Angeles with "several cannery workers: Japanese, Mexicans, Filipinos, and white Americans" and coming to the realization that "there was the same thing in each of them that possessed me: their common faith in the working man. . . . Then it came to me that we are all fighting against one enemy: Fascism. It was in every word and gesture, every thought."[50] Indeed, the image that brings about Bulosan's final reverie upon the promise of America is the sight of "Filipino pea pickers in the fields" stopping to wave as the bus that Bulosan is riding passes by.

The history of Native American autobiography sets these two forms in a developmental relation, while re-enacting the shift from ethnography to ethnic self-history. The first full-length autobiography published by a Native American, William Apess's *A Son of the Forest. The Experience of William Apes, a Native of the Forest* (1829), is quite literally a conversion narrative that concludes with Apess's receiving a license to preach.[51] George Copway, a Canadian Ojibwa who moved to the United States in 1846 after becoming a Methodist minister, mixes ethnography with conversion narrative in *The Life, History, and Travels of Ka-ge-ga-gah-bowh* (1847), which contains detailed, if slightly romanticized, accounts of Ojibwa tribal customs as well as the story of Copway's conversion to Christianity. Charles Eastman's two autobiographies, *Indian Boyhood* (1902) and *From the Deep Woods to Civilization* (1916), stress the formative influence not of the Santee Sioux customs according to which he was raised by his paternal grandmother and uncle, but rather the Christian humanism that he learned at U.S. universities.

Apess, Copway, and Eastman are exceptions rather than the rule for nineteenth- and early twentieth-century Native American autobiography. They write rather than speak their autobiographies. The bulk of nineteenth-century Native American personal narratives were transcriptions of oral accounts, and they were presented to the white reading public as specimens of ethnography. Prominent examples include J. B. Patterson's *Life of Black Hawk* (1833), S. M. Barrett's *Geronimo's Story of His Life* (1906), and perhaps the most famous of these accounts, *Black Elk Speaks, Being the Life Story of a Holy Man of the Oglala Sioux, as told through John G. Neihardt* (1932). Although scholars believe that Neihardt sought to capture the Lakota chief's narrative as faithfully as he could, he nevertheless took liberties with the oral account, including the addition of the text's famous opening and closing paragraphs. Instead of Neihardt serving as Black Elk's amanuensis, we have Black Elk serving as the vehicle for Neihardt's vision of Native America. In contrast to these personal narratives, in which both the individuality and the representativeness of the subject are effaced by the mediation of a white interpreter, late-twentieth-century autobiographical texts like N. Scott Momaday's *The Way to Rainy Mountain* (1969) and *The Names* (1976) and Leslie Marmon Silko's *Storyteller* (1981) begin with the individual voices of their authors, but quickly expand to incorporate the polyvocality of tribal traditions.

Autobiography and autobiographical fiction have also played a formative role in the emergence of gay and lesbian American literature. With the advent of the gay liberation movement in the aftermath of the Stonewall Rebellion came a new literary genre: the "coming-out" narrative. Anthologies of personal accounts like *The Lesbian Path* (1980) and *The Coming Out Stories* (1980) found an immediate audience within the gay community, while Audre Lorde's "biomythography," *Zami: A New Spelling of My Name* (1982), and Paul Monette's *Becoming a Man* (1992) gained national critical attention. The early 1980s saw the rise of what might be called the gay male *Bildungsroman*, whose central act was often a boy's coming out to his parents. Prominent examples of the genre include Edmund White's *A Boy's Own Story* (1980) and Robert Ferro's *The Family of Max Desir* (1983), as well as David Leavitt's *The Lost Language of Cranes* (1986), in which a son and father come out to one another. Like many ethnic autobiographies, coming-out narratives map the individual onto the collective: they tell individual and occasionally idiosyncratic stories that often turn on the realization that the narrator's experience is shared by a broad community of other individuals. The act of coming out is often performative rather than constitutive; that is, the act of coming out to one's family and friends is often the very act that signals and brings about the embracing of one's homosexual identity. Likewise, the emergence of the coming-out narrative as a major genre of writing has helped to bring about the existence of an openly gay American literature and to provide crucial encouragement to gay Americans still locked in their closets. The fact that literary coming-out narratives may have practical effects is made evident at the end of the anthology *Growing Up Gay/Growing Up Lesbian* (1994), which includes one appendix listing "books, magazines, and videos that may be of special interest to young adults" and a second appendix listing such "resources" as hotlines and support groups for gay youth. The collective nature of gay personal narrative and autobiographical fiction has only been strengthened with the advent of a second major genre, the AIDS narrative, which includes both non-fictional accounts such as Monette's *Borrowed Time* (1988), an account of the death of his lover, Roger Horwitz, and novels such as Ferro's *Second Son* (1988) and Monette's *Afterlife* (1990).

Perhaps because many Native American tribal cultures are matriarchal, matrilineal, and traditionally tolerant of homosexuality and transvestism, Native American feminist writers like Leslie Marmon Silko, Louise Erdrich, or Paula Gunn Allen have not been subjected to the kind of withering attacks that Asian American and Mexican American feminists and gay writers have received from their straight male counterparts. In the work of writers like Maxine Hong Kingston or the gay Chicano novelist John Rechy, the claims of ethnicity occasionally come into conflict with the claims of gender or sexuality. These writers are doubly marginalized: by mainstream U.S. culture on the basis of ethnicity, and by both mainstream U.S. culture and their own ethnic subcultures on the basis of gender or sexuality. The playwright and novelist Frank Chin has bitterly attacked Kingston for choosing the claims of feminism over the claims of ethnicity in *The Woman Warrior*. He accuses her of betraying her culture and of playing to Western stereotypes that undermine Chinese masculinity. Similarly, in an autobiographical collection of poems, essays, and stories entitled *Loving in the War Years* (1983), the lesbian Chicana feminist Cherríe Moraga takes aim at the misogyny that prevents a true sense of "Chicano community" from being achieved: "There is a deeper love between and amongst our people that lies buried between the lines of the roles we play with each other. . . . Family is *not* by definition the man in a dominant position over women and children. . . . The strength of our families never came from domination. It has only endured in spite of it—like our women." [52]

Misogyny, however, is not the only problem for writers like Moraga who are multiply marginalized. Women of color encounter discrimination from men of color on the basis of gender, and from other women on the basis of color. The groundbreaking anthology *This Bridge Called My Back: Writings by Radical Women of Color* (1983), which Moraga edited together with Gloria Anzaldúa, began as "a reaction to the racism of white feminists."[53] Dedicated to the task of demonstrating that "we are not alone in our struggles nor separate nor autonomous but that we—white black straight queer female male—are connected and interdependent," the anthology brings together prose and poetry by straight and gay African American, Asian American, Chicana, Latina, and Native American women. Moraga and Anzaldúa describe *This Bridge Called My Back* "as a revolutionary tool falling into the hands of people of all colors."[54] It is a text that demonstrates that the goal of setting emergent American literatures into a comparative framework— a framework that highlights similarity without losing sight of difference—is not just a scholarly imperative, but also a cultural necessity: it is the necessary precursor to the reconception of the idea of "America" that is the goal of emergent writers in the United States.

Anzaldúa has written what, in both formal and thematic terms, is arguably the most radical autobiography produced by a late-twentieth-century American emergent writer. *Borderlands/La Frontera: The New Mestiza* (1987) is a hybrid text written partly in prose and partly in poetry, partly in English and partly in Spanish, and it brings the issue of hybridity immediately to the fore. "I am a border woman," writes Anzaldúa in the book's preface: "I grew up between two cultures, the Mexican (with a heavy Indian influence) and the Anglo (as a member of a colonized people in our own territory). I have been straddling that *tejas*-Mexican border, and others, all my life. It's not a comfortable territory to live in, this place of contradictions. Hatred, anger and exploitation are the prominent features of this landscape." Motivated by her "preoccupations with the inner life of the Self, and with the struggle of that Self amidst adversity and violation," Anzaldúa's text demonstrates that for someone like her—the book's jacket describes her as "a Chicano *tejana* lesbian-feminist poet and fiction writer"—personal narrative is political narrative: to understand her personal identity she must unearth the mythic and historical foundations upon which it is built, and explore a complex cultural inheritance drawn from the civilizations of the Aztec, the Spaniard, and the Anglo. Hers is an identity wracked by the contradictions of race, ethnicity, gender, and sexuality, but—like Walt Whitman before her—she embraces these contradictions. Anzaldúa imagines the borderlands as a space where mainstream systems of classification break down: "To live in the Borderlands means you are neither *hispana india negra españa / ni gabacha, eres mestiza, mulata,* half-breed." *Borderlands/La Frontera* depicts the borderlands as a place of unspeakable violence, but also a place of incredible promise, a place that cannot be tamed by hegemonic culture, a place where new selves and kinds of selves can be born: "To survive the Borderlands / you must live *sin fronteras* / be a crossroads."[55]

For writers and critics of late-twentieth-century emergent U.S. literatures, the borderlands would become a powerful trope. What these literatures have in common is the desire to negotiate the borderlands between traditional cultures, to live without frontiers, to become a crossroads where Wittman Ah Sing (Chinese American *and* American playwright) can meet Walt Whitman (American bard *and* gay American) in order to collaborate in the making of what Whitman called "the greatest poem"—America itself.

2

Nineteenth-Century Roots

In N. Scott Momaday's *House Made of Dawn* (1968), the Native American protagonist, Abel, is brutally beaten without provocation by a Chicano policeman named Martinez. Richard Rubbio, the Chicano protagonist of José Antonio Villarreal's *Pocho* (1959), first learns about racism by observing the way his friends discriminate against a Japanese boy named Thomas. And midway through John Okada's *No-No Boy* (1946), a young Japanese American veteran named Kenji realizes that instead of finding ways to unite to achieve common goals, America's minority cultures continually find ways to discriminate against one another and even against their own members:

> the Negro who was always being mistaken for a white man becomes a white man and he becomes hated by the Negroes with whom he once hated on the same side. And the young Japanese hates the not-so-young Japanese who is more Japanese than himself, and the not-so-young, in turn, hates the old Japanese who is all Japanese and, therefore, even more Japanese than he.

Kenji tries to find a "pattern" that can be "studied" so that "answers" can be "deduced," but all he is able to conclude is that "the world was full of hatred."[1] What he does not manage to articulate is the fact that the disunity of America's marginalized cultures evident in these three novels is no accident. It is, instead, the result of a divide-and-conquer strategy of comparative racism, in which racial and ethnic groups are measured against not only the gold standard of Anglo-Saxon "whiteness" but also against one another, so that they can be assigned positions of relative inferiority. These positions shift over time depending on the threat that these groups are seen to pose to the mainstream. For example, from the mid- to the late nineteenth century, the Chinese were seen as a "degraded" race while the Japanese were held in relative esteem; by the end of World War II, these positions had been reversed. Comparative racism has been an abiding feature of popular discourse and (until relatively recently) of legislation in the United States, and nowhere more evident than in the late-nineteenth-century debates and acts surrounding the question of which non-white immigrants and resident aliens should be allowed to become citizens of the United States.

The writer Frank Chin's autobiographical essay, "Confessions of a Chinatown Cowboy" (1972), opens with a description of one of his cultural heroes, an old-timer named Ben Fee: "His hometown, Chinatown San Francisco, has forgotten the name of Ben Fee and the man he was, for its own good. In New York he's what he was in Frisco, but more so, a word-of-mouth legend, a bare-knuckled unmasked man, a Chinaman loner out of the old West, a character out of Chinese swordslingers, a fighter. The kind of Chinaman we've been taught to ignore and forget if we don't want America to drive Chinatown out of town" [2] Eager to assimilate into mainstream U.S. culture, Chinese Americans, according to Chin, traded in heroism for humility. They have forgotten the role that their ancestors played in the heroic settling of the American West. Vilified from the late nineteenth century until World War II as unassimilable aliens, Chinese Americans would be cast in the role of the "model minority" after the war, in contradistinction to those minorities—particularly African Americans and Chicanos—who were growing increasingly militant in their calls for social equality. According to literary scholar Elaine Kim, Asian Americans were portrayed by the white mainstream during the 1960s as "restrained, humble, and well-mannered, a people who respect law, love education, work hard, and have close-knit, well-disciplined families." [3] For Chin, the price for this acceptance was exorbitant: it meant the feminization of Chinese American men, who are depicted by mainstream

U.S. culture as obedient, passive, and effeminate. "We are the Uncle Toms of the nonwhite peoples of America," writes Chin, "the despicable Shortys, a race of yellow white supremacists, yellow white racists. We're hated by the blacks because the whites love us for being everything the blacks are not. Blacks are a problem: badass. Chinese are not a problem: kissass."[4]

Chin's writing is all about transforming yourself from a kissass into a badass. His general strategy is twofold. First, Chin achieves a style that is often violent and jarring by drawing on the models provided by the Black Power movement of the 1960s. Describing Chin's first two plays and his collection of short stories, Sau-ling Cynthia Wong writes that Chin's "verbal pyrotechnics impressed even as its hybridity baffled mainstream critics and outraged some Chinese readers."[5] Second, Chin—like the natives manipulating the Westerner's Bible in Homi Bhabha's famous essay "Signs Taken for Wonders" (1994)—takes the dominant tradition of U.S. liberal individualism and shifts its meaning.[6] In describing himself as a "Chinatown Cowboy" and using archetypes of rugged individualism drawn from the literature of the American West, Chin not only reasserts the vitality of Chinese American masculinity, but also roots that masculinity deep within a cherished archetype from U.S. cultural mythology. By focusing on the image of the Chinese worker building the railroad and opening up the American West, Chin argues that Asian American masculinity has been a crucial aspect of U.S. history all along.

Chin has devoted his writing to refuting the idea that Asian Americans are necessarily the victims of an "identity crisis" in which they are forced to choose between two opposed and incompatible identities—the Asian and the American. Chin's stories and plays depict a Chinatown that is dying because it provides no models of "manhood" for its younger generation. Chin's dramas of beseiged Asian American manhood look back to a more heroic era in which Chinese men were men. Asserting that the cultural mythologies of China, with its "swordslingers," and the United States, with its gunslinging loners, are fundamentally alike, Chin claims a place for Asian American men within the archetype of the American rugged individualist. In denying the opposition between American and Asian forms of masculinity, Chin moves away from the choice implicit in the idea of an "identity crisis" toward a conception of cultural hybridity in which the Asian and the American fuse into a seamless whole.

The problem, however, is that this account of identity is still a drastic oversimplification. For Chin, the only identities that matter are the "American" and the "Asian," and he vilifies those Asian Americans who try to assert the primacy of other categories such as gender or sexuality. Chin's aim is not to reconceptualize American identity but simply to reconfigure it, to enable it to accommodate his vision of Asian masculinity. Not only has Chin accepted the general premise of binary thinking, but he has also accepted some of the particular premises of the opposition he is seeking to refute, namely its misogyny and homophobia.

I invoke Frank Chin's writing here to serve as an emblem of the fact that the roots of many of the problems and strategies that mark U.S. emergent literatures from the 1960s on lie in nineteenth-century U.S. cultural dynamics. The task of showing what nineteenth-century U.S. history looked like to those pushed to the margins of U.S. culture was central to the project of late-twentieth-century U.S. emergent writing. For example, in describing his "first impulse" in writing the young-adult novel *Morning Girl* (1992), which portrays the lost Taino tribe, Michael Dorris argues that "if we concede the explication of our past, on any level, to those who have no investment in its accurate and sympathetic portrayal, we are giving up much more than the exploration of roots. We are abandoning the future to which we are uniquely entitled."[7] The project of creating the emergent, which by definition is all about the future, turns out also to be very much about the past.

The Origins of "Homosexuality"

Ironically, the image that Chin chooses as a counterweight to the portrayal of Asian American men as "effeminate closet queens like Charlie Chan" or "homosexual menaces like Fu Manchu" may not be as free from associations with same-sex desire as he thinks. In his study *Queer Cowboys* (2005), Chris Packard argues that the association of the cowboy with a certain kind of "ruggedness"—"unrestricted freedom, crafty self-reliance, familiarity with wilderness and horses, good with guns"— is primarily the effect of Hollywood's recreation of the archetype. "If you

look a little closer" at the image of the cowboy, Packard writes, "you'll
see another figure, the cowboy's sidekick—his partner and loyal friend,"
and in nineteenth-century representations of the cowboy, the relationship between partners is frequently marked by erotic affection: "Before
1900, that is to say before the modern invention of the 'homosexual'
as a social pariah, cowboy narratives represented male-male affection
quite a bit more freely than Westerns produced after 1900, when male-
male sex was classified as abnormal."[8] Packard cites Badger C. Clark's
cowboy poem "The Lost Pardner" (1915) as an example of this kind of
male-male affection:

> We loved each other in the way men do
>   And never spoke about it, Al and me,
> But we both *knowed,* and knowin' it so true
> Was more than any woman's kiss could be.
>
> . . . .
>
> The range is empty and the trails are blind,
>   And I don't seem but half myself today.
> I wait to hear him ridin' up behind
>   And feel his knee rub mine the good old way.
> He's dead—and what that means no man kin tell.
>   Some call it "gone before."
> Where? I don't know, but God! I know so well
>   That he ain't here no more!

The poem tries to capture an unspoken aspect of the relationship
between the narrator and his partner, Al, something that was "more
than any woman's kiss could be," yet captured in the feel of knees rub-
bing together.[9]

The term "homosexuality" first appeared in 1869 in a pamphlet entitled "An Open Letter to the Prussian Minister of Justice" by the Aus-
trian-born Hungarian journalist Karl Maria Benkert. Writing under
the pseudonym "Karl Maria Kertbeny," Benkert urged that sodomy be
decriminalized in the penal code that was about to come into force in
the North German Confederation and, two years later, in a unified German state, the so-called Second Reich. Although what we would today
call "homosexuality" existed in the ancient Greek world, classical Greek

has no word for "homosexual." Ancient Greek culture understood sexuality as a matter of preference rather than orientation, liable to change from occasion to occasion—at least as far as men were concerned. Describing the sexual practices of ancient Greece in *The Use of Pleasure* (1984), Michel Foucault argued that "the notion of homosexuality is plainly inadequate as a means of referring to an experience, forms of valuation, and a system of categorization so different from ours. The Greeks did not see love for one's own sex and love for the other sex as opposites, as two exclusive choices, two radically different types of behavior."[10]

The idea of "homosexuality" is also inadequate to describe the sexual practices of many Native American cultures whose languages contain words that express sexual categories for which there are no equivalents in European cultures. The term *berdache* has been used by anthropologists to describe morphological males who do not play the traditional male roles within their tribes. In his study of sexual diversity in Native American culture, the anthropologist Walter L. Williams writes that a berdache has

> a clearly recognized and accepted social status, often based on a secure place in the tribal mythology. Berdaches have special ceremonial roles in many Native American religions, and important economic roles in their families. They will do at least some women's work, and mix together much of the behavior, dress, and social roles of women and men. Berdaches gain social prestige by their spiritual, intellectual, or artistic contributions, and by their reputation for hard work and generosity. They serve a mediating function between women and men, precisely because their character is seen as distinct from either sex. They are not seen as men, yet they are not seen as women either. They occupy an alternative gender role that is a mixture of diverse elements.

Williams concludes that "berdachism is a way for society to recognize and assimilate some atypical individuals without imposing a change on them or stigmatizing them as deviant."[11]

In contrast, the history of the term "homosexual" indicates that it was used precisely to stigmatize some people as deviant and to attempt to impose change on them. The course of Western scientific research into the nature of homosexuality was profoundly influenced by Richard von Krafft-Ebing's treatise *Psychopathia Sexualis* (1886), which depicted homosexuality as a pathological condition. Krafft-Ebing devoted a hundred pages in the first edition of the treatise to a discussion of "antipathic sexual instinct"; he would adopt Kertbeny's term *homosexualität* in subsequent editions. Rejecting the contention that homosexuality was in any way "natural," he argued that the only "natural" sexuality was procreative, heterosexual sexuality. A prominent dissenter from Krafft-Ebing's position was Sigmund Freud, who wrote in his "Letter to an American Mother" (1935) that "homosexuality assuredly offers no advantage[,] but it is nothing to be ashamed of, no vice, no degradation, it cannot be classified as an illness; we consider it to be a variation of the sexual function produced by a certain arrest in development. Many highly respectable individuals of ancient and modern times have been homosexuals, several of the greatest men among them (Plato, Michelangelo, Leonardo da Vinci, etc.)."[12] Freud never formulated a coherent, fully developed theory of homosexuality, and the fact that the homosexuals who came to him for treatment were suffering from mental illness led many of his followers to ignore his belief that "homosexual persons are not sick," a statement written in 1903 in a letter to the Viennese newspaper *Die Zeit*.

One such follower was the immigrant novelist and literary critic Ludwig Lewisohn (1882–1955), who was a champion of Freudian approaches to literature. In his memoir, *Up Stream: An American Chronicle* (1922), Lewisohn described his assimilation into U.S. culture, which he criticized for its "Neo Puritan barbarism."[13] In his critical work, Lewisohn sought to reinterpret the U.S. literary tradition through a Freudian lens, which led him to describe "the whole of our modern literature" as "a single act of rebellion" against Puritan doctrines.[14] A Jewish American scholar, Lewisohn argued strenuously for the transformative impact that immigrants should and would have on U.S. culture, declaring in *Up Stream* that "the notion of liberty on which the Republic was founded, the spirit of America that animated Emerson and Whitman, is vividly alive to-day only in the unassimilated foreigner, in that pathetic pilgrim to a forgotten shrine."[15] And yet, in formulating his canon of great American literature seven years later in *Expression in America* (1929), Lewisohn saw fit to exclude Whitman's poetry, which he described as "enervating . . . and unendurable," primarily on account of what he took to be its author's immorality:

> I, at least, range myself morally—if not aesthetically and philosophi-
> cally—with those who out of a sound and necessary instinct, the instinct
> after all of life and its continuance, rejected the barren homosexual and
> his new-fangled manner of neither speech nor song. [16]

For Lewisohn, rebellion against Puritanism had its limits, and these were marked by homosexual practice. Lewisohn's objections antici-pated the cultural situation of the late twentieth century, in which U.S. culture largely accepted the tenets of multiculturalism except when it came to gay culture.

Occupied America

The first U.S. Naturalization Act (1790) enabled "free white persons" who had been in the United States for as little as two years to be nat-uralized in any U.S. court.[17] Immigrant blacks—and later immigrant Asians—were not intended to be naturalized, and the act made no citi-zenship provisions for non-whites who were born in the United States. Whether or not a free black could be a citizen depended upon the state in which he or she was living, until the ratification of the Fourteenth Amendment in 1868 established uniform national citizenship.

Mexican Americans, however, had already learned that mere citizen-ship did not guarantee the protection of rights for those who are non-whites. As a result of the Treaty of Guadalupe Hidalgo, which ended the Mexican-American War in 1848, Mexico ceded all of its territories north of the Rio Grande to the United States—territories that spanned the present-day states of Arizona, California, Nevada, New Mexico, Utah, and half of Colorado. Although approximately 2,000 of the area's Spanish-speaking residents chose to relocate to Mexico, more than 80,000 remained on their lands and automatically became American citizens, though they were allowed to maintain their language and cul-tural traditions. Article IX of the treaty guaranteed Mexicans remain-ing in the Southwest "the enjoyment of all the rights of citizens of the United States according to the principles of the Constitution; and in the meantime shall be maintained and protected the free enjoyment of their liberty and property, and secured in the free exercise of their religion."[18] Commenting on the signing of the treaty, the Mexican diplomat Manuel Crescion Rejón gloomily predicted that "our race, our unfortunate people will have to wander in search of hospitality in a strange land, only to be ejected later. Descendants of the Indians that we are[,] the North Americans hate us, their spokesmen depreciate us, even if they recognize the justice of our cause, and they consider us unworthy to form with them one nation and one society."[19]

The Mexicans who stayed to become American citizens were treated as second-class citizens: they constituted an ethnic minority within American national culture, and they were soon victimized by unscrupulous white Americans. "A pre-Civil War type of carpetbagger moved into the territory to make his fortune," writes the Chicano fiction writer and scholar Américo Paredes, "preying upon the newly created Americans of Mexican descent. The Mexican's cattle were killed or stolen. The Mexican was forced to sell his land; and if he did not, his widow usually did after her husband was 'executed' for alleged cattle rustling. Thus did the great Texas ranches and the American cattle industry begin."[20] Naturalized Mexicans in California also found themselves treated as second-class citizens. Though they outnumbered Anglos in the territory at first, the discovery of gold near John Sutter's mill led to a massive influx of migrants to California. In 1849, the Mexican population of California was 13,000, while the Anglo population had ballooned to 100,000. As a result, Anglos were able to control the state legislature and enacted discriminatory laws aimed at Mexicans. An anti-vagrancy act popularly referred to as the "Greaser Act" defined as "vagrants" all persons "commonly known as 'Greasers' or the issue of Spanish or Indian blood . . . and who [were] armed and not peaceable and quiet persons"; a foreign miner's license tax of twenty dollars per month was in effect a tax on miners perceived to be Mexicans, since the bulk of the fees collected were taken from Spanish-speaking miners, including those who were in fact U.S.-born citizens of Mexican extraction.[21]

The roots of twentieth-century Chicano literature lie in the tradition of resistance that originated during this period as a response to what Mexican Americans still consider to be the "occupation" of America by the U.S. government. The period that began with the Texas uprising and closed with the Mexican Revolution of 1910 was the heyday of the Mexican American *corrido*, a form of folk song that came to dominate the popular culture of the Southwest. The *corrido* is a narrative ballad, usually anonymously composed, and sung or spoken to musical accompaniment. Related to ballad forms such as the *copla*, the *décima*, and the *romance*, which had been brought by the Spanish to Mexico, the *corrido* flourished during the hundred years that followed the Texas uprising, particularly in the border region south of Texas where relations between Mexican and Anglo-Americans were particularly troubled. In contrast to earlier ballad forms, which generally dealt with incidents from daily life, the *corrido* emphasizes drama and conflict, particularly the resistance of an individual to forces of oppression.

True to its name, which is derived from the verb *correr*, "to run," the *corrido* generally offers a swiftly paced story, most often told in stanzas of four eight-syllable lines. In his groundbreaking study of the *corrido*, *"With His Pistol in His Hand": A Border Ballad and Its Hero* (1958), Américo Paredes argues that the "balladry of the Lower Border [was] working toward a single type: toward one form, the *corrido*, toward one theme, border conflict; toward one concept of the hero, the man fighting for his right with his pistol in his hand."[22] Paredes's study, which is often cited by the first generation of Chicano writers as a major influence, focuses on the most famous of these ballads, "El corrido de Gregorio Cortéz," which attacks the racism and lawlessness of Anglo-Americans by recounting the story of a Mexican American cowboy—a *vaquero*—who avenges his brother's murder at the hands of an Anglo sheriff. These verses demonstrate the way in which this representative *corrido* contrasts the intelligence and courage of the *vaquero* with the stupidity and cowardice of the Anglo cowboy:

> In the ranch corral
> they managed to surround him.
> A little more than 300 men
> and there he gave them the slip.
> There around Encinal
> from all that they say
> They had a shoot-out
> and he killed another sheriff.

Gregorio Cortéz said,
with his pistol in his hand,
"Don't run, you cowardly Rangers
from one lone Mexican."
He turned toward Laredo
without a single fear,
"Follow me, you cowardly Rangers,
I am Gregorio Cortéz."[23]

Taken together, the various variants of the Cortéz *corrido* have been described by the critic Raymund Paredes as "a kind of Mexican American epic that pulls together the basic themes of contemporary Mexican American writing: ethnic pride, a forceful rejection of unflattering Anglo stereotypes, and, through celebration of Cortéz's marvelous *vaquero* skills, an affirmation of the Mexican American's rootedness in the Southwest."[24]

In 1876 Porfirio Díaz engineered a coup and became president of Mexico. In order to help finance the industrialization of agriculture, mining, and transportation, the Díaz government encouraged investment by North Americans, who were benefiting from the expansion of the U.S. economy during the decades after the Civil War. Industrialization and in particular the building of 15,000 miles of railroad track between 1880 and 1910 transformed the Mexican economy, bringing about the decline of the communal village and forcing many peasants to become migrant workers; increasingly these workers—called *braceros*—traveled across the border to work in the United States. These *braceros* often competed with freed slaves for work, and like the Chinese, they were identified by white Americans as equivalent to blacks and treated in a similarly discriminatory fashion. In addition, they shared with Chinese sojourners the sense that they were merely transient residents of the United States: according to Américo Paredes, "the Mexican immigrant's sense of continuing to 'pass through' after twenty years or more of residence in the United States contributed to his problems, since he remained a perennial visitor in a foreign country, without children born in the Uiteed States in his own way of thinking."[25] The sufferings of the *bracero* were also captured in the stanzas of the *corrido*, which began to bear titles like "Los Deportados" ("The Deported

Ones"), "La Discriminación," "Los Enganchados" ("The Work Gang"), and "Tristes Quejas de Un Bracero" ("A Bracero's Complaint").

The outbreak of the Revolution of 1910 produced what Paredes calls "the Greater Mexican heroic *corrido*," but the theme of border conflict continued to dominate Mexican American balladry. What the Mexican Revolution did produce was a massive influx of new *braceros* who would fill the need for cheap foreign labor created after the Chinese Exclusion Acts of 1882, 1892, and 1902 and the U.S. government's "Gentleman's Agreement" with Japan in 1907—all of which combined to curtail the flow of working-class Asians into the Western states.

It is thought that as many as 100,000 Mexican immigrants entered the United States during the years surrounding the Mexican Revolution; with the outbreak of World War I in 1914, a second wave of immigration began that would bring over one million Mexican immigrants to the United States by the end of the 1920s.

> I'm going to tell you, gentleman,
> all about my sufferings.
> Since I left my country,
> to come to this nation.
> It must have been about ten at night,
> the train began to whistle.
> I heard my mother say,
> "There comes that ungrateful train
> that is going to take my son."
> "Good-bye to my beloved mother.
> Give me your blessings.
> I am going abroad,
> where there is no revolution."[26]

These lines from the *corrido* "El Deportado" ("The Deportee"), recorded by Los Hermanos Buñuelos in 1929, are typical of the shift that occurred in the border ballad during this period of immigration. Throughout this period, as its subject shifted from the *vaquero* to the *bracero*, the *corrido* remained the primary cultural form through which the suffering of Mexicans in United States found expression. "El Deportado" concludes with these verses addressed to the people of Mexico:

Oh my beloved countrymen
I suffered a lot.
The light skinned men are very wicked.
They take advantage of the occasion.
And all the Mexicans
are treated without compassion.
There comes a large cloud of dust,
with no consideration.
Women, children and old ones
are being driven to the Border.
We are being kicked out of this country.
Good-bye beloved countrymen,
we are being deported.
But we are not bandits,
we came to work.
I will wait for you in my homeland,
there is no more revolution.
Let's leave my dear friends,
we will be welcomed
by our beautiful nation.

Taken together, what "El corrido de Gregorio Cortéz" and "El Deportado" demonstrate is that the abiding theme of the Mexican American *corrido* is the racial oppression suffered at the hands of Anglo-Americans who sought to deny Mexican American citizens their rights and to exploit poor Mexicans seeking to better their fortunes in the United States.

Detribalization

In 1871 the federal government passed the first in a series of laws designed to assimilate Native Americans by weaning them from their tribal orientation, a process that would lead to the conferral of citizenship rights by the Dawes Act sixteen years later. What Congress did in 1871 was to endorse a policy that treated Native Americans as individuals and wards of the government, and ceased to recognize the legal standing of tribes. The weaning process continued in 1883 when the judicial powers of chiefs were dissolved and transferred to a system of federal courts. Finally, in 1887, the Dawes Act, which Theodore Roosevelt described as "a mighty pulverizing engine to break up the tribal mass," formally dissolved tribes as legal bodies and redistributed tribal lands among families and unmarried individuals.[27] Heads of families were allotted 160 acres, individuals eighty acres, with the stipulation that the lands were to be held in trust for twenty-five years without taxation, so that the Native Americans could learn to profit from the land and to assume the responsibilities that land-holding entailed, including the payment of taxes. Once the twenty-five years had elapsed, the Native Americans would become full owners of their allotments, free to sell or lease them, or—if they could not pay their taxes—to lose them.

The Dawes Act was passed in response to the efforts of reformers like Helen Hunt Jackson, whose 1881 tract, *A Century of Dishonor*, and 1884 novel, *Ramona*, had publicized the unjust treatment of Native Americans. Most reformers had decided by 1887 that the only alternative to assimilation for the Native American was extermination. The Dawes Act was intended to speed that process of assimilation by bringing to an end the Native tribal system, with its economy based on hunting and gathering, and introducing Native Americans to an individualistic conception of social life and a capitalistic understanding of land use and agriculture. Addressing the Lake Mohonk Conference of the Friends of the Indians in 1886, the president of Amherst College, Merrill E. Gates, argued that "to bring him out of savagery into citizenship we must make the Indian more intelligently selfish before we can make him unselfishly intelligent. We need to awaken in him wants. . . . Discontent with the teepee and the starving rations of the Indian camp in winter is needed to get the Indian out of the blanket and into trousers—and trousers with a pocket in them, and with a pocket that aches to be filled with dollars."[28] During the debate over the Dawes Act, Texas senator Samuel Bell Maxey objected to the bill's provision for Native American citizenship: "Look at your Chinamen, are they not specifically excepted from the naturalization laws?" Maxey hoped that the treatment of Chinese immigrants might serve as a precedent for reining in the rights of Native Americans. The provision stood, however, because natives—unlike the Chinese—were considered capable of eventual assimilation.

According to the historian Frederick Hoxie, the Dawes Act was "made possible by the belief that Indians did not have the 'deficiencies' of other groups [such as the Chinese]: they were fewer in number, the beneficiaries of a public sympathy and pity, and [were considered] capable of advancement."[29] In other words, like African Americans, Natives were considered re-educable. Being capable of advancement means being capable of learning the lessons of individualism and laissez-faire capitalism necessary for assimilation into mainstream U.S. culture.

The ultimately devastating effect of the Dawes Act upon Native American tribal culture is dramatized in Louise Erdrich's novel *Tracks* (1988), the third novel in the tetralogy that includes *Love Medicine* (1984), *The Beet Queen* (1987), and *The Bingo Palace* (1994). *Tracks* is a "historical novel" in the conventional sense of the term: the dated chapters carefully establish the time of the novel as the years 1912–1924 and the events of the novel correspond to documented historical occurrences: the outbreaks of tuberculosis that afflicted North Dakota from 1891 to 1901 and the battles over Native American land rights that erupted after the implementation of the Dawes Severalty Act. Unlike Kingston, Erdrich never names the pieces of legislation that set in motion the events of the novel. In *China Men*, Kingston discusses legislation explicitly in order to get across the idea that standard national history and ethnic self-history tell very different stories, and the book throws its weight behind ethnic self-history, by relegating its overtly historical material to a single interchapter. *Tracks* emphasizes ethnic self-history even further by suppressing standard national history, including it only by implication.

Like many novels written by Native American writers, *Tracks* dramatizes the collision of two different ways of understanding the nature of history and time. The dating of its chapter by season and year juxtaposes the Western linear sense of time that assigns sequential numbers to each year with the cyclical conception of time identified with the changes of season and stressed in many Native American cultures. In addition, the time period covered in each chapter is also described by its specific Native American name. Thus, the first chapter is called "Winter 1912: *Manitou-geezisohns*: Little Spirit Sun." The opening paragraph also dramatizes the collision of these two conceptions of time and history:

We started dying before the snow, and like the snow, we continued to fall. It was surprising there were so many of us left to die. For those who survived the spotted sickness from the south, our long fight west to Nadouissioux land where we signed the treaty, and then a wind from the east, bringing exile in a storm of government papers, what descended form the north in 1912 seemed impossible.[30]

Erdrich's narrator, Nanapush, links each of the events he describes to traditional Native American creation myths, which stress the role played by the four directions, a link that proves ironic because what he is describing is the destruction of his tribe. The paragraph's description of written materials such as "the treaty'" and the "storm of government papers" points to another distinction between native and Western modes of historiography: Native self-history is transmitted orally through storytelling, while Western history is transmitted through written accounts. Moreover, Western history is to a large extent a history of the written word and of the ways in which writing has been used to effect cultural change. *Tracks* dramatizes the defeat of the native culture of storytelling by a Western culture of documents. Native historiography must give way to Western historiography, a pattern embodied by the use of the date "1912" at the end of the novel's first paragraph to puncture the sense of mythical time with which the paragraph begins. Erdrich shares this understanding of the difference between Native American culture and U.S. culture with a great many other Native American authors. For example, Paula Gunn Allen argues that "there is some sort of connection between colonization and chronological time. There is a connection between factories and clocks, and there is a connection between colonial imperialism and factories. There is also a connection between telling Indian tales in chronological sequences and the American tendency to fit Indians into the slots they have prepared for us." And she notes that she had difficulty with publishers because she "chose Indian time over industrial time as a structuring device" in *The Woman Who Owned the Shadows* (1983), her first novel.[31]

It is no accident that *Tracks* begins in 1912, twenty-five years after the Dawes Act, for though the novel does not mention the act by name, its plot revolves around the struggles of the Turtle Mountain Chippewa to maintain a sense of tribal identity and to keep their allotments from falling into the hands of timber companies. *Tracks* focuses particularly on the plight of Nanapush's adopted daughter, Fleur Pillager, whose choice allotment on the banks of Lake Matchimanito is ultimately lost, in part through the connivance of "government Indians" like Bernadette Morissey who are eager to assimilate and to profit from the misfortunes of fellow tribe-members. Intended to bolster Native American land ownership, the Dawes Act ended up sabotaging it, inadvertently opening up areas previously reserved for Native Americans to white settlement. Many Native Americans, like Fleur Pillager, lost their allotments because they could not pay their taxes; others lost their allotments after pledging them as security for loans to buy goods, while others were conned into selling their allotments well below fair market value. The U.S. government abetted the erosion of Native American ownership with the 1906 Burke Act, which shortened the twenty-five-year trust period for Native Americans deemed "competent," enabling them to sell (or lose) their lands that much more quickly, and in 1917 the ironically named Commissioner of Indian Affairs, Cato Sells, issued a "Declaration of Policy" stipulating that all Native Americans with more than one-half white blood would be automatically defined as competent, given U.S. citizenship, and required to pay taxes on their allotments. Linda Hogan's first novel, *Mean Spirit* (1990), dramatizes the aftermath of the Dawes Act in Oklahoma, where white oilmen, acting in tandem with government agents, cheat and if necessary murder Native Americans whose allotments happen to have become valuable due to the discovery of oil. "They had ideas about the Indians," Hogan writes about the government clerks distributing land royalty checks, "that they were unschooled, ignorant people who knew nothing about life or money." The U.S. government has imposed the lessons of individualism and capitalism upon Native culture, but whites resent it when the Native Americans are not only willing but able to implement those lessons: "In the background, a surly clerk in a white shirt piped up and said to another one, out loud, 'Hell, some of them buy three cars. We don't have that kind of money, and we're Americans.'" Hogan uses moments of magical realism to embody the wonder and power of Native culture, but these moments are no match for the realism that embodies the hypocrisy of white culture, whose mean spirit reduces the culture and life of Native America—quite literally—to "nothing more than a distant burning."[32]

It is estimated that between 1887 and 1934, when the Wheeler-How-ard Indian Reorganization Act ended the policy of allotment and once again recognized tribal ownership of lands, more than 60 percent of tribal lands were lost to railroads, cattlemen, timber companies, and land corporations: before 1887, 139 million acres were held in trust for Native Americans in the form of reservations; by 1934 only 48 million acres of land were still under Native control, and many Natives were left landless.[33]

Gold Mountain

When gold was discovered at Sutter's Mill in 1849, white Easterners and European immigrants began to flock to California, but they weren't the only ones: 325 Chinese migrants arrived in California that year to par-ticipate in the Gold Rush, followed the next year by 450 of their com-patriots. Starting in 1851, however, the number of Chinese emigrating to California began to rise dramatically, with more than 2,500 arriving that year and more than 20,000 arriving in 1852, bringing the total of Chinese immigrants to about 25,000. By 1870 there were approximately 63,000 Chinese in the United States, the majority of them (77 percent) living in California. By 1890, three years after the Dawes Act, there were 107,488 "Chinese" living in the United States.[34] (In the U.S. Census, "Chinese" was a racial definition that included both immigrants from China and their descendants.)

The Chinese men who first emigrated to the United States in the mid-nineteenth century were known as *gam saan haak*, "travelers to the Gold Mountain," and they thought of themselves as "sojourners." Initially, these Chinese men were welcomed as visitors who could assist in fostering California's economic growth; mid-nineteenth-century accounts referred to these Chinese migrants as "Celestials" (since China was often called the "Celestial Empire"). California's leading newspaper, the San Francisco *Daily Alta California*, wrote in 1852 that "quite a large number of the Celestials have arrived among us of late. . . . Scarcely a ship arrives that does not bring an increase to this worthy integer of our population. The China boys will yet vote at the polls, study in the same schools and bow at the same altar of our own countrymen." The gover-nor of California, John McDougal, told the legislature at the beginning of 1852 that the Chinese constituted "one of the most worthy classes of our newly adopted citizens—to whom the climate and the character of these lands are peculiarly suited"—apparently failing to remember that Chinese were prohibited from becoming American citizens by the 1790 Naturalization Act, which restricted the privilege of naturalization to "white" immigrants. Throughout the 1850s, California's popular press contained numerous articles presenting favorable portraits of Chinese immigrants.[35]

These views, however, were not shared by white workers with whom the Chinese were competing for jobs. As early as the spring of 1852, there was considerable anti-Chinese sentiment among white miners, and their agitation led to the passage of a new foreign miners' license tax, which appeared to apply to all immigrant miners but was in reality aimed specifically at the Chinese. It stipulated that a monthly tax of three dollars was to be paid by any miner who did not intend to become an American citizen; Chinese were prohibited from having this intent. "In California," wrote Mark Twain in *Roughing It* (1872), a Chinese man "gets a living out of old mining claims that white men have abandoned as exhausted and worthless—and then the officers come down on him once a month with an exorbitant swindle to which the legislature has given the broad, general name of 'foreign' mining tax, but is usually inflicted on no foreigners but Chinamen."[36] This miner's tax remained in place until it was theoretically abolished by the Civil Rights Act of 1870.

In "The Grandfather of the Sierra Nevada Mountains," from *China Men* (1980), Maxine Hong Kingston imagines the sojourner's life that her grandfather Ah Goong led while working for the Central Pacific. It was one of Ah Goong's "peculiarities," Kingston writes, "that he heard the crackles, bangs, gunshots that go off when the world lurches; the gears on its axis Snap. Listening to a faraway New Year, he had followed the noise and came upon the blasting in the Sierras. . . . The Central Pacific hired him on sight; chinamen had a natural talent for explosions." Chinese migrants had begun to work in greater and greater numbers for the Central Pacific Railroad when profits from mining started to decrease in the early 1860s. By 1867, there were 12,000 Chinese working for the line (representing 90 percent of its entire work force).[37]

Kingston's story depicts Ah Goong's experiences during the strike of 1867, which took place after the railroad proposed to raise wages four dollars per month (to thirty-five) while requiring Chinese workers to work ten-hour shifts. Five thousand Chinese workers walked out, demanding wages of forty-five dollars (a raise of fourteen dollars) and a work-day equal in length to that of white workers: "Eight hours a day good for white man, all the same good for Chinamen" was their slogan. Because the white workers did not join the strike and because the railroad managed to cut off the strikers' food supply, the matter was settled in nine days, and the final compromise was a four-dollar raise and the same eight-hour shift. "The China Men went back to work quietly," writes Kingston. "No use singing and shouting over a compromise and losing nine days' work." What was a cause for celebration was the completion of the railroad in 1869; Kingston describes the scene at Promontory Point when the two tracks were connected at last: "A white demon in top hat tap-tapped on the gold spike, and pulled it back out. Then one China Man held the real spike, the steel one, and another hammered it in."[38] Contemporary commentators noted the contribution made to the project by the Chinese: "The dream of Thomas Jefferson, and the desires of Thomas Hart Benton's heart," wrote one magazine writer in an essay called "Manifest Destiny in the West," "have been wonderfully fulfilled, so far as the Pacific Railroad and the trade with the old world of the East is concerned. But even they did not prophesy that Chinamen should build the Pacificward end of the road."[39] Ah Goong has misguidedly purchased worthless papers from a "Citizenship Judge," but it is "having built the railroad" that makes him feel truly American.[40]

Although Chinese workers were first hired by the railroad in February of 1865, Kingston places Ah Goong with the railroad in the spring of 1863, allowing her to write that Ah Goong was also hired "because there were not enough workingmen to do all the labor of building a new country" and to add wryly that "some of the banging" that Ah Goong heard "came from the war to decide whether or not black people would continue to work for nothing."[41] The link between Chinese and blacks here is not idle, for as Ronald Takaki has argued, racial characteristics previously associated only with blacks were easily transferred to the Chinese, because many of the Europeans and Americans who were coming to California from the East had never seen a Chinese person before. They therefore simply assumed that the Chinese were equivalent to the non-white peoples with whom they *were* familiar: Indians and blacks.[42] After a change in editorial leadership, the *Daily Alta California* proclaimed in 1853, "we have a class here . . . who have most of the vices of the African and they are numerous in both town and country. We allude to the Chinese. Every reason that exists against the toleration of free blacks in Illinois may be argued against that of the Chinese here."[43] White miners often referred to the Chinese as "nagurs" and described them along with blacks as savage, childlike, lustful—in short, physically and morally inferior. The black population in California in 1852 was approximately 2,200, less than a tenth of the Chinese population, and it is thought that the stereotypes of blacks found in the popular press were imported by white Southerners who moved to California during the Gold Rush and who represented approximately one-third of the total population of California at this time. But because anti-black racism had been a part of the national consciousness for so long, it provided a ready-made template for the description and judgment of other peoples of color.[44]

This use of anti-black racism as a standard of reference occurred not only in the popular press but in legal discourse as well. California law treated blacks, Native Americans, and Chinese equally—equally inferior to whites. Mark Twain, that keen critic of American slavery, also documented the systematic racism directed at Chinese in *Roughing It*: "Any white man can swear a Chinaman's life away in the courts, but no Chinaman can testify against a white man. Ours is the 'land of the free'—nobody denies that—nobody challenges it. (Maybe it's because we won't let other people testify.) As I write, news comes that in broad daylight in San Francisco, some boys have stoned an inoffensive Chinaman to death, and that although a large crowd witnessed the shameful deed, no one interfered."[45]

In the 1854 case of *People v. Hall*, the California Supreme Court based its opinion on section fourteen of an 1850 law regulating criminal proceedings according to which "no black or mulatto person, or Indian, shall be allowed to give evidence in favor of, or against a white man." Attempting to include Chinese under the rubric of the term "Indian," the court argued first that the term "Indian" originated in Columbus's mistaken belief that he had reached one of the "Islands of the Chinese

Sea" when he arrived at Hispaniola and was therefore always intended to signify inhabitants of Asia, and second that it was a common belief among ethnologists that the Indian and "the Mongolian, or Asiatic," belonged to "the same type of the human species." In other words, said the Court, "the name of Indian, from the time of Columbus to the present day, has been used to designate, not alone the North American Indian, but the whole of the Mongolian race, and that the name, though first applied probably through mistake, was afterward continued as appropriate on account of the supposed common origin."[46]

The court, however, did not stop there. It bolstered its argument by speculating about the intentions of the original Naturalization Act of 1790 when it used the term "free white persons," stating, "We are of the opinion that the words 'white,' 'Negro,' 'mulatto,' 'Indian,' and 'black person' wherever they occur in our Constitution and laws, must be taken in their generic sense, and that, even admitting the Indian of this continent is not of the Mongolian type, that the words 'black person' in the 14th section [of the 1850 law], must be taken as contradistinguished from white, and necessarily excludes all races other than the Caucasian."[47] As a result of this twisted logic, Chinese were prevented from being able to give testimony for or against whites until 1872, when the 1850 law was repealed. What is important to note is that "black" here is an inclusive category constructed on the basis of physical characteristics. As we shall see, both the definition and the construction of this category will have shifted by the time of the Chinese Exclusion Act in 1882.

Chinese immigrants protested being equated with Indians and free blacks. In 1855, a merchant named Lai Chun-Chuen, writing on behalf of the San Francisco Chinese business community, upbraided white Americans for describing Chinese people as if they were "the same as Indians and Negroes." Arguing that Native Americans knew "nothing about the relations of society," since they wore neither clothes nor shoes and lived in caves, Lai pointed out that the Chinese had a wealthy civilization that dated back more than a thousand years, with long traditions of civil government and philosophy. "Can it be possible," he asked, "that we are classed as equals with this uncivilized race of men?" Three years earlier, a Chinese community leader named Norman Asing had asked a similar question in the pages of the *Daily Alta California*. Writing an open letter to the third California governor, John Bigler, who had just given a special message to the legislature on the evils of Chinese immigration, Asing "remind[ed]" Bigler that "when your nation was a wilderness, and the nation from which you sprung *barbarous*, we exercised most of the arts and virtues of civilized life; that we are possessed of a language and a literature, and that men skilled in science and the arts are numerous among us; that the productions of our manufactories, our sail, and workshops, form no small commerce of the world. . . . We are not the degraded race you would make us."[48]

Yet white Americans not only continued to depict the Chinese as a degraded race, but also began to present blacks as far less degraded in comparison. For example, in 1877, the California legislature sent a "memorial" to the United States Congress offering advice on the question of limiting Chinese immigration. Comparing blacks in the eastern states with Chinese immigrants in California, the memorial notes that "the free Negro speaks our language, . . . grows up among us, worships the same God as ourselves, and is accustomed to our institutions." The Chinese, on the other hand, constitute a race that "is utterly a stranger to our language, to the fundamental principles of enlightened religion, to our consciousness of moral obligations, and, with a few individual exceptions, even to a sense of the most common proprieties of life." Blacks, in other words, are well-behaved and well-acculturated compared to the Chinese, and yet the eastern states find "the presence of a comparatively small population of [free blacks] exceedingly annoying, and fraught with dangers not only to the peace of their own community, but to the harmony between their laws and the constitutional policy of the National Legislature." How much worse then is California's plight, the memorial asks, confronted as she is by the "unlimited influx of a race which already comprises the eighth part of her entire population," a race that seems completely alien.[49] So alien, in fact, that at the California Constitutional Convention in 1887—the year of the Dawes Act—a delegate named John F. Miller could declare: "Were the Chinese to amalgamate at all with our people, it would be the lowest most vile and degraded of our race and the result of that amalgamation would be a hybrid of the most despicable, a mongrel of the most detestable that has ever afflicted the earth."[50] Miscegenation between blacks and whites is bad, apparently, but miscegenation between Chinese and whites would be a horror.

Things had looked promising for Chinese immigrants in 1868, when the United States and China signed the Burlingame Treaty, in which the two nations agreed that they would "cordially recognize the inherent and inalienable right of man to change his home and allegiance, and also the mutual advantage of the free migration and emigration of their citizens and subjects respectively from the one country to the other for purposes of curiosity, of trade, or as permanent residents." Maxine Hong Kingston uses this excerpt from the Treaty as the headnote for "The Laws" section of *China Men*, but her first entry immediately undercuts this seemingly idealistic piece of governmental rhetoric, juxtaposing it to the fact that 1868 was also the year in which "40,000 miners of Chinese ancestry were Driven Out."[51] Although the Fourteenth Amendment was also enacted in 1868 to guarantee that "naturalized Americans have the same rights as native-born Americans," Kingston points out that this guarantee was soon denied to Asian Americans by the Naturalization Act of 1870, which limited naturalization to "white persons and persons of African descent." In broadening the 1790 Naturalization Act, which had been rendered anachronistic by the abolition of slavery, Congress pointedly rejected the more general, color-blind phrase "persons," which was advocated by a group of radical Republicans led by Senator Charles Sumner of Massachusetts. The debates over the 1870 act made it clear that the new phraseology was designed to exclude Chinese from citizenship. The act thus created a third category to which Chinese immigrants were relegated: "aliens ineligible to citizenship," a category that was reinforced by the provisions of the Chinese Exclusion Act twelve years later, which made the Chinese the only ethnic group that could not immigrate freely to the United States. They would remain ineligible until 1943, when the Chinese exclusion laws were finally repealed by Congress.

African Americans and Native Americans were not the only ethnic groups to whom Chinese and Chinese Americans were unfavorably compared. Many white Americans believed that the Japanese were a far superior race to the Chinese, a fact borne out by the writing careers of the Eaton sisters, Edith and Winnifred. Using the pseudonym Sui Sin Far, Edith Eaton (1865–1914) became the first writer to attempt an "inside" representation of Chinese American lives. Eaton was the daughter of an English merchant named Edward Eaton and a Chinese woman named Grace Trepesis, who was abducted from home at the age of three or four and eventually adopted by an English missionary family in Shanghai. She emigrated with her parents and five siblings from Macclesfield, England, to the United States in 1874, because her father's family disapproved of his marriage to a Chinese woman, and the family eventually settled permanently in Montreal, Canada, where Edith's sister Winnifred was born in 1875. Ultimately, the Eatons had sixteen children, two of whom died during childhood. Edith herself contracted rheumatic fever as a child; the disease weakened her constitution and eventually contributed to her early death at the age of forty-nine. She nevertheless pursued a career in journalism, publishing her first article, "A Trip in a Horse Car," in the Montreal magazine *Dominion Illustrated* in 1888. Eaton adopted the pseudonym Sui Sin Far (literally, "water fragrant flower") when she began publishing short stories in the mid-1890s. Her short fiction was collected into a volume entitled *Mrs. Spring Fragrance* (1912), which received generally favorable reviews. The New York *Independent* wrote that "the conflict between occidental and oriental ideals and the hardships of American immigration laws furnish the theme for most of the tales" and suggested that a reader "has his mind widened by becoming acquainted with novel points of view."[52] Generally more conservative, the *New York Times* wrote that "Miss Eaton has struck a new note in American fiction," though its praise was qualified with the suggestion that this note had not been "struck . . . very surely, or with surpassing skill." Admitting, however, that "it has taken courage to strike it at all," the *Times* reviewer argued that Eaton's goal of "portray[ing] for readers of the white race the lives, feelings, sentiments of the Americanized Chinese on the Pacific coast, of those who have intermarried with them, and of the children who have sprung from such unions" is "a task whose adequate doing would require well-nigh superhuman insight and the subtlest of methods."[53] This sentiment indicates just how resistant white Americans were to the idea that they shared a common humanity with the "Chinese," who were routinely vilified as being subhuman.

Further evidence of this vilification can be found in an anecdote that Sui Sin Far recounts in her autobiographical essay, "Leaves from the Mental Portfolio of an Eurasian" (1909). Sitting at a dinner party given by the man who employs her as a stenographer, she listens, aghast, to this exchange:

> My employer shakes his rugged head. "Somehow or other," says he, "I cannot reconcile myself to the thought that the Chinese are humans like ourselves. They may have immortal souls, but their faces seem to me to be so utterly devoid of expression that I cannot help but doubt."
>
> "Souls," echoes the town clerk. "Their bodies are enough for me. A China man is, in my eyes, more repulsive than a nigger."
>
> "They always give me such a creepy feeling," puts in the young girl with a laugh.
>
> "I wouldn't have one in my house," declares my landlady.
>
> "Now, the Japanese are different altogether. There's something bright and likeable about those men," continues Mr. K.[54]

It was, of course, highly unlikely that a Midwestern man like Mr. K. would actually have encountered anyone of Japanese extraction. Although a few Japanese nationals had entered the United States after the Civil War, Japanese immigration did not begin in earnest until 1885, when the Japanese government began to give its citizens official permission to emigrate. Before 1890 there were approximately 3,000 immigrants from Japan to the mainland United States, but between 1891 and 1900 that number jumped up to 27,000; by 1924 (when the Asian Exclusion Act was passed) a total of 275,000 Japanese had emigrated to the U.S. mainland. It is important to put these numbers in perspective, however, by noting that the Japanese constituted a very small minority during the period between 1890 and World War II, never more than 2.1 percent of the California population or more than 0.02 percent of the total U.S. population (which numbered 130 million in 1940).[55]

Eventually, Sui Sin Far finds the courage to speak out against the racism of her dinner companions, though her first impulse is to remain quietly incognito:

> A miserable, cowardly feeling keeps me silent. I am in a Middle West town. If declare what I am, every person in the place will hear about it the next day. The population is in the main made up of working folks with strong prejudices against my mother's countrymen. The prospect

before me is not an enviable one—if I speak. I have no longer an ambition to die at the stake for the sake of demonstrating the greatness and nobleness of the Chinese people.

Mr. K. turns to me with a kindly smile.

"What makes Miss Far so quiet?" he asks.

"I don't suppose she finds the 'washee washee men' particularly interesting subjects of conversation," volunteers the young manager of the local bank.

With great effort, I raise my eyes from my plate. "Mr. K.," I say, addressing my employer. "The Chinese people may have no souls, no expression in their faces, be altogether beyond the pale of civilization, but whatever they are, I want you to understand that I am—I am Chinese."

There is silence in the room for a few minutes. Then Mr. K. pushes back his plate and standing up beside me, says:

"I should not have spoken as I did. I know nothing whatever about the Chinese. It was pure prejudice. Forgive me!"

I admire Mr. K.'s moral courage in apologizing to me; he is a conscientious Christian man, but I do not remain much longer in the little town.[56]

This story both captures the depth of white American prejudice against the "Chinese" and also conveys a sense of the nature of Sui Sin Far's activism: her speech tacitly accepts the superiority of white civilization. Earlier in the essay, Eaton has described a childhood fight against white children who yell epithets like "yellow-face, pig-tail, rat-eater" at her and her brother: "they pull my hair, they tear my clothes, they scratch my face, and all but lame my brother; but the white blood in our veins fights valiantly for the Chinese half of us," and they are able to report later on to their mother that they have "won the battle."[57] The assumption that the white blood is stronger than the Chinese underwrites Sui Sin Far's activism; she seems to believe that her hybrid identity makes her better able to champion the cause of the Chinese in America: later in the essay, she writes, "I meet many Chinese persons, and when they get into trouble am often called upon to fight their battles in the papers. This I enjoy."[58] Eaton's syntax here embodies her cultural situation: she is sympathetic to "Chinese persons," wishes to fight their battles, but writing primarily for a white audience and feeling empowered by her white blood, she describes other Chinese Americans in the third person, as "they" rather than "we."

The title of Eaton's essay, "Leaves from the Mental Portfolio of an Eurasian," recalls the title of an extremely popular book by Fanny Fern (Sara Willis Payson), *Fern Leaves from Fanny's Portfolio* (1853), and it indicates Eaton's affinity with nineteenth-century women writers of domestic fiction. Her writings expose the hardships suffered not only by Chinese Americans, but also by women, particularly women of the working class. It is this characteristic that has led scholars of Asian American literature to see her as a forerunner of Maxine Hong Kingston, whose writing also offers a two-pronged critique of U.S. culture. At the same time, however, the title of her book, *Mrs. Spring Fragrance*, suggests a hint of the exoticism that Sui Sin Far manipulates throughout her writings, particularly in the flowery language with which she translates Chinese names and expressions into English, and in the physical appearance of the book, which was printed on paper embossed with a design that any reader would deem "Chinese" and featured a vermilion cover stamped with gold letters and representations of the moon, lotus flowers, and a dragonfly. While such devices might seem to be at odds with Eaton's often bitterly ironic representations of the hardship of Chinese American life, we might compare Eaton's use of these strategies to the deployment of sentimentality in novels like Fern's *Ruth Hall* (1854) and Harriet Beecher Stowe's *Uncle Tom's Cabin* (1852). Eaton lures white readers in by catering to their Orientalist expectations, which are then not dashed but cunningly reoriented as the stories unfold.

Later in the essay, Eaton takes up the idea suggested in the anecdote by her employer that "the Japanese are different altogether." Once its ports had been forcibly opened to Western trade by Admiral Perry in 1854, Japan (in contrast to China) embraced the idea of modernization on the Western model and drew upon the scientific and technological expertise of experts from the West; Japan's military would force China to cede both Korea and Taiwan in 1895, and ten years later it defeated Russia. These victories gained Japan the respect of Western nations, and the country's domestic prosperity meant that relatively few of its citizens were seeking to emigrate to the United States. Americans like Eaton's employer could idealize the Japanese because they had practically no contact with them. Eaton notes that because "Americans [have] for many years manifested a much higher regard for the Japanese than for the Chinese, several half Chinese young men and women, thinking to advance themselves, both in a social and business sense, pass as Japanese."[59] In fact, Eaton's younger sister, Winnifred, would do precisely that—at least as a writer—adopting an ostensibly Japanese pseudonym, Onoto Watanna, and inventing a suitable biography, which claimed that she was born in Nagasaki, the daughter of a Japanese noblewoman. Winnifred had a longer career than her sister: after writing what is thought to be the first novel published by an Asian American, *Miss Nume of Japan* (1899), she would write a dozen more novels, a fictionalized autobiography, and a biography of her sister Sara. Winnifred did not restrict herself to Asian or Asian American subjects: for example, *The Diary of Delia: Being a Veracious Chronicle of the Kitchen with Some Sidelights on the Parlour* (1907) purports to be the journal of one Delia O'Malley, housekeeper to the Wooley family and is written in Irish American dialect, while Eaton's final novel, *His Royal Nibs* (1925), recounts the adventures of Cheerio, an English painter on a ranch in Alberta, who finds himself inspired by Native American subjects and ultimately gains the love of the rancher's daughter. In contrast to her sister Edith, Winnifred's goal was not to challenge the expectations of her readers but to write popular fiction, and her novels and autobiography both reflect and take advantage of popular stereotypes of both Asians and women.[60]

The fact that China was held in relatively low esteem by the U.S. government in comparison to Japan during this period can be seen in the different responses offered by the United States to rising immigration from the two countries. The Burlingame Treaty was eventually suspended in 1881, and the following year Congress passed the first Chinese Exclusion Act, which prevented Chinese laborers, whether skilled or unskilled, from entering the continental United States for ten years. This ban was extended for another ten years in 1892 by the Geary Act, and then extended indefinitely in 1904 with the prohibition enlarged to include Hawai'i and the Philippines.

In contrast to this unilateral attempt to limit immigration from China, the United States sought to work with the Japanese government to regulate the flow of immigrants. Unlike China, Japan at the end of the nineteenth century was an emerging world power, and during the 1890s, when Japanese immigrants began to be perceived as a threat by labor leaders on the West Coast, the Japanese government began to monitor the treatment of Japanese nationals in the United States, believing Japan's prestige as a nation would be damaged if it allowed its emigrants to be exploited as the Chinese and other Asians had been. By 1900 each of the three major political parties in California—Democrat, Populist, and Republican—publicly opposed immigration from Asia. In 1905 President Theodore Roosevelt, though privately sympathetic to many of the arguments made in favor of Japanese exclusion, nevertheless informed the government in Tokyo that "the American Government and the American People have not the slightest sympathy with the outrageous agitation against the Japanese," adding that "while I am President the Japanese will be treated just exactly like . . . other civilized peoples."[61] When the flow of immigrants from Japan rose precipitously to 127,000 in 1907, Roosevelt sought a political solution that could mollify both the Japanese government and anti-Japanese public opinion in California. Roosevelt negotiated the so-called "Gentleman's Agreement" with Japan, which consisted of six notes exchanged between the two governments in late 1907 and early 1908, in which the Japanese agreed to limit immigration to the United States.

What made the Chinese seem so alien to white Americans? In the second volume of his 1893 study, *The American Commonwealth*, the British historian James Bryce wrote that "the circumstance of colonial life, the process of settling the western wilderness, the feelings evoked by the struggle against George III, all went to intensify individualism, the love of enterprise, and the pride in personal freedom" in the United States. In Bryce's analysis, individualism and its related values are not uniquely American; he argues that the American "State governments of 1776 and the National government of 1789 started from ideas, mental habits, and administrative practice generally similar to those of contemporary England." Americans, however, do not acknowledge the origins of this aspect of their social thought. "From that day to this," wrote Bryce, "individualism, the love of enterprise, and the pride in personal freedom, have been deemed by Americans not only their choicest, but their peculiar and exclusive possessions."[62]

Bryce was, essentially, confirming the analysis offered half a century earlier by another famous European observer of U.S. culture, Alexis de Tocqueville. In the second volume of *Democracy in America*, published in 1840, Tocqueville wrote that "'individualism' is a word recently coined to express a new idea. Our fathers only knew about egoism." Henry Reeve, the translator of the American edition, felt obliged to comment on his use of the term: "I adopt the expression of the original," he wrote in a footnote, "however strange it may seem to the English ear, . . . because I know of no English word exactly equivalent to the expression."[63] The term *individualisme* had been coined in France during the 1820s, and it was deployed by both counter-revolutionary and socialist thinkers as a critique of Enlightenment thought. It is in this negative sense that Tocqueville uses the term "individualism" in the second volume of *Democracy in America*. Tocqueville defines it as "a calm and considered feeling which disposes each citizen to isolate himself from the mass of his fellows and withdraw into the circle of family and friends; with this little society formed to his taste, he gladly leaves the greater society to look after itself." According to Tocqueville, egoism "springs from a blind instinct," while "individualism is based on misguided judgment rather than depraved feeling." The distinction, however, ultimately becomes moot: "Egoism sterilizes the seeds of every virtue; individualism at first only dams the spring of public virtues, but in the long run it attacks and destroys all the others too and finally merges in egoism."[64]

American thinkers, however, were already in the process of appropriating and redefining the term "individualism." In 1839, the year before Tocqueville's second volume appeared, the anonymous author of a piece in the *Democratic Review* entitled "The Course of Civilization" described the "history of humanity" as "the record of a grand march . . . at all times tending to one point—the ultimate perfection of man. The course of civilization is the progress of man from a state of savage individualism to that of an individualism more elevated, moral and refined."[65] Two years later, in the first American review of *Democracy in America*, which appeared in the *Boston Quarterly Review*, an anonymous author inverts Tocqueville's argument in order to appropriate the term "individualism" and endow it with a positive connotation. Regarding individualism as the driving force behind American society, the reviewer describes it as "that strong confidence in self, or reliance upon one's own exertion and resources." The author applauds what Tocqueville laments, arguing that "it is the artificial classification of mankind, into certain unfounded castes of the high and the low, the learned and the ignorant, patricians and plebeians, priests and laymen, princes and subjects . . . rather than the free scope of personal or individual peculiarities, which has enfeebled, and thereby corrupted the race." Individualism, by destroying the chains forged by aristocratic society and forcing each individual to rely on "the inherent and profound resources of his own mysterious being," has actually created a new "organic unity of the collective race."[66] Individualism is thus perceived not as a destructive vice that dams the spring of public virtues but rather as the source of all public virtue and, ultimately, as the mechanism through which America will fulfill its promise.

According to the logic of this rhetoric, then, blacks and Indians can be assimilated into the white race if they can learn the lessons of individualism. And thus what makes the Chinese so alien is not their particular physical or genetic characteristics but their refusal to accede to the principles of individualism. Lai Chun-Chuen and Norman Asing argue that the Chinese are a civilized race with a long history and that they should therefore be distinguished from blacks and Indians. And their wish is granted, though not in the way that they hoped. For that long history of civilization is, in fact, precisely the problem. Unlike African Americans or Native Americans, the Chinese have too much civilization. The Chinese "race," concludes an 1885 report by the San Francisco Board of Supervisors, "is one that cannot readily throw off its habits and customs" and the "fact that these customs are so widely at variance with our own, makes the enforcements of our laws and compulsory obedience to our laws necessarily obnoxious and revolting to the Chinese." In other words, unlike blacks and Indians, the Chinese have a culture that puts them at odds with American individualism, and it is a culture that cannot simply be "pulverized," to recall Teddy Roosevelt's expression. And this, I suggest, is why the supervisors' report describes Chinese "customs" as "so widely at variance with our own."[67]

Some thirty years earlier, in 1853, the *Daily Alta California* complained that the Chinese were more clannish than American blacks and morally inferior to them, as if being "clannish" were a sign of moral inferiority.[68] The same logic can be found in the California Legislature's 1877 memorial to the U.S. Congress. The self-sacrifice and co-operation necessary for the Chinese to survive in a culture hostile to them are portrayed as signs that the Chinese are a "degraded" race: "Chinese labor ranks no higher in the public respect than slave labor. Its compensation is so low in proportion to the necessities of life in California that the white laborer cannot compete with the Chinaman." Noting that "the larger portion of the Chinese has been engaged in mining," the memorial states that "during the early years after the discovery of gold in this State, when our population was sparse, and when there was no lack of rich surface mines, the American and European miner experienced no hardship from the presence of the Chinese." Later, however, as "the rich surface diggings became more and more exhausted, and the chances of generous reward for individual labor in mining claims became rare, the antipathies of our own race against the Mongolians were aroused, and grew daily stronger in proportion as the mines occupied by Mongolians became of increasing importance to American citizens or Europeans, who sought the means of a modest and toilsome subsistence for a permanent settlement upon our soil." Competition is the name of the game in American individualism, but the Chinese get no credit for competing well because they are not motivated by "the chances of generous reward for individual labor." Their willingness to settle for less and pursue communal rather than individual goals have given them, seemingly, an unfair advantage. And, the memorial continues, "in the cities too hostility toward the Chinese is increasing because in several industries white workingmen cannot compete with the Chinese": white workers, "being unable to maintain a decent and civilized subsistence upon wages which afford the Chinaman a comfortable living, were compelled, in every case where Chinese competition made its appearance, to retire from their profession and abandon its exercise to their Chinese competitors."[69] The frugality of the Chinese is thus depicted as not as a form of Franklinian virtue but rather as a vice.

In the 1885 San Francisco Board of Supervisors report, the depiction of this supposed vice is intensified to the point of hyperbole. The report likens frugality to opium-smoking, gambling, and prostitution. "Compel the Chinamen," the report recommends, "by municipal laws which are not only enacted but enforced, to live like our own race; prevent them from burrowing and crowding together like vermin; enforce cleanliness in mode of life; break up opium dens and gambling hells; restrict the number of inhabitants in any given block in the city; enforce upon this people, so far as may be possible by every legitimate method that can be devised, a cost of living that shall approach as nearly as possible that of the ordinary white laborer."[70] What lies behind this hyperbole is a fear that is implicit in both the memorial and the supervisors' report: that Chinese frugality and communitarianism will turn out to foster a vice within American individualism itself, a vice that could ultimately destroy the American way. According to the memorial, Chinese practices bring about the "degradation of labor and the impoverishment of the laboring classes," both of which it describes as "poisons which destroy the lifeblood of a republic." A few pages later it becomes clear how this happens, as the memorial admits that "the presence of hordes of Mongolians would at present undoubtedly be advantages to the capitalists and manufacturers. These classes, although very necessary to the development of a young State, are generally not as careful of the preservation of the principles of freedom and of the exclusion of every element dangerous to the maintenance and the purity of republican institutions, as they are anxious of reaping immediate and unusual profits." In other words, the writers of the memorial argue that the availability of cheap Chinese labor will inevitably lead the capitalist and the manufacturer to become greedy, thereby proving Tocqueville right about the idea that selfishness lies at the heart of American individualism. Chinese communitarianism will prove to be a "poison" that will destroy American individualism from within.[71]

Deemed incapable as a race of understanding or practicing individualism, the Chinese were denied the ability to become naturalized citizens and as a result denied the ability to be fully fledged bearers of individual rights. The right to be considered an "individual citizen" is inextricably linked to the ways in which race is defined, and then redefined by the U.S. courts. There is perhaps no better illustration of the intimate link between American individualism and American racism than the 1869 case of the *People v. Washington*, in which a mulatto was indicted for the robbery of a Chinese man named Ah Wang, on the basis of testimony from Chinese witnesses. The Civil Rights Act of 1866 had guaranteed all citizens equality before the law with respect to their personal liberty. Included in the definition of citizens were all persons born within the United States and not subject to a foreign power. The main thrust of the act was to guarantee blacks the same rights as whites. The law stipulated that citizens of every race and color, without regard to previous condition of servitude, should have "the same right, in every State and Territory, to the full and equal benefit of all laws and proceedings for the security of person and property as is enjoyed by white citizens." On appeal, the Supreme Court overturned the mulatto Washington's conviction, reasoning that since California law explicitly excluded Chinese testimony against whites, then extending equality to blacks meant giving them the same right—the same right to be protected from Chinese testimony. In this case, "black" was no longer a category that signified all non-whites, as it had in the earlier case of the *People v. Hall.* Now "white" was a category that signified those whose rights would be protected, a category that pointedly excluded the Chinese.[72] When the Dawes Act conferred citizenship rights upon Native Americans in 1887, "white," rather than "black," would prove to be the more inclusive term. In both popular and legal discourse, then, where "black" once signified "all non-whites," white came to signify—at least, temporarily—"all non-Chinese." What this analysis suggests, of course, is not that blacks had a legal or cultural standing equal to those of whites, since this was also an era of virulent anti-black discourse in which black citizenship rights gained after the Civil War were significantly eroded. Instead what is demonstrated by this pattern of rhetoric—with its unthinkable equation of whites and blacks—is the depth of white hatred for the Chinese.

The Chinese Exclusion Act lessened but did not stop the flow of Chinese to the United States: new immigrants managed to enter the country through illegal border crossings and, after 1906, through an elaborate system of immigration fraud that took advantage of the conjunction of a loophole in American law and a natural disaster. The Fourteenth Amendment had stipulated that "all persons born . . . in the United States" were to be citizens, including people of Chinese ancestry. The great San Francisco earthquake and fire of 1906 destroyed nearly all of the birth records pertaining to Chinese immigrants, enabling many Chinese aliens to claim American citizenship fraudulently. Some of these "paper sons" returned to China to bring their sons back to the United States, but a great number of them stayed in China and sold their forged certificates of return to other Chinese, who could then bring their sons, nephews, and cousins to the United States.[73]

The idea of the "paper son" whose identity is constructed from half-truths designed to circumvent U.S. immigration laws becomes a major motif in Chinese American fiction. In *China Men*, Kingston imagines her father's first trip to the United States: "BaBa would go with two sets of papers: bought ones and his own, which were legal and should get him into the Gold Mountain according to American law. But his own papers were untried, whereas the fake set had accompanied its owners back and forth many times. These bought papers had a surname which was the same as our own last name—unusual luck: he would be able to keep the family name. He would carry his diplomas, and if they did not work, he would produce the fake papers."[74] Leila, the narrator of Ng's *Bone*, writes that her stepfather "saved every single scrap of paper. I remember his telling me about a tradition of honoring paper, how the oldtimers believed all writing as sacred." She reflects that her stepfather was "right to save everything. For a paper son, paper is blood."[75] Family history thus exists in two versions, the official public history of paper sons and the secret private history of true familial relations, though frequently the versions mingle so that what is true and what is made-up are no longer separable: "I'm the stepdaughter of a paper son," Leila says, "and I've inherited this whole suitcase of lies. All of it is mine. All I have are those memories, and I want to remember them all."[76]

Kingston's BaBa is detained at San Francisco's Angel Island, where he is repeatedly interrogated by the "Immigration Demons," who ask about the number of pigs his family owned in 1919, the number of steps on the back stoop of the family house, when he cut off his queue, what his relatives' addresses in the United States had been—all the while "look[ing] into his eyes for lies." Because "he had an accurate memory" and thus manages to keep his answers consistent from session to session, he is finally allowed into the United States. BaBa's experience is meant to be representative: after the passage of the Exclusion Act, all prospective Chinese immigrants arriving at San Francisco Bay were led to the "Tongsaan Matau," the China Dock, were they were processed for immigration in a notorious detention center that they referred to as the "Muk uk" or "Wooden Barracks"; the miserable condition of the facility led to its replacement in 1910 by the Angel Island facility. It was not uncommon for those who were awaiting processing to be detained for several weeks, months, or even longer, and detainees were prohibited from leaving the compound or meeting any visitors from the outside. To express their feelings of loneliness and despair, many of these detainees wrote lines of poetry on the walls of the barracks, which were copied down in the 1930s by two detainees and thus survive today. The two poems that follow are typical:

> So, liberty is your national principle;
> Why do you practice autocracy?
> You don't uphold justice, you Americans,
> You detain me in prison, guard me closely.
> Your officials are wolves and tigers,
> All ruthless, all wanting to bite me.
> An innocent man implicated, such an injustice!
> When can I get out of this prison and free my mind?

> A weak nation can't speak up for herself.
> Chinese sojourners have come to a foreign country.
> Detained, put on trial, imprisoned in a hillside building;
> If deposition doesn't exactly match: the case is dead and in a bind.
> No chance for release.
> My fellow countrymen cry out injustice:
> The sole purpose is strict exclusion, to deport us all back to Hong
>   Kong.
> Pity my fellow villagers and their flood of tears.[77]

What many of these poems demonstrate is an understanding not only of the principles of American democracy but also the stipulations of the Burlingame Treaty, and they voice the despair of discovering that they were foolish to believe that either would be upheld.

Kingston's description of U.S. officials as "Immigration Demons" alludes to the counter-mythology that Chinese immigrants developed in response to their own demonization by white Americans. Many of the sojourners who returned to China represented their trip to the Gold Mountain as a difficult and dangerous errand into a wilderness peopled by savages. Indeed, much as William Bradford did in his *History of Plymouth Plantation* (1630), Chinese sojourners mythologized the harshness of life in America. Lee Chew, whose personal narrative was included in Hamilton Holt's *Life Stories of (Undistinguished) Americans, As Told by Themselves* (1906), refers to "Chinese prejudice against Americans" and recalls "the wild tales that were told about them in our village." Described by Holt as a "representative Chinese business man of New York," Chew protests that "the treatment of Chinese in this country is all wrong and mean," but argues nonetheless that "Americans are not all bad, nor are they wicked wizards." He notes, however, that not all Chinese immigrants share his opinion: "some of the Chinese, who have been here twenty years and who are learned men, still believe that there is no marriage in this country, that the land is infested with demons and that all the people are given over to general wickedness."[78]

The idea that marriage did not exist in the United States was, however, effectively true for Chinese men. From the mid-nineteenth century through at least the end of World War II, the Chinese population in the United States was overwhelmingly male: for example, there were 11,794 Chinese in California in 1852, but only seven of them were women. In 1870, the ratio of Chinese men to women in the United States was fourteen to one; by 1920, it had improved to seven to one, and twenty years later it was slightly under three to one.[79] Women were left behind because the expense of paying their passage would have decreased the profitability of the sojourn, and women from the better classes tended to have bound feet that would prove to be a severe handicap on an arduous journey. In addition, wives who stayed behind were thought to provide a form of insurance for the families who depended on the money that husbands and sons sent back to China. According to one Chinese woman, "The mother wanted her son to come back. If wife go to America, then son no go back home and no send money."[80] Chinese American men also suffered from U.S. culture's obsession with miscegenation: they were prohibited by law from marrying white women. As a result, the Chinese Exclusion Act of 1882 caused the Chinese American population to undergo a long decline by freezing its lopsided gender ratio in place, essentially creating a population of bachelors in which young men were always outnumbered by old.

In contrast, though it was presented to Californians as the equivalent of an exclusion act, the Gentleman's Agreement that Roosevelt negotiated with the Japanese government actually allowed the Japanese American population to more than double during the next twenty years, as well as shifting the gender balance of the Japanese American population from being overwhelmingly male in 1908 to nearly even by 1924. The Japanese American community referred to the years following the Gentleman's Agreement as *yobiyose-jidai*, "the period of summoning": the agreement not only enabled married Japanese men resident in the United States to send for their wives and children, but also permitted resident Japanese bachelors to acquire "picture brides" by proxy.[81]

U.S. immigration laws had the effect of masculinizing Chinese American culture; at the same time, however, U.S. naturalization laws had the effect of feminizing Chinese Americans: with the granting of citizenship to non-white groups in the 1870s and 1880s, men of Chinese extraction—and indeed of Asian extraction generally—were treated by the United States as if they were women. This legal conception was reinforced by popular stereotypes that portrayed "chinamen" as naturally (in other words, racially) suited only to feminized, service-oriented jobs such as laundry-washing and table-waiting. "The Chinese laundryman does not learn his trade in China," Lee Chew complained: "There are no laundries in China. The women there do the washing in tubs and have no washboards or flat irons. All the Chinese laundrymen here were taught in the first place by American women just as I was taught."[82] With the enfranchisement of women by the Nineteenth Amendment in 1919, the legal standing of Asian American men was further eroded, and even after the enfranchisement of Chinese Americans in 1943, the stereotype of the effeminate Asian American man would continue to be pervasive and damaging. Frank Chin argues that throughout the period leading up to World War II, "the stereotype came out of the laws, out of the schools, out of the white literary lights of the time, out of the science, out of the comics, movies, and radio night and day." As a result, not only white Americans but also many Chinese Americans came to internalize it, and according to Chin, early Chinese American writing represented "Chinese men" almost exclusively as "emasculated and sexually repellent."[83]

The Power of Invidious Distinctions

The public culture of late-nineteenth-century America produced ways of thinking about those who deviate from the norm of the heterosexual white American that remain powerful even in the aftermath of the civil rights movements of the 1960s and the triumph of multiculturalism in the 1980s and 1990s. Homophobia and comparative racism are unmistakable elements of the cultural landscape that serves as the backdrop for late-twentieth-century emergent writing in the United States. The latest group to which the template of anti-black racism has been applied are Arab Americans, who hear themselves called "sand niggers." The Arab American poet, essayist, and law professor Lawrence Joseph captures the anger and frustration that are part of a young Lebanese American's life in Detroit in his poem "Sand Nigger":

> Outside the house my practice
> is not to respond to remarks
> about my nose or the color of my skin.
> "Sand nigger," I'm called,
> and the name fits: I am
> the light-skinned nigger
> with black eyes and the look
> difficult to figure—a look
> of indifference, a look to kill—
> a Levantine nigger
> in the city on the strait
> between the great lakes Erie and St. Clair
> which has a reputation
> for violence. . . . [84]

A counterweight to Joseph's bleak vision of life as a young Lebanese American can be found in *The Night Counter* (2009), the first novel by the Palestinian American writer Alia Yunis. A sprawling family saga about two Lebanese American immigrants and their descendants, the novel ultimately finds hope in the mingling of ethnicities and races that modern American life makes possible. The final pages of the novel find the family matriarch reconciled to the lifestyle of her gay grandson and to the existence of an illegitimate great-granddaughter who is half African American. The joke that one character makes about a radio station—"A bunch of crazy, liberal, Arab-loving, Spanish-speaking, Jewish homosexuals"—serves as an emblem for the possibility that America's minority cultures might become less divided and thereby less easily conquered.[85]

3

The Politics of Early Twentieth-Century U.S. Literary History

In the first chapter of *Tripmaster Monkey*, Wittman Ah Sing tries to impress his date, Nanci, by reading her some of his poetry. She isn't exactly impressed:

> "You sound black," she said. "I mean like a Black poet. Jive. Slang. Like LeRoi Jones. Like . . . like Black."
>
> He slammed his hand—a fist with a poem in it—down on the desk—fistful of poem. He spit in his genuine brass China Man spittoon, and jumped on top of the desk, squatted there, scratching. "Monkey see, monkey do?" he said. "Huh? Monkey see, monkey do?" Which sounds much uglier if you know Chinese.[1]

But Nanci is right: in the course of the novel, Wittman must cease applying templates developed by others and find a voice and a literary form of his own.

As I suggested in Chapter 2, however, Wittman conceives of his primary problem as something else: the oppressiveness of a literary canon dominated by the work of "white guys" like Whitman and Melville. After Nanci makes her escape, he fumes:

> He whipped around and began to type like mad. Action. At work again.

And again whammed into the block question: Does he announce now that the author is—Chinese? Or, rather, Chinese-American? And be forced into autobiographical confession. Stop the music—I have to butt in and introduce myself and my race. "Dear reader, all these characters whom you've been identifying with—Bill, Brooke, and Annie—are Chinese—and *I* am too." The fiction is spoiled. You who read have been suckered along, identifying like hell, only to find out that you'd been getting a peculiar, colored, slanted p.o.v. "Call me Ishmael." See? You pictured a white guy, didn't you? If Ishmael were described—ochery ecru amber umber skin—you picture a *tan* white guy.[2]

Wittman's goal is to "spoil all those stories coming out of and set in New England Back East," and his first thought is to make use of the strategies for resistance pioneered by African American writers like LeRoi Jones and Richard Wright. The first chapter of *Tripmaster Monkey* thus alerts us to two of the problems that face late-twentieth-century emergent writers: their marginalization by those who make the canons of literature that are celebrated and taught, and the lure of the literary solutions that earlier emergent literatures seem to offer to the problem of canonization.

The canon of "American Literature" to which Wittman is responding was largely the product of America's participation in the twentieth century's two world wars. In *The Cambridge History of American Literature* (1996), Evan Carton and Gerald Graff note that before World War I "American literature had distinctly second-rate status in the eyes of most literary critics, some of whom believed the very idea was a contradiction in terms." After the war, however, "American literature, which had come to be identified with a strong tradition of moral idealism, seemed even better suited than English literature to the task of strengthening the bonds of citizenship in the face of enemies abroad and disorder at home."[3] The novelist and Freudian critic Ludwig Lewisohn argued that World War I had forced Anglo-Americans to confront "the later immigrant strains: the German, the Jewish, the Latin, and the Slav."[4] Immigration was a major issue in American politics both before and after the war. In 1919, writes Paul Lauter,

what many native-born Americans viewed as a "deluge" of immigration, interrupted by the war, resumed. Between 1901 and 1920 over

14.5 million immigrants came to these shores, particularly from Italy, the Austro-Hungarian Empire, and Czarist Russia. Although the foreign-born and their children, together with African Americans, did most of the hard work in mining, manufacture, and construction, they remained—with their presumptively curious dialects, strange religions, and exotic cultures—alien if not positively menacing to established classes of Americans.[5]

It was in this context that an all-but-forgotten writer named Herman Melville began to move to the center of American literary studies and that American literary studies themselves began to become an important part of college curricula.

The critic F. O. Matthiessen, who began his teaching career as an instructor at Yale in the late 1920s, noted that until 1930 Melville's great novel *Moby-Dick* had been classified in the Yale University library as a treatise on cetology.[6] American literature, according to a study published by Ferner Nuhn in the March 1928 edition of H. L. Mencken's *American Mercury*, "was about equal in importance to Scandinavian literature [and] one-tenth as important as English literature." At the undergraduate level, Nuhn reported, one out of eleven English courses was in American literature on average; at the graduate level, the ratio was worse—one out of thirteen—and there were as many courses devoted to Chaucer as there were to American literature as a whole. "It seems little enough to ask," Nuhn concluded, "that the national literature be granted a status equal to that now generally accorded such subjects as journalism, the Spanish language and literature, band instruments, horticulture, animal husbandry, and military science and tactics."[7]

By the time Nuhn's article was published, the "Melville Revival" had already begun. Lauter argues that American intellectuals sought "a new champion" of culture, whose work might "uphold against British condescension American claims to an equality in culture which would be consonant with America's established title to military and diplomatic parity" and "sustain certain established American values now at contest." The "Melville" whom we know today as the exemplar of "classic" American literature was, Lauter writes, "constructed in the 1920s as part of an ideological conflict which linked advocates of modernism and of traditional high cultural values—often connected to the academy against a social and cultural 'other,' generally, if ambiguously, portrayed as feminine, genteel, exotic, dark, foreign, and numerous."[8] As we will see, the debate over realism and other literary terms had implications not only for the shape of U.S. literature in general, but also for the shape of ethnic literatures specifically.

Melville's canonization, and the solidification of an American canon of classics around him, was not complete until after World War II, and Matthiessen would play a large role in that process. In *F. O. Matthiessen and the Politics of Criticism* (1988), William E. Cain argues that "American literature as we know it today is a masterly achievement of modernism, an imaginative enterprise on a grand scale that was undertaken by writers and critics inside and outside the university." Cain cites Malcolm Cowley's observation that "perhaps the principal creative work of the last three decades in this country has not been any novel or poem or drama of our time, not even Faulkner's Yoknapatawpha saga or Hemingway's *For Whom the Bell Tolls* or Hart Crane's *The Bridge*; perhaps it has been the critical rediscovery and reinterpretation of Melville's *Moby-Dick* and its promotion, step-by-step, to the position of national epic."[9] Matthiessen set Melville, along with Emerson, Thoreau, Whitman, and Hawthorne, at the heart of what he called the "American Renaissance," a term that he used as the title of the magisterial study that he published in 1941 and that would be come a commonplace of American literary scholarship shortly thereafter.[10] (Matthiessen omitted Poe from *American Renaissance*, but would contribute an article on Poe to the landmark *Literary History of United States* [1948] that had the effect of adding Poe to the canon of American Renaissance writers.) Matthiessen had begun writing the book during the 1930s, seeking in American literature an antidote to the German fascism that was threatening Europe, and what he considered to be distinctive about the American Renaissance authors was their commitment to democracy, even if it meant (as it did for Hawthorne and Melville) recognizing democracy's shortcomings.

At the same time that Matthiessen was at work on *American Renaissance*, a group of scholars was attempting to create a new collaborative literary history of the United States, which would supersede the *Cambridge History of American Literature* that had been published from

1907 to 1921. Jay B. Hubbell had proposed to the editors of the journal *American Literature* in 1931 the idea of its affiliated American Literature Group's undertaking "a comprehensive literary history of American literature."[11] Although accepted in principle by the advisory council of the group, it took until 1939 for what became the Committee on a Cooperative Literary History, chaired by Robert E. Spiller, to meet. There the foundations for the *Literary History of the United States* were laid. Spiller and his co-editors would ultimately make the project independent of the American Literature Group to avoid the institutional politics that might prevent the new history from becoming an "interpretive synthesis" with a strong editorial point-of-view, which Spiller hoped to create in contrast to the miscellaneous quality of the *Cambridge History*.[12] Ultimately, what guided the overall narrative of the *Literary History of the United States* was Spiller's conviction that American literary history was cyclical, and that there were two great periods in American literature—the American Renaissance of the mid-nineteenth century and the modernist period of the 1930s, which constituted a second renaissance. For Spiller, the great artists of the second renaissance were Dreiser, Frost, Fitzgerald, Hemingway, Steinbeck, Wolfe, and—above all—Faulkner. Looking back at this period from the vantage point of a third-edition postscript in 1963, Spiller (and his co-editor Willard Thorp) reiterated the belief that the second renaissance had faded by the time that *Literary History of the United States* was published in 1948.

The critical response to Spiller's *History* was mixed, and most critics failed to comment on Spillers's cyclical delineation of a second renaissance, in part because the contributors who worked on that section of the *History* produced pieces that were less attuned to his vision than those who contributed to the section on the American Renaissance.[13] The first review of the *History*, written by Norman Holmes Pearson for the *Saturday Review of Literature*, praised it for its "autocratic editorial bravery," which he felt had been missing in the *Cambridge History*.[14] Impressed by many of the chapters on individual authors, Pearson was even more impressed by the regional and international influences traced in the chapters featuring multiple authors and contexts. Whether by design or by accident, Pearson's review cut against the grain of Spiller's larger vision. To single out the regional elements in the *History* was to assert that the book was strongest when it was aligned with the larger realist vision with which regionalism had long been associated. But it was precisely against realism that Spiller, as editor, was taking a stand: in Spiller's view, "only a romantic movement can create great literature."[15]

There was little room for ethnic writers either in Spiller's consensus or in the narrative of modernist emergence that had become a commonplace by 1948. As Werner Sollors points out in *Ethnic Modernism* (2008), the story of modernism's rise "always moved from a premodern, Victorian, realist code to the formal explosion of style and color that marked the achievement of each modern artist." Ethnic literature has typically not been included in accounts of modernism, in part because "ethnic literatures of the first half of the twentieth century developed a repertoire of ethnic themes" and "offer[ed] many details, large and small, that have been of interest of sociologists, anthropologists, and ethnic historians." As a result, ethnic literatures were associated with realism rather than the formal experimentalism of high modernism, and works like Jean Toomer's *Cane* (1923) and Henry Roth's *Call It Sleep* (1934) were viewed as exceptions that proved the rule.[16]

Sollors seeks to emend the story that is typically told about the rise of Anglo-American modernism. He demonstrates that modernism comprises a much richer and more contradictory set of attitudes and points out that "a given writer's views of modernity could be at variance with his or her attitudes toward modernism." High modernists such as T. S. Eliot were often critical of many aspects of modernity, but employed formally experimental modernist literary techniques; ethnic writers, too, could be critical of modernity, but tended to use "premodernist prose and plotlines" to describe the phenomena of modern life. What interests Sollors particularly, however, is the writing that is both "promodern and modernist," including works by "ethnic and minority writers . . . from groups who look back to pasts that offer too little invitation for sustained nostalgia (e.g. slavery, persecution, or severe class oppression)." For Sollors "ethnic literature" during the period 1910–1950 means writing by African Americans, Jewish Americans, and other European immigrants. He draws a distinction between the writing produced by these groups and that produced by Native Americans, Asian Americans, and Mexican Americans during this period. Noting that the word "multicultural" was launched by Edward F. Haskell's little-known *Lance: A Novel about Multicultural Men* (1941), Sollors argues that "the foundation for modern multicultural literature was being laid in those decades," but these precursors of multiculturalism—writers like John Joseph Matthews, D'Arcy McNickle, Sui Sin Far, Younghill Kang, Carlos Bulosan, Toshio Mori, Hisaye Yamamoto, Mario Suárez, John Rechy, and José Antonio Villarreal—do not play a major role in Sollors's account of "ethnic modernism." In many respects, the tradition that Sollors documents reaches its fruition after 1968, in the work of writers like N. Scott Momaday, Maxine Hong Kingston, and Leslie Marmon Silko.[17]

The association of ethnic writing with realism predates the start of the twentieth century. It was Howells who was the most prominent standard-bearer for realist writing in the latter part of the nineteenth century, and he took a keen interest in the works of writers like the African American Charles Chesnutt and the Russian-Jewish immigrant Abraham Cahan, whose writings investigated race-oriented and ethnic themes. Maintaining that realism "is nothing more and nothing less than the truthful treatment of material," Howells understood the pressing project of American fiction at the end of the nineteenth century to be taking up the work that romanticism could no longer do.[18] In *Criticism and Fiction* (1891), a collection of editor's columns from *Harper's Weekly*, Howells wrote:

> Romanticism then sought, as realism seeks now, to widen the bounds of sympathy, to level every barrier against aesthetic freedom, to escape from the paralysis of tradition. It exhausted itself in this impulse; and it remained for realism to assert that fidelity to experience and probability of motive are essential conditions of a great imaginative literature. It is not a new theory, but it has never before universally characterized literary endeavor. When realism becomes false to itself, when it heaps up facts merely, and maps life instead of picturing it, realism will perish too.[19]

In seeking to escape the paralysis of tradition, romanticism had, in the view of Howells and other realists, become too concerned with abstractions. One strategy for the would-be realist was to become a regionalist and to write "local-color fiction." According to Howells's contemporary, the novelist and critic Hjalmar Hjorth Boyesen, "Nothing could testify with more force to the fact that we have outgrown romanticism than this almost unanimous desire to chronicle the widely divergent phases of our American civilization. There are scarcely a dozen conspicuous States now which have not their own local novelist."[20]

For Boyesen, romanticism is at odds with the reality of nineteenth-century life in the United States. Hawthorne, he argued, was at a disadvantage because he "labored as a romancer in a world ostensibly devoid of romance," though his writing bears touches of the realist sensibility in the "exquisite delicacy with which he reproduces the tone and color of any locality which forms the settings of his more important scenes." Boyesen praised Harriet Beecher Stowe's *Oldtown Folks* (1869) for its "minute power of observation and an appreciation of local color which might almost entitle her to the name of a realist." Crediting Howells above all for the "triumph of realism in American fiction," Boyesen argues that it is "because Realism has ousted or is ousting Romanticism from all its strongholds that we have a literature worthy of serious consideration, and growing every year more virile, independent, and significant."[21]

Realism, however, has always been a capacious and rather nebulous term. Critics regularly include James and Twain with Howells as major realist writers of the late nineteenth century, though neither of them used the term to describe his practice or openly took part in what Howells called the "realist war" that began in the 1880s.[22] This grouping alone suggests that realism might best be defined in this period as simply writing that takes issue with some tenet of American romanticism. The realism of Howells turns on his attention to the dynamics of class and their embodiment in material details, while James's *Portrait of a Lady* (1881) is often described as an example of "psychological" realism. In contrast, Twain's *Huckleberry Finn* (1884) seems "realistic" because of its use of dialect and its Southern setting, as well as its attention to the ways in which class, race, and the institution of slavery affect its characters. In addition, critics argue over whether the term *naturalism*, which is typically applied to the writings of Stephen Crane, Frank Norris, and Theodore Dreiser, should be conceived as a repudiation of realism or an extension of it. Reviewers typically referred to Crane as a "realist."[23]

Realism paved the way for Charles Chesnutt to become the first African American author to be published by an upmarket, literary publisher. The "conjure tales" that were first published in the *Atlantic* and then collected in *The Conjure Woman* (1899), which was published by Houghton, Mifflin, were examples of regionalist fiction, local color tales that followed literary conventions established in Joel Chandler Harris's successful collection *Uncle Remus: His Songs and Sayings* (1881). Each tale features a prologue by the white narrator, John, who then yields to the storytelling voice of a freedman named Uncle Julius, who (like Harris's Uncle Remus) then proceeds to tell a story in black dialect from his years on the plantation. As Uncle Julius tells his stories about conjuring to John and his wife, Annie, he plays on their expectations and at the end of each story manages to get something of value from them. At the end of the first story, "The Goophered Grapevine," ostensibly told by Julius to dissuade John from buying the vineyard on which Julius happens to live, we realize that Julius has made a sly case for his own indispensability in the event that John ignores his advice and buys the grapevine: only Julius can tell which vines have been "goophered" and which have not. John reveals that he did indeed buy the vineyard and hired Julius as a coachman afterward. This story and others offers an allegory of Chesnutt's own position as a storyteller, able to manipulate his Northern white readership by giving them local color fiction, full of hokey magic, but made to seem "realist" through the use of black dialect.

In Chesnutt's case, however, this regionalist form of realism came to seem like a strait jacket. The first three stories from *The Conjure Woman* had been published between August 1887 and June 1889, and in the fall of 1889, Chesnutt wrote in a letter, "I think I have about used up the old Negro who serves as a mouthpiece, and I shall drop him in future stories, as well as much of the dialect."[24] Although Chesnutt would continue to use Uncle Julius as a character in stories written over the next seven years, the new stories did not feature conjuring and downplayed elements of the marvelous. When Chesnutt submitted a group of stories to Houghton, Mifflin in 1897, his proposed collection was rejected by a senior member of the company, Walter Hines Page, who was also an editor at the *Atlantic*. Page, however, proposed an alternative:

> "There is yet a possibility of Mssrs. Houghton, Mifflin and Company's doing something for you along this line—if you had enough 'conjure'

stories to make a book, even a small book. I cannot help feeling that that would succeed. All the readers who have read your stories agree on this—that 'The Goophered Grapevine' and 'Po' Sandy,' and the one or two others that have the same original quality that these show, are stories that are sure to live—in fact, I know of nothing so good of their kind anywhere. For myself, I venture unhesitatingly the prediction of a notable and lasting success with them, but the trouble at present is there are only about three of these stories which have this quality unmixed with other qualities. If you could produce five or six more like these, I think I am safe in making you a double promise—first, of magazine publication, and then the collection, I think would make a successful book."[25]

Chesnutt responded by writing six additional tales, which were added to the first three to make up *The Conjure Woman*.

With the success of that volume, Chesnutt sought once again to move away from the regionalist mode. The stories in his next collection, *The Wife of His Youth and Other Tales of the Color Line* (1899), were designed (as Chesnutt wrote to his publisher) "to depict life as it is, in certain aspects that no one has ever before attempted to adequately describe," but also to "throw a light upon the great problem on which the stories are strung; for the backbone of this volume is not a character, like Uncle Julius in *The Conjure Woman*, but a subject, as indicated in the title—*The Color Line*."[26] He explored the color line again in his novel *The House behind the Cedars* (1900), which dramatized the attempts of a brother and a sister to pass for white.

His next novel, however, explored a politically charged incident that had taken place in November 1898, in which a disputed election in Wilmington, North Carolina, led to a riot and an outbreak of mass violence against African Americans. Chesnutt wrote to Page that he was "deeply concerned and very much depressed at the conditions in North Carolina," and he described the riot as "an outbreak of pure, malignant and altogether indefensible race prejudice, which makes me feel personally humiliated, and ashamed for the country and the state."[27] *The Marrow of Tradition* (1901) was Chesnutt's response to this event, a fictionalized account of the riot. Howells had praised Chesnutt's earlier work: he called the stories in *The Wife of His Youth* "new and fresh and strong, as life always is, and fable never is," adding that "the stories of

The Conjure Woman have a wild, indigenous poetry, the creation of sincere and original imagination, which is imparted with a tender humorousness and a very artistic reticence."[28] But he was disappointed by *The Marrow of Tradition*: in his review of the novel, Howells recognized the justice of Chesnutt's cause but regretted the bitterness with which Chesnutt chose to dramatize it. Chesnutt, he wrote, "stands up for his own people, with a courage which has more justice than mercy in it. The book is, in fact, bitter, bitter."[29] The publication of the novel caused a rift between Howells and Chesnutt that was never repaired. Chesnutt turned away from literature to devote himself to the stenography firm that he had established in Cleveland in 1887, the year that he had passed the bar exam and published his first story, "The Goophered Grapevine." What Chesnutt discovered was that an African American author could be a "realist" so long as he produced conjure tales or seemingly apolitical stories about the color line, but the realism of *The Marrow Tradition* crossed a line beyond which his white readership was loathe to go.

Another young writer in whom Howells took an interest was the Russian-Jewish immigrant Abraham Cahan, who had come to the United States in 1881 in order to avoid being arrested as a revolutionary in the aftermath of the assassination of Tsar Alexander II. A dedicated socialist, Cahan sought to interpret U.S. culture to his fellow immigrants. He had become a fan Howell's writing during the 1880s, when Howells was writing a series of novels that addressed the problems of class difference and poverty; in 1889, Cahan delivered a lecture on "Realism" before the New York Labor Lyceum, in which he presented Tolstoy and Howells as practitioners of realism in literature. Cahan was a "walking delegate," a union representative seeking to organize sweatshop workers, and Howells sought him out as part of his research for his Utopian novel, *A Traveler from Altruria* (1894). Howells encouraged Cahan to write fiction and sought to help him have his first novel, *Yekl*, published. Howells's own publisher rejected the book, saying that "the life of an East-Side Jew wouldn't interest the American reader." One editor wrote to Howells that "our readers want to have a novel about richly-dressed cavaliers and women, about love which begins in the fields while they are playing golf. How can a novel about a Jewish immigrant, a blacksmith who became a tailor here, and whose wife is ignorant interest them?"[30] Cahan later recalled in his autobiography that Howells comforted him by saying that "even though he had the big-gest name, cheap trashy novels sold better than Howells's best works, and reviews of his writings showed that the critics had a quite primitive view of literature."[31] Cahan translated *Yekl* into Yiddish, and it was published in 1895 in *Arbeiter Zeitung*, the Yiddish-language newspaper that Cahan edited from 1891 to 1895. Howells made a final attempt, submitting the manuscript to D. Appleton, who accepted it. *Yekl* was published during the summer of 1896, and Howells reviewed it for the New York *World*.

Howell's review was titled "New York Low Life in Fiction" and paired Cahan's novel with Stephen Crane's latest novel, *George's Mother* (1896). Printed between the byline and the text was a special sub-headline: "The Great Novelist Hails Abraham Cahan, the Author of 'Yekl,' as a New Star of Realism, and Says that He and Stephen Crane Have Drawn the Truest Pictures of East Side Life." Howells praises Cahan as "a writer of foreign birth who will do honor to American letters, as Boyesen did," but his review replicates the distinction between "Americans" and Jews that ran through the various editorial rejection letters that Cahan had received. Cahan is a "Russian," and because "romanticism is not consid-ered literature in Russia, his story is, of course, intensely realistic" just as Crane's are. Yet, although "the artistic principle which moves both writers is the same," Howells implies that Cahan's writing is more powe-ful because "the picturesque, outlandish material with which Mr. Cahan deals makes a stronger appeal to the reader's fancy." Howells adds, "He has more humor than the American, too, whose spare laughter is apt to be grim, while the Russian cannot hide the relish of the comic incidents of his story." Implicit in Howell's review is a kind of cultural essential-ism, in which many of Cahan's strengths as a writer are the result of "the far and rich perceptions of his Hebraic race"; Cahan's English is "marvelous" because it has the "simplicity and purity" of "a man born to write Russian."[32]

Howell's praised Cahan's next book, *The Imported Bridegroom and Other Stories* (1898), equally enthusiastically, and he begins his review by asserting that Cahan is a regionalist writer:

Abraham Cahan's last book bears the same topographical relation to the East Side of New York that Miss Wilkins' bears to New England, or Miss Nicholas' to Indiana, or Miss Bell's to the South, or Mr. Gray's to Western

New York. No American fiction of the year merits recognition more than this Russian's stories of Yiddish life, which are so entirely of our time and place, and so foreign to our race and civilization.

Once again, Cahan's subject is represented as un-American, and much of its interest lies precisely in the fact that it *is* un-American, that it is "so foreign to our race and civilization." Like Chesnutt with his conjure stories, Cahan is being praised for treating an "outlandish" subject realistically. The comparison to regionalist writers, who are typically bringing stories about provincial life to the attention of a metropolitan audience, suggests that there is something provincial about the Lower East Side, even though it lies in the heart of one of the oldest districts of the metropolis. Indeed, Howells concludes the review by wondering whether Cahan will ever tackle a truly American subject: "It will be interesting to see whether Mr. Cahan will pass beyond his present environment out into the larger American world , or will master our life as he has mastered our language."[33] Cahan would write only one more literary fiction in English, his 1917 novel, *The Rise of David Levinsky*, which tells the story of the Americanization of a Jewish businessman and was inspired by Howells's novel *The Rise of Silas Lapham* (1884). Howells called the book an "artistic triumph," though privately he felt that the book was "too sensual."[34]

Cahan would turn away from literature for reasons similar to Chesnutt's, concentrating his efforts on the the Yiddish newspaper the *Jewish Daily Forward*, which he helped found in 1897 and edited from 1902 until his death in 1951. The landmarks in Jewish American fiction published after Cahan's *David Levinsky* and before the beginning of World War II tended, however, to follow that novel's model, adopting realist modes of representation and being very frequently autobiographically inflected. Michael Gold's autobiographical novel *Jews without Money* (1930), published at the outset of the depression, was an indictment of capitalism that touched a nerve with its vivid depictions of the degrading conditions in the Lower East Side. The book had eleven printings in its first year of publication and made Gold a national figure. Even Henry Roth's *Call It Sleep* (1934), long viewed as the sole example of a Jewish American text in the modernist tradition, begins in a realistic autobiographical mode before it veers away into formal experimentation.

The foremost proponent of realism among African American writers during the first half of the twentieth century was Richard Wright. Prompted by the publication of Wright's first novel, *Native Son* (1940), the prominent African American intellectual leader Alain Locke wrote in the January 1941 issue of *Opportunity* about the difficulties that face writers who belong to groups deemed to be minorities in the United States: "Minorities have their artistic troubles as well as their social and economic ones, and one of them is to secure proper imaginative representation, particularly in fiction and drama. For here the warped social perspective induces a twisted artistic one." Echoing Samuel Johnson's description of Shakespeare's genius at characterization, Locke argues that in fiction and drama, "characterization must be abstract enough to be typical, individual enough to be convincingly human." He then goes on, however, to delineate the way in which this problem of representation, difficult as it is for any writer, is made more difficult in a culture of prejudice: "The delicate balance between the type and the concrete individual can be struck more easily where social groups, on the one hand, have not been made supersensitive and morbid by caste and persecution, or on the other, where majority prejudice does not encourage hasty and fallacious generalization." In such cultural situations, "an artist is free to create with a single eye to his own artistic vision." Locke argues that when Shakespeare depicts Macbeth murdering his king, the audience will not believe that "all Scotchmen [are] treacherous hosts"; but he continues, "it is often a different matter with Shylock, and oftener still with Uncle Tom or Porgy."[35] Because Jews were a vilified minority in Shakespeare's time, an English audience is likely to believe that Shylock's greed and vengefulness are typical of all Jews, rather than examples of an individual's failing. The submissiveness of Stowe's Uncle Tom might be taken as a trait common to all Americans of African descent.

Locke quickly turns his attention to Richard Wright's *Native Son* (which provided the occasion for his essay), with the implicit assumption that in order for minorities to assure that they are properly represented, they must represent themselves. But once again the culture of prejudice that surrounds them creates problems, as the minority author must contend with questions that are never posed to non-minority authors. *Native Son* is a naturalist novel, which examines unflinchingly a young African American man's fall into crime and murder. "What about Bigger?" Locke asks: "Is he typical, or as some hotly contest, mis-representative? And whose 'native son' is he anyway?"[36] Locke's piece raises the question of the relationship between minority writing and literary realism. Is it the minority writer's responsibility to use realism as a means to combat deleterious stereotypes such as the submissive darky or the greedy Jew? But what happens when realistic representa-tion involves unflattering depictions of members of a minority group? Is it irresponsible for a writer to portray an individual from a minor-ity group realistically in this case, if there is a risk that the audience will take a character's vices and failings to be representative rather than individual and idiosyncratic? Locke's comment about Shylock suggests that it might be (assuming, of course, that it is not Shakespeare's intent to foment prejudice). Should the minority writer avoid realism, por-traying things as they should be rather than they are, if realistic repre-sentation is likely to reinforce stereotypes rather than undermine them? Was it irresponsible of Wright to create Bigger Thomas, knowing that many of Wright's readers would see in Bigger confirmation of all their worst fears about African Americans?

Locke sidesteps this question by arguing that *Native Son* must be understood not primarily in the context of African U.S. culture, but rather "in the context of contemporary American literature, its view-points and trends." Only then "is it possible to get a sound and objective appraisal of *Native Son*." Locke characterizes twentieth-century Ameri-can literature as a progressive endeavor: "Year by year, we have been noticing the rising tide of realism, with its accompanying boon of social honesty and artistic integrity. Gradually it has transformed both the fic-tion of the American South and of the Negro." Writers like Faulkner have, in Locke's view, "released us from the banal stereotypes—where all Southern ladies were irreproachable and all Southern colonels paragons of honor and chivalry." In this context, "another sort of Negro hero and heroine" are required, and Locke declares that "it is to Richard Wright's everlasting credit to have hung the portrait of Bigger Thomas alongside in this gallery of stark contemporary realism." In Locke's view, Bigger is not a portrait of the African American but rather a mirror held up to a racist white culture: "Wright's portrait of Bigger Thomas says more about America than it does about the Negro, for he is the native son of the black city ghetto, with its tensions, frustrations and resentments."

Ultimately, Locke believes that Wright's novel is a "timely and incisive analysis of the core dilemmas of the situation of race and American democracy."[37]

Wright and Locke both believe that literary realism is the most effective and most responsible technique for the minority author. Their commitment to realism led them to disparage Zora Neale Hurston's novel *Their Eyes Were Watching God* (1937) in what has become known as the "Hurston-Wright debate." In her 1928 essay, "How It Feels to Be Colored Me," Hurston had distanced herself from what she called "the sobbing school of Negrohood":

> I am not tragically colored. There is no great sorrow dammed up in my soul, nor lurking behind my eyes. I do not mind at all. I do not belong to the sobbing school of Negrohood who hold that nature somehow has given them a lowdown dirty deal and whose feelings are all hurt about it. Even in the helter-skelter skirmish that is my life, I have seen that the world is to the strong regardless of a little pigmentation more of less. No, I do not weep at the world—I am too busy sharpening my oyster knife.
>
> Someone is always at my elbow reminding me that I am the granddaughter of slaves. It fails to register depression with me. Slavery is sixty years in the past. The operation was successful and the patient is doing well, thank you. The terrible struggle that made me an American out of a potential slave said "On the line!" The Reconstruction said "Get set!" and the generation before said "Go!" I am off to a flying start and I must not halt in the stretch to look behind and weep. Slavery is the price I paid for civilization, and the choice was not with me.[38]

Hurston's first book, *Jonah's Gourd Vine* (1934), was described by the *New York Times* as "the most vital and original novel about the American Negro that has yet been written by a member of the Negro race. It is to be hoped," the reviewer concluded, "that Miss Hurston will give us other novels in the same colorful idiom."[39] For Wright, this "colorful idiom," which he believed to be the source of Hurston's appeal to white audiences, was a symptom of her retrograde romanticism. In a scathing review of Hurston's *Their Eyes Were Watching God* (1937), which the

New York Times had described as "beautiful," Wright castigated Hurston for her "highly charged language":

> Miss Hurston can write; but her prose is cloaked in that facile sensuality that has dogged Negro expression since the days of Phillis Wheatley. Her dialogue manages to catch the psychological movements of the Negro folk-mind in their pure simplicity, but that's as far as it goes.
>
> Miss Hurston *voluntarily* continues in her novel the tradition which was *forced* upon the Negro in the theater, that is, the minstrel technique that makes the "white folks" laugh. Her characters eat and laugh and cry and work and kill; they swing like a pendulum eternally in that safe and narrow orbit in which America likes to see the Negro live: between laughter and tears.
>
> . . . The sensory sweep of her novel carries no theme, no message, no thought. In the main, her novel is not addressed to the Negro, but to a white audience whose chauvinistic tastes she knows how to satisfy. She exploits the phase of Negro life which is "quaint," the phase which evokes a piteous smile on the lips of the "superior" race.[40]

Hurston responded by reviewing Wright's first collection of stories, *Uncle Tom's Children* (1938), and describing it as "a book about hatreds." No doubt believing that the book belongs to the "sobbing school of Negrohood," Hurston wrote that "Mr. Wright serves notice by his title that he speaks of people in revolt, and his stories are so grim that the Dismal Swamp of race hatred must be where they live. Not one act of understanding and sympathy comes to pass in the entire work." Despite her reservations about Wright's command of dialect, Hurston allows that "the book contains some beautiful writing. One hopes that Mr. Wright will find in Negro life a vehicle for his talents."[41]

Alain Locke, who had been one of Hurston's supporters, voiced his opinion in a round-up of the previous year's African American writing for the June 1, 1938, issue of *Opportunity* magazine. He described *Their Eyes* as "folklore fiction at its best, which we gratefully accept as an overdue replacement for so much faulty local color fiction about Negroes." He goes on, however, to chastise Hurston for squandering her gifts:

> When will the Negro novelist of maturity, who knows how to tell a story convincingly—which is Miss Hurston's cradle gift, come to grips with motive fiction and social document fiction? Progressive southern fiction has already banished the legend of these entertaining pseudo-primitives whom the reading public still love to laugh with, weep over and envy. Having gotten rid of condescension, let us now get over oversimplification![42]

Locke believed that Hurston, who was trained in anthropology, was writing from folklore rather than life and thereby reducing the representation of African American life to a species of local color fiction. What he wanted—and what he believed that African American letters needed—was realism.

Native Son proved to be a watershed in both African American literature and in U.S. ethnic writing more generally. The novel pushed African American literature onto new ground: no longer would an African American author have to shy away from creating a character like Wright's Bigger Thomas for fear of reinforcing a negative stereotype. As the Jewish critic Irving Howe put it in a widely read 1963 essay, "The day *Native Son* appeared, American culture was changed forever. No matter how much qualifying the book might later need, it made impossible a repetition of the old lies."[43]

In his autobiographical narrative, *America Is in the Heart* (1943), the Filipino American writer Carlos Bulosan recalls finding a literary role model in Wright:

> I was fortunate to find work in a library and to be close to books. In later years I remembered this opportunity when I read that the American Negro writer, Richard Wright, had not been allowed to borrow books from his local library because of his color. I was beginning to understand what was going on around me, and the darkness that had covered my present life was lifting. I was emerging into sunlight, and I was to know, a decade afterward in America, that this light was not too strong for eyes that had known only darkness and gloom.[44]

Later on, in an autobiographical piece entitled "My Education" (1979), Bulosan recalls the American writers whose work he read:

Hemingway was too preoccupied with himself, and consequently he wrote of himself and his frustrations. I was also disappointed with Faulkner. Why did he give form to decay? And Caldwell, Steinbeck— why did they write in costume? And Odets, why only middle class disintegration? Am I not an immigrant like Louis Adamic? Perhaps I could not understand America like Richard Wright, but I felt that I would be ineffectual if I did not return to my own people. I believed that my work would be more vital and useful if I dedicated it to the cause of my own people.[45]

Noting the "affinities" between *Native Son* and *America Is in the Heart*, Oscar Campomanes and Todd S. Gernes suggest that Bulosan's book "acknowledges an artistic and spiritual debt" to Wright, whose life and work may have "sparked [Bulosan's] own social and intellectual awakening."[46] What Bulosan seems to recognize in Wright is a kindred spirit: both men are writing from within a national culture that treats peoples of color like second-class citizens and devalues the intellectual work of minority writers. The publication of *Native Son* made Wright one of the most visible and vocal opponents of U.S. culture's oppression of its minorities, and his work offered a natural template to a young minority writer like Bulosan.

In 1964, the critic Daniel Aaron responded to Howe's defense of Wright with an astute essay entitled "The Hyphenate Writer and American Letters" in which he tried to delineate a trajectory that both Jewish American and African American writing had followed—and that most minority literatures in the United States were likely to follow.[47] Aaron describes a three-stage process "by which the 'minority' writer [passes] from . . . 'hyphenation' to 'dehyphenation.'" In the first stage, "the pioneer spokesman for a hitherto unspoken-for minority—ethnic, racial, or cultural—writes about his Negro or Jewish compatriots in an effort to overcome—or better, to blur—the antiminority stereotype already stamped in the minds of the old-stock Americans." In the second stage, "the hyphenate writer tends to be less conciliatory, less willing to please. . . . As he personalizes the consequences of discrimination and exploitation, he incurs the risk of a double criticism: from the official voices of the status quo, who resent his unflattering or even 'un-American' image of American life, and from his own ethnic or racial fellows who would prefer a genteel and uncantankerous spokesman and who accuse him of misrepresenting his own people." Finally, Aaron argues,

> in the third stage, the minority writer passes from the periphery to the center of his society, viewing it no less critically, perhaps but more knowingly. He no longer feels hyphenated, because he has appropriated its culture and linked himself with his illustrious literary predecessors to the degree that he can now speak out uninhibitedly as an American. . . . Without renouncing his ethnic or racial past, he has translated his own and his minority's personal experiences . . . into the province of the imagination.[48]

Aaron's essay argues that the process of dehyphenation is both desirable and inevitable for ethnic writers who seek to be literary artists. For Aaron, dehyphenation is not only a process of Americanization, but also a process of individuation and universalization. Aaron argues that dehyphenation is "not hostile to the democratic dream of diversity, or to the foreign bodies in national life that have invigorated American language and literature." Moreover, the dehyphenated writer "is not "necessarily conciliatory and apolitical. His protest or revolt, however, is made as a man and as a writer—not as a self-appointed spokesman for a minority, a class, a race. It is the human condition and the human predicament, finally, that engage him."[49] Aaron's either/or logic suggests that you can be either "hyphenate" or "American," but not both, and that ultimately, to be a literary artist, you must be neither. The solution to the problem of hyphenation is, for Aaron, ultimately a universalist humanism.

Aaron is careful to note that what he is describing should not be viewed as "a chronological process with each of the three stages clearly demarcated from the others," because "literary periods and groups and developments never work out so patly in actuality as they appear to do in the summaries of literary historians." Indeed, he suggests that at a given moment a single minority group may provide examples of writers who fit each of the stages that he has outlined.[50]

Aaron felt confident in 1963 that Jewish American literature fit the pattern he had discerned. "Abraham Cahan's fine novel *The Rise of David Levinsky* (1917), Michael Gold's *Jews Without Money* (1930), Saul

Bellow's *The Victim* (1947), and Bernard Malamud's *The Assistant* (1957) all deal with Jews, but the last two books are by writers who feel more at home in their country than did their ghetto-bred forerunners. Their characters are people who also happen to be Jews." What has changed in Bellow and Malamud is not "the subject matter," but rather the writer's "attitude, his mental stance, his way of looking at his friends and relatives, at himself and the world. . . . He no longer peers out from behind the minority barricade. In fact, he is no longer the *conscious* 'representative' of a national or racial group, but a writer, a disaffiliate. Race and religion and ethnic origin are merely so many colors for his writer's palette."[51]

Aaron rightly wonders, however, whether the opportunities for dehyphenation that are presented to white minority writers—whether Jewish, Irish, Italian, or something else—are, at the time that he is writing, also open to African Americans. By 1980, however, Maxine Hong Kingston can cite African American literature's ability to transcend the association between realism and ethnic writing, telling an interviewer: "There is an expectation among readers and critics that I *should* represent the race. I don't like hearing non-Chinese people say to a Chinese person, 'Well now I know about you because I have read Maxine Hong Kingston's books.' Each artist has a unique voice. Many readers don't understand that. The problem of how representative one is will only be solved when we have many more Chinese American writers. Then readers will see how diverse our people are. Black writers have already surmounted the problem."[52] In their different ways, writers like James Baldwin, Ralph Ellison, and Toni Morrison are able to mediate between the claims of "universalization" and "individuation," producing novels that become staples not only of courses in "African American Literature" but also of courses in "American Literature." Morrison's winning of the Nobel Prize in 1993 might serve as a way of marking the end of African American literature's status as an emergent literature in the context of U.S. literary culture. The citation from the Swedish academy praised Morrison as a writer "who in novels characterized by visionary force and poetic import, gives life to an essential aspect of American reality."[53]

One of the goals of emergent writing is to induce the second type of change that Hans Robert Jauss describes in theorizing the "horizon of expectations," in which a later work causes readers to see an earlier work with fresh eyes. The Spokane/Coeur d'Alene writer Sherman Alexie exemplifies this shift in his poem "Defending Walt Whitman" (1996), which uses humor to pay homage to Whitman but also to put him in his place:

> Basketball is like this for Walt Whitman. He watches these Indian boys
> as if they were the last bodies on earth. Every body is brown!
> Walt Whitman shakes because he believes in God.
> Walt Whitman dreams of the Indian boy who will defend him,
> trapping him in the corner, all flailing arms and legs
> and legendary stomach muscles. . . .
>
> . . . .
> There is no place like this. Walt Whitman smiles.
> Walt Whitman shakes. This game belongs to him.

These whimsical lines dramatize the predicament faced not only by Native American writers, but also by all U.S. writers who belong to emergent literary traditions. As a Spokane/Coeur d'Alene Native American, Alexie is playing a game in which he is the underdog and Whitman the favorite: Whitman dominates the landscape of U.S. poetry; his powerful shots "strike[e] the rim so hard that it sparks"; the "game belongs to him." The poem imagines "Indian boys" who must defend against Whitman, who must prevent him from scoring by blocking his shots. Yet it also imagines other Native Americans, those who are Whitman's teammates: "Some body throws a crazy pass," Alexie writes, "and Walt Whitman catches it with quick hands." These Native Americans work with Whitman; they defend *him* against those who oppose him. The poem pays homage to Whitman by adopting his free verse idiom and by describing the game from his perspective. At the same time, however, it shows us a Whitman who is out of place, who is awed by the "twentieth-century warriors" surrounding him, whose "beard is ludicrous on the reservation," who "stands / at center court while the Indian boys run from basket to basket," who "cannot tell the difference between / offense and defense." The poem's title is a pun, simultaneously with Whitman and against him. The poem celebrates Whitman, even as it seeks to contain him within the context of "a reservation summer basketball court." At the same time, the poem luxuriates in homosociality:

Walt Whitman dreams of the Indian boy who will defend him,
trapping him in the corner, all flailing arms and legs
and legendary stomach muscles. . . . [54]

"Defending Walt Whitman" asks us to reread Walt Whitman, that most canonical of U.S. poets, and to recall that as a gay man writing about sexuality, Whitman was—and, in this respect, still is—an emergent writer.

Melville gets similar treatment in Alexie's novel *Flight* (2007), which begins: "Call me Zits."[55] If Kingston's *Tripmaster Monkey* adopts an attitude of resentment toward Melville, with its protagonist suggesting that the dilemma of whether or not to introduce one's race was not something that Melville faced, Alexie's opening line resituates Melville as a disaffected young writer whose works are misunderstood. When *Moby-Dick* appeared in 1851, it was an emergent text: with its opening "Etymology" and "Extracts" sections, its enigmatic, encyclopedically minded narrator, Ishmael, and its portrayal of Ishmael and the South Seas harpooneer Queequeg as a "cosy, loving pair," *Moby-Dick* openly challenged the dominant horizon of expectations for a novel. Melville negotiated with both the dominant literary culture and dominant national culture—and lost, only to be revived some seventy years later as an exemplar of the dominant culture, the centerpiece of an American national literature that, its proponents argued, could match the European national traditions for excellence.

The model of cultural interaction implicit in the novel seems to anticipate both Williams's and Appiah's descriptions of cultural conversation and negotiation. Melville's narrator calls himself "Ishmael," a reference to Abraham's illegitimate son, the biblical outcast traditionally believed to be the progenitor of the Arabs. The name "Ishmael" thus signifies someone who stands outside of the dominant Western biblical tradition. As Lauter suggests, in valorizing *Moby-Dick*, its early twentieth-century champions focused on one aspect of the novel's emergent perspective—its formal experimentation—but excluded what was emergent about the novel thematically, namely its interest in "social and culture 'other[s]'"—in my terms, its cosmopolitan perspective. Ishmael is an outsider throughout the novel, a first-time whaleman who hails not from a traditional whaling town, but from New York. I believe that

Melville opens the novel in the "city of the Manhattoes" in order to align Ishmael's perspective with what the intellectual historian Thomas Bender calls "the historic cosmopolitanism of New York." Unlike New England Puritanism and Jeffersonian agrarianism, which Bender describes as "the most influential myths of America," New York's cosmopolitanism does not "reject the idea of difference"; indeed, according to Bender, "Very early in the city's history, difference and conflict among interests were acknowledged as not only inevitable but perhaps of positive value."[56] Later in the novel, Ishmael writes, "I freely assert, that the cosmopolite philosopher cannot, for his life, point out one single peaceful influence, which within the last sixty years has operated more potentially upon the whole broad world, taken in one aggregate, than the high and mighty business of whaling."[57] Ishmael here aligns himself with the cosmopolite philosopher by providing that philosopher with the salient example that he has been missing: for Ishmael it is not too outlandish to believe that the way to what Immanuel Kant called "perpetual peace" might be pioneered by whaleships.

The cosmopolitan experience is all about finding sameness across gulfs of difference: it's not about eradicating gaps in cultural experience but rather about bridging them. This is the experience that Ishmael craves at the end of the "Loomings" chapter: describing himself as "tormented with an everlasting itch for things remote," Ishmael tells us, "I love to sail forbidden seas, and land on barbarous coasts. Not ignoring what is good, I am quick to perceive a horror, and could still be social with it—would they let me—since it is but well to be on friendly terms with all the inmates of the place one lodges in."[58] Two chapters later he will meet the man who will become his "bosom buddy," the "wild cannibal" Queequeg. When Ishmael is saved at the end of the novel because he is able to hang onto a life buoy that Queequeg had intended to be his coffin and had carved with the likeness of the tattoos on his body, it is symbolically his relationship with Queequeg, his ability to reach out across cultural difference, that has saved him. In the epilogue, we learn that, as the Pequod is being dragged down into a vortex, Ishmael is saved precisely by being at "the margin of the ensuing scene."[59] *Moby-Dick* thus dramatizes the power of writing from the margins, of being in the *emergent* literary position.

Like Melville's Ishmael, the name of the narrator in Alexie's novel *Flight* marks him as an outsider, in this case a teenager whose facial disfigurement defines his identity even more than his mixed Native American and Irish background—unless, of course, his disfigurement is *caused* by his background. As Zits puts it:

> I'm dying from about ninety-nine kinds of shame.
>
> I'm ashamed of being fifteen years old. And being tall. And skinny. And ugly.
>
> I'm ashamed that I look like a bag of zits tied to a broomstick. I wonder if loneliness causes acne.
>
> I wonder if being Indian causes acne.[60]

Zits is a chatty narrator, but unlike Ishmael, he doesn't have encyclopedic aims, and *Flight* is brief novel. But its plot twists vertiginously as Zits—who may have just committed a mass murder—suddenly finds himself unstuck in time and space, inhabiting the bodies and subjectivities of a corrupt FBI agent, a mutilated Native American boy whose tribe is present at Custer's last stand, an old Native American scout leading U.S. Cavalry soldiers on a punitive raid to an Native American camp, a white flight instructor whose friend and pupil has used a plane to commit a terrorist act, and finally his own derelict father. Zits's body-hopping allows him to experience difference in a unique way: not only inhabiting the lives of others but inhabiting lives on opposite sides of violent cultural confrontations.

At the end of *Moby-Dick*, Ishmael is rescued from the seas by a ship called the *Rachel* which is searching for some crewmen, including its captain's son, who have fallen overboard: "It was the devious-cruising Rachel, that in her retracing search after her missing children, only found another orphan."[61] At the end of *Flight*, Zits is adopted by a white family and rescued from his past—and his name. We never learn whether Ishmael's real name is Ishmael, but we do learn Zits's name: no longer an outcast, Zits reveals and embraces his given name. It is "Michael," the archangel—a sign that Alexie's novel, for all of its anger, ultimately believes in the possibility of redemption.[62] That is one way to sum up the project of U.S. emergent literatures after 1968.

4

Liberation Movements

On May 17, 1954, the U.S. Supreme Court paved the way for the Civil Rights movement of the 1960s by issuing its landmark decision in *Brown v. Board of Education.* The Court overturned its ruling in *Plessy v. Ferguson* (1896), which had legalized segregation according to race. In a unanimous decision, the Court declared that "separate educational facilities are inherently unequal" and therefore violated the Equal Protection Clause of the Fourteenth Amendment of the Constitution. No longer would states be allowed to create public schools that were segregated according to race. Ten years later, the Civil Rights Act of 1964 mandated that voter registration requirements be applied equally to all individuals, regardless of race, and outlawed racial segregation not only in schools, but also at workplaces and public facilities. The bill had been introduced by President John F. Kennedy on June 11, 1963, in a television and radio speech to the nation in which he described the "moral crisis" facing the United States "as a country and as a people." Arguing that "it ought to be possible . . . for every American to enjoy the privileges of being American without regard to his race or his color," Kennedy declared "it is time to act in the Congress, in your State and local legislative body and, above all, in all of our daily lives."[1]

Emergent writing became a crucial part of the liberation movements of the 1960s. The Native American poet Simon Ortiz (Acoma Pueblo) describes the decade as "inspirational," "creative," and "invigorating," because it was a "worldwide phenomenon of third-world peoples decolonizing themselves and expressing their indigenous spirit, especially in Africa and the Americas." And, Ortiz argues, this "process of decolonizing includes a process of producing literature."[2] Describing "the condition of the Chicano" in 1972, Luis Valdez, the director of the radical Teatro Campesino, wrote, "Our people are a colonized race, and the root of their uniqueness as Man lies buried in the dust of conquest. In order to regain our corazon, our soul, we must reach deep into our people, into the tenderest memory of their beginning." And then he quotes the poet Alurista's poem "Mis ojos hichados":

>   razgos indígenas
>   the scars of history on my face
>   and the veins of my body
>   that aches
>   vomita sangre
>   y llora libertad
>   I do not ask for freedom
>   I AM freedom.[3]

What many Native American, Asian American, and Chicano writers learned from the experiences of the 1960s is that literature has a crucial role to play in the formation of ethnic identity and the creation of ethnic pride. Asked to compare the so-called "Native American Renaissance" to the "Harlem Renaissance in black writing," N. Scott Momaday points to Dee Brown's best-selling revisionist historical account, *Bury My Heart at Wounded Knee* (1970), researched and written during the 1960s, as a watershed; according to Momaday, the publication of Brown's book created "a sudden disposition to understand the experience of the Native American. The kind of burgeoning that we're talking about really happened in the publishing world rather than in any sort of social or political arena."[4] The early stages of both Asian American literature and Chicano/a literature were also marked by encounters with a "publishing world" that had paid little attention to these emergent literary traditions.

Hispanic American Literature

Hispanic American literature began to flower during the 1960s, led by a vibrant group of Chicano/a writers who saw themselves as part of a tradition of literature by Hispanic authors (written most often in Spanish but occasionally also in English) that existed on what is now U.S. soil as far as back as the sixteenth century. The expedition of Juan de Onate (1598–1608) produced the first New World example of the European tradition of epic poetry, *Historia de la Nueva Mexico* (1610), written by Gaspar Perez de Villagrá (1555–1620). The poem's thirty cantos, full of allusions to Classical epic and Christian doctrine, culminate with the brutal suppression of the Acoma pueblo. In the aftermath of the conquest of Nueva España (which later became Mexico), Spanish speakers created a vibrant oral culture that was a New World descendant of the medieval Spanish peninsular tradition of ballads and dramas. In the mid-nineteenth century, this Spanish culture, which had displaced the indigenous Native American culture, was itself displaced as a result of the Mexican-American War, which ended in 1848 with the Treaty of Guadalupe Hidalgo. The history of Chicano/a expression begins with the resulting Americanization of a vast area that had once been part of Mexico; U.S. Puerto Rican literature was shaped by the cultural aftershocks of Spain's loss of Puerto Rico to the United States in 1898.

In the genre of poetry, these two dominant strains of twentieth-century Hispanic American writing have much in common: Chicano/a literature and U.S. Puerto Rican literature share a Latin American heritage, a deep connection to Spanish language and culture, the experience of being a minority within U.S. culture, and an abiding interest in racial and ethnic mixing *(mestizaje)*. Both poetic traditions make frequent use of "code-switching" between English, Spanish, and other vernacular forms, a kind of linguistic *mestizaje* that serves not only to represent accurately the sociocultural situations of their communities but also to empower bilingual readers. Spanish represents the most visible and viable challenge to the hegemony of the English language in the United States, and the debates over bilingual education have been driven largely by the issue of classroom instruction in Spanish. The use of Spanish by U.S. Hispanic writers, either exclusively or in combination with English, serves as a challenge to the idea that "American literature" should be written in English.

There are, however, significant differences between these two dominant traditions of Hispanic American writing. Chicanos/as have a far more conflicted attitude toward their Spanish heritage, due in part to the fact that Mexican culture underwent two periods of anti-hispanism, once after independence in 1821 and then again during the Revolution of 1910. Many of the important early Chicano/a writers sought to stress their Native American heritage as the key to Chicano/a identity. In contrast, many Puerto Rican writers rebelled against the process of Americanization that began in 1898 when Spain ceded Puerto Rico to the United States and continued with the granting of U.S. citizenship to Puerto Ricans in 1917. A Hispanist strain of Puerto Rican writing arose that sought to achieve a "pure" poetry of lyricism, metaphor, and strong identification with Spanish culture. In addition, Chicano/a literature is grounded in a continental sense of geography, oriented in northern Mexico, while U.S. Puerto Rican literature is very much part of a Caribbean tradition of island writing. The history of European imperialism transforms this geographic distinction into a racial distinction: Chicano/a culture views itself primarily as a mixture of Native American and Spanish heritages, while Puerto Rican culture stresses its mixture of Spanish and black.

The flowering of Chicano/a literature is often considered to be the result of the Chicano Movement, which arose during the early 1960s in tandem with other movements aimed at gaining civil rights for disenfranchised minority groups. As a result, Chicano/a critics like Juan Bruce-Novoa, Raymund Paredes, and Ramón Saldívar tend to conceive of Chicano/a literature as an emergent literature that consciously defines itself against mainstream Anglo-American culture. Saldívar argues that "the narrative writings of Chicano women and men must be understood as different from and in resistance to traditional American literature, yet must also be understood in their American context, for they take their oppositional stance deliberately, in order to offer readers a reformulation of historical reality and contemporary culture." Most agree, too, with Bruce-Novoa's suggestion in the introduction to his study *Chicano Authors: Inquiry by Interview* (1980) that the "emergence" of "Chicano literature is a recent phenomenon" that was to a large extent "a by-product of the Chicano Movement, the socio-political civil rights struggle begun in the mid-1960's by and on behalf of people of Mexican descent living in the United States."[5]

José Antonio Villarreal's *Pocho* (1959), the first novel by a Mexican American author to be published by a mainstream American publishing house, uses the world of the *corridos* like "Gregorio Cortéz" as its point of departure. Taking its title from the Mexican epithet for an Ameri-canized Chicano/a, the novel is a *Künstlerroman* that tells the story of Richard Rubbio, a Mexican American boy growing up in California, whose father, Juan, was a companion of the legendary Pancho Villa and a hero of the Mexican Revolution. When the novel opens, however, the Mexican Revolution is long past—if not in years then in spirit: Villa has retired, his rival General Alvaro Obregón has become President of Mexico, and Juan Rubbio feels a disillusionment that embodies the loss of revolutionary fervor. Rubbio is a figure from the heroic *corrido*: the first scene of the novel presents him striding into a cantina in Ciudad Juárez, flirting with a young woman, and then deliberately insulting and shooting her lover. Once his identity is discovered by the soldiers who arrest him, Rubbio is treated with respect, even reverence, by the general in command at Juárez, an older man who feels emasculated and useless in the post-revolutionary political climate. By the end of the chapter, however, it is clear that the day of the heroic *corrido* and of men like Rubbio is over: when Rubbio learns that Villa has been killed, he resigns himself to eking out a living in the United States, "mourn[s] deeply for the loss of his god," and dreams of the day that he and his family can return to Mexico, while realizing with each passing year that he is now "one of the lost ones."[6]

After the first chapter, the novel shifts its focus almost exclusively to Rubbio's son, Richard, leaving behind the world of the *corrido* for the world of the *pocho*. Left behind too is the fusion of individual and communal values that characterizes the *corrido*: the culture into which Richard is born is a culture that valorizes individualism above all. Grow-ing up among Anglos in Santa Clara, California, Richard experiences what sociologists call *structural assimilation*: most of Richard's close friends are Anglos and his steady girlfriend is a white girl from Nordic and Portuguese stock. Like Joyce's *Portrait of the Artist as a Young Man* (1916), upon which it was modeled, *Pocho* presents a protagonist who attempts to forge an identity for himself, first by exploring his heritage as a Roman Catholic, then by attempting to understand his historical situation as a member of a colonized people (which for Richard means first-hand knowledge of union halls, strikes, and strike-related violence, as well as racial discrimination), and of course by coming to terms with the sexual feelings that accompany adolescence and young adulthood. Richard's development into a young man who decides that he wants to become a writer is set against the gradual disintegration of his family, and Richard comes to realize that he cannot "give [the] institution [of marriage] the importance it had falsely taken on through the centuries. Marriage, per se, was not life, nor could it govern life." Richard's process of assimilation is complete when he rejects both the "codes of honor" by which his father lives, and the Catholic faith that is so important to his mother, substituting instead a set of ideas about honor and faith that arise from his own personal experience. This "cultural assimilation" culminates when Richard declares to himself, "I can be a part of everything" late in the novel, "Because I am the only one capable of controlling my destiny. . . . Never—no, never—will I allow myself to become a part of a group—to become classified, to lose my individuality." At the end of *Pocho*, Richard takes up his father's old vocation—he joins the U.S. armed forces—but it is a gesture that represents the final break with the culture of Mexico that his father still embraces.[7]

Chicano/a critics disagree about the role that *Pocho* has played in Chicano/a literary history. Because of its obvious embrace of the tradition of the *Künstlerroman,* its linguistic style (which is firmly rooted in standard American English), and its assimilative stance (which resembles the one that Richard Rodriguez would later adopt), *Pocho* has been called "an American book with Mexican American characters and themes" and disparaged as "the kind of book" that subsequent "Mexican American writers neither admired nor wanted to write."[8] On the other hand, because subsequent landmark Chicano/a novels like Anaya's *Bless Me, Ultima* (1972) and Acosta's *The Autobiography of a Brown Buffalo* (1972) would also adopt the framework of the story of the writer's apprenticeship and because it treats themes that would become staples of later Chicano/a writing—immigration, Catholic culture, Mexican sexual taboos, the effects of assimilative pressure upon the traditional Mexican family—*Pocho* has also been called "the first

Chicano novel" and "a paradigmatic Chicano narrative," an example of a shift in the horizon of expectations.[9]

The etymology of the term "Chicano" is still hotly disputed among Chicano/a scholars. The most likely derivation is from "Mexicano," with the "x" pronounced the way it was at the time of the Spanish Conquest, as "sh." The term "Chicano," which came to prominence during the student movements of the 1960s, was eventually adopted by literary scholarship, which subsequently adopted the locution "Chicano/a" to mitigate gender bias. The term was not universally accepted by those whom it was intended to describe, however. According to the critic José Limón, "Almost immediately after . . . [its] public appearance within the student movement, the term set off controversy and debate within the larger U.S.-Mexican community. The general reaction ranged from indifference to outright rejection and hostility."[10] Various other terms gained currency in different regions, however: for example, "Hispano" and "Spanish American" were preferred terms in southern Colorado and northern New Mexico, while "Mexicano" was widely accepted in South Texas and in many of the border regions.

Equally hard to define is the so-called "Chicano Movement"—"La Causa"—which arose during the early 1960s in tandem with other movements aimed at gaining civil rights for disenfranchised minority groups. We might locate the origins of this widespread and diffuse set of social issues in the strike that became known as "La Huelga" a word that originally signified rest, repose, relaxation from work. In 1962, César Chávez founded the National Farm Workers Association in Delano, California; the NFWA would eventually become the United Farm Workers (UFW). On September 16, 1965, the *campesinos* of the NFWA voted to join the Filipino grape pickers who were on strike. La Huelga would last for five years and gain national attention with the grape boycott begun in New York in 1968. On a 250-mile pilgrimage to the state capitol, Sacramento, Chávez and his fellow strikers issued a document called "The Plan of Delano," which declared "the beginning of a social movement in fact and not in pronouncements. We seek our basic, God-given rights as human beings." It was a moment of solidarity among oppressed groups: "The strength of the poor," declared the plan, is "in union. We know that the poverty of the Mexican or Filipino worker in California is the same as that of all farm workers across the country, the

Negroes and poor whites, the Puerto Ricans, Japanese and Arabians; in short, all of the races that comprise the oppressed minorities of the United States."[11]

Out of the UFW came El Teatro Campesino, a bilingual theater company established by Luis Valdez in 1965 "to teach and organize Chicano farm workers." In an account contained in an anthology of Chicano/a writing entitled *Aztlán: An Anthology of Mexican American Literature* (1972) that he co-edited with Stan Stiner, Valdez recalled starting "in a broken-down shack in Delano, California, which was the strike office for César Chávez'[s] farm workers' union" by hanging "signs around people's necks, with the names of familiar character types: scab, striker, boss, etc. They started to act out everyday scenes on the picket line. These improvisations quickly became satirical. More people gathered around and started to laugh, to cheer the heroes and boo the villains; and we had our first show." In plays such as *Los Vendidos* (1967), *The Militants* (1969), and *Soldado Raso* (1971), Valdez updated Mexican and Spanish dramatic forms to dramatize issues that were important to the membership of the UFW. Their preferred form was the comic *acto*, a one-act play of less than half an hour that, according to Valdez, dealt "with the strike, the union and the problems of the farm worker." Satirizing the opponents of the UFW, the Teatro toured across the country in 1967 "to publicize the strike, performing at universities, in union halls and civic auditoriums, at New York's Village Theater, at the Newport Folk Festival and in the courtyard of the U.S. Senate Building in Washington, D. C.," receiving an Obie award in 1968 "for creating a workers' theater to demonstrate the politics of survival."[12] Valdez argued that "Chicano theater must be revolutionary in technique as well as content. It must be popular, subject to no other critics except the pueblo itself; but it must also educate the pueblo towards an appreciation of social change, on and off the stage."[13] In 1969, the Teatro filmed a version of *I am Joaquín*, an epic poem written in 1967 by another hero of the Chicano Movement, Rodolfo "Corky" Gonzales, who founded the Crusade for Justice in Colorado.

In 1970, Valdez introduced a second genre, the *mito* (myth), which Valdez describes as "a parable that unravels like a flower Indio fashion to reveal the total significance of a certain event." With its combination of parable and ritual, the *mito* allowed the Teatro to present longer narratives and to explore the Native American elements of Chicano/a identity. In 1971, Valdez published *Actos: The Teatro Campesino*, a collection of *actos* written between 1965 and 1971. "We will consider our job done," he wrote the next year, "when every one of our people has regained his sense of personal dignity and pride in his history, his culture, and his race."[14]

Drawing on the cultural energies let loose by El Teatro Campesino, a group of Chicano/a academics at the University of California, Berkeley, founded Quinto Sol Publications in 1969 to make works by Chicano/a authors available. Seeking to foster the growth of an identifiable Chicano/a literature, Quinto Sol began by publishing a journal called *El Grito*, which the novelist Tomás Rivera described in 1980 as the "one milestone" to date in Chicano/a literature.[15] Two years later it produced the first anthology of Chicano/a creative writing, *El espejo / The Mirror* (1st ed., 1969), edited by Octavio Romano-V. and Herminio Rios-C., leading Rivera to remark to the critic Juan Bruce-Novoa that the Chicanos/as were the first people to have an anthology before they had a literature.[16] The writers who became associated with Quinto Sol were self-conscious experimenters, who sought to break down boundaries between fiction and nonfiction, poetry and prose in order to capture the modern-day Chicano/a experience, while remaining true to the folk traditions that arose in Mexico and the Southwest. Many Chicano/a poets sought to take advantage of their bilingualism, blending Spanish and English in their poetry. The very existence of Quinto Sol gave Chicano/a authors a sense of empowerment.

In 1970, the publishers established El Premio Quinto Sol, a cash prize designed to establish a canon of Chicano/a novels; the project lasted for three years and its recipients—Tomás Rivera, Rudolfo Anaya, and Rolando Hinojosa-Smith—would become what Juan Bruce-Novoa calls "the Chicano Big Three," still the most widely read and studied of Chicano/a novelists. As inspirational as Villarreal's *Pocho* was to a generation of Chicano/a writers, by 1970 its assimilationist vision had come to seem problematic and even outdated. The blurb on the back cover of the paperback edition published in 1970 offers this apology: "To many young Mexican-Americans who seek an identity rooted in their own cultural heritage, the pocho represents much of what they, the chicanos, are trying to change." In his introduction to the paperback edition,

Ramón Ruiz damns the novel with faint praise, arguing that *Pocho* "has immense historical value for today's reader," because it "documents the intellectual-emotional evolvement of Mexican-Americans in a chronological sense." For Ruiz, Villarreal's handling of his protagonist's plight is outdated, and he concludes his introduction by championing the ideological point of view espoused by the newly christened Chicanos:

> In rebellion against his dual heritage, Richard stands defenseless, an insecure and beaten young man. Here Villarreal reveals the gulf that time and events have built between his generation of Mexican-Americans and chicanos. No longer are chicanos "lost" Richards. The militant and not-so-militant young with Spanish surnames have started to build, not just a regional political movement, but an identity to replace that sense of inferiority that settled down upon Richard in his lonely battle with reality.[17]

The scholar Raymund Paredes argued that "to its largely Anglo readership, *Pocho* was a moving portrait of a necessary if painful process of assimilation. To a Mexican American audience, awash in a rising tide of ethnic pride, however, *Pocho* was a story of terrible loss. . . . [It] was precisely the kind of book a new generation of Mexican American writers neither admired nor wanted to write."[18]

The first Quinto Sol prize was awarded to Tomás Rivera's novelistic collection of sketches about migrant workers, . . . *y no se lo tragó la tierra* (. . . *and the Earth Did Not Part*, 1971), which epitomized the Quinto Sol sensibility. Unlike *Pocho,* which depicts the displacement of traditional Chicano/a values by the individualist ideology of Anglo-America, *Tierra* portrays the survival of those values in the face of discrimination and economic hardship. According to Rivera, while he was writing *Tierra*, "The Chicano Movement was una fuerza total ya [a complete power already] in the university and so forth. I wanted to document, somehow, the strength of those people I had known"—the migrant workers of the period 1945 to 1955.[19] Influenced by the writings of such experimentalists as William Faulkner, James Joyce, John Dos Passos, and Juan Rulfo,[20] *Tierra* is a novel in the sense that Sherwood Anderson's *Winesburg, Ohio* (1919) might be considered a novel, and it begins on a note that briefly recalls the magical realism of Rulfo or

Latin American "Boom" writers like Jorge Luís Borges and Gabriel García Márquez:

> Aquel año se le perdió. A veces trataba de recordar y ya para cuando cría que se estaba aclarando todo un poco se le perdían las palabras. Casi siempre empezaba con un sueño donde despertaba de pronto y luego se daba cuenta de que realmente estaba dormido. Luego ya no supo is lo que pensaba había pasado o no.

> That year was lost to him. At times he tried to remember and, just about when he thought everything was clearing up some, he would be at a loss for words. It almost always began with a dream in which he would suddenly awaken and then realize that he was really asleep. Then he wouldn't know whether what he was thinking had happened or not.[21]

Magical realism is not the dominant mode of *Tierra*, however: what Rivera learns above all from the Rulfo of *El llano en llamas* (*The Burning Plain*, 1953) or *Pedro Páramo* (1955) is a sense of irony, detachment, and spareness.

The rest of *Tierra* consists of twelve sketches, each representing a month of the narrator's "lost year" and each preceded by an interchapter in the manner of Hemingway's *In Our Time* (1925), with a concluding sketch in which the narrator attempts to "discover and rediscover and piece things together." The sketches portray the harshness of the Chicano migrant's life: in "Los niños no se aguantaron" ("The Children Couldn't Wait"), a foreman accidentally shoots a young boy who has taken an unauthorized water break; in "Los quemaditos" ("The Little Burn Victims"), three children burn to death while left alone in a migrant worker's shack because "the owner didn't like children in the fields doing mischief and distracting their parents"; in "Cuando lleguemos" ("When We Arrive"), we hear the thoughts of workers crammed into a truck: "When we get there I'm gonna see about getting a good bed for my vieja. Her kidneys are really bothering her a lot nowadays. Just hope we don't end up in a chicken coop like last year, with that cement floor. Even though you cover it with straw, once the cold season sets in, you just can't stand it. That was why my rheumatism got so bad, I'm sure of that." Although *Tierra* seems, at first, to resemble Villarreal's *Pocho* in portraying one young man's search for self-understanding, Rivera's narrator ultimately bears more resemblance to Sherwood Anderson's George Willard: he floats through the different sketches, some of which are told in the first person, others in the third. The effect is less that of the traditional *Bildungsroman* than the portrayal of collective experience. What happens to the Chicano/a *Bildungsroman* as it moves from Villarreal to Rivera is that it becomes a form in which what is stake is the development not simply of the individual protagonist but also of the community and culture to which he or she belongs. In novels of development like *Tierra* and Sandra Cisneros's *The House on Mango Street* (1983), as well as autobiographies like Ernesto Galarza's *Barrio Boy* (1971), individual identity and communal identity develop simultaneously and are inseparably intertwined.[22]

The winner of the third Quinto Sol prize, Rolando Hinojosa's *Estampas del valle y otras obras (Sketches of the Valley and Other Works*, 1973), shares certain features with Rivera's *Tierra*: it is written in Spanish, makes use of the *estampa*, or sketch form, popularized by Julio Torri in Mexico, and takes as its setting southern Texas. Unlike Rivera's irony, which is always tinged with melancholy and bitterness, Hinojosa's irony is tinged with humor, as he describes human behavior that ranges from the heroic to the depraved. Where Rivera limited himself to the experience of migrant farm workers, Hinojosa aims to portray a far more representative version of Chicano/a life.

Set in Klail City, a fictional town in the Río Grande Valley, *Estampas del valle* consists of four different kinds of narrative: twenty portraits of the valley and its inhabitants by Jehú Malacara; six accounts of Badleamar Cordero's stabbing to death of Ernesto Tamez; a chronicle devoted to the lives of Texas Mexicans; and Rafa Buenrostro's recollections of his schooling and of his experiences in the Korean War. *Estampas* would prove to be the first in a series of novels—the *Klail City Death Trip* series—devoted to the depiction of "Belken County." Hinojosa's second novel, *Klail City y sus alrededores* (1976) was awarded the prestigious award for best novel of the year by the Cuban publishing house La Casa de las Américas; it was published in English in the United States in 1977 with the Spanish title *Generaciones y semblanzas* (Generations and Biographies). The series continued in 1978 with an extended verse narrative entitled *Korean Love Songs*, followed by *Mi querido Rafa (Dear*

Rafe, 1981), *Rites and Witnesses* (1982), *Partners in Crime* (1985), *Claros varones de Belken* (*Fair Gentlemen of Belken County* 1986), *Becky and Her Friends* (1989), and *Ask a Policeman* (1998).

Influenced by the narrative styles of both Faulkner and García Márquez, the *Klail City Death Trip* series continues the project begun by Américo Paredes in his study of "The Ballad of Gregorio Cortez": it offers a critique of the Anglo cultural mythologies surrounding the Texas Rangers in particular and the borderlands of the Southwest in general, while creating a massive historical fiction that has the effect of ennobling Chicano/a history. It also dramatizes the linguistic evolution of the cultures that it depicts: the Spanish of *Estampas del valle* gives way to the explicit bilingualism of *Mi querido Rafa*, which is followed by the English of *Rites and Witnesses*, whose protagonists—Jehú Malacara and Rafa Buenrostro—are enmeshed in the larger culture of the United States: "In the first two or three works," Hinojosa told an interviewer, "I focus mainly on the Texas-Mexican. But as both Rafa Buenrostro and Jehú Malcara grow up and go into the Army, the University of Texas and the workplace, they're coming into the Anglo world." In a sense, the *Klail City Death Trip* series also continues the project of Rivera's *Tierra*: it emerges, finally, as a massive *Bildungsroman* in which both the young boys and the valley community introduced in *Estampas del valle* reach maturity in the midst of an individualistic dominant culture without sacrificing their ties to collective history and identity.[23]

Sandwiched between Rivera and Hinojosa as winners of the Quinto Sol prize was Rudolfo A. Anaya, whose *Bless Me, Ultima* (1972) is written in English. Like *Pocho*, *Bless Me, Ultima* focuses on the experiences of a young boy who aspires to be a writer. Set in New Mexico just after World War II, the novel also maps the ways in which a community responds to cultural change both within and without. Antonio Marez is a boy who embodies liminality, torn as he is between the two different subcultures from which his parents hail. His father is a *llanero*, a man of the plain who "had been a vaquero all his life, a calling as ancient as the coming of the Spaniard to Nuevo Méjico." His mother, however, is the "daughter of a farmer," who "could not see the beauty in the llano and . . . could not understand the coarse men who lived half their lifetimes on horseback." The novel's first-person narrative includes italicized passages depicting the dreams of the young Antonio, whose boyhood is profoundly influenced by his friendship with the old *curandera* (folk-healer) Ultima, who comes to stay with the family as the novel opens. Through Ultima, Antonio learns about pre-Christian forms of spirituality and knowledge that do not supplant but instead supplement the Christian teachings that he learns in school and at church. Both Ultima and her apprentice Antonio are mediating forces in the novel: through them, the novel's oppositions—between father and mother, *llanero* and farmer, Christian and non-Christian—are synthesized into a dialectical relationship. Towards the end of the novel, we see signs of the encroachment of Anglo culture onto the Chicano/a world of Antonio's youth, most pressingly in the form of the apocalyptic threat of the atomic bomb, being tested by the U.S. government in New Mexico. What Antonio feels he has learned from Ultima is "that the tragic consequences of life can be overcome by the magical strength that resides in the human heart." Although early critics of the novel faulted it for its seeming evasion of the materiality of history, *Bless Me, Ultima* proves to be as deeply political as either Rivera's or Hinojosa's writings. What the novel ultimately suggests is that the fusion of spiritual traditions will enable Antonio not only to mediate conflicts within his community but also to help that community maintain its sense of identity and coherence in the face of a consuming Anglo culture.[24]

The Quinto Sol prize project succeeded in establishing the core of a Chicano/a canon, but as the critic Juan Bruce-Novoa has argued, it was a canon constructed around the desire to present a positive image of Chicanos/as and their culture. Excluded were the works of writers like John Rechy, whose novels focus on questions of gay rather than Chicano/a identity, or Oscar Zeta Acosta, whose social satire refuses to limit itself to flattering portraits of Chicanos. Even Tomás Rivera fell victim to the desire to promote communally correct portraits of Chicano life: the Quinto Sol editors are thought to have rejected "El Pete Fonseca" (1970), now considered to be one of his finest stories, because they believed it to present an unflattering portrait of Chicanos.

Critics who justified omitting Rechy's best-selling novel *City of Night* (1963) from a list of Chicano/a classics because the novel's perspective and subject matter are far more influenced by Rechy's sexuality than by his ethnicity could not use the same logic to exclude Acosta's writings. Acosta was born in El Paso, Texas, in 1935, but moved with his family to Riverbank (now part of Modesto), California, at the age of five. After attending Oakdale Joint Union High School, Acosta turned down a music scholarship to the University of Southern California, instead enlisting in the United States Air Force (as a member of the Air Force Band), primarily so that he could continue to be involved with an Anglo woman whose parents disapproved of him. After their relationship ended a year later, Acosta sought solace in religion, converting from Catholicism to the Baptist faith and becoming a preacher. Shipped to Panama in part because of his overzealous attempts to convert other Catholic soldiers, Acosta became a minister at a leper colony and was honorably discharged from the Air Force in 1956. After a suicide attempt prompted by his loss of faith, Acosta met Betty Daves in a Modesto hospital and married her shortly thereafter. In 1965, the now-divorced Acosta began studying law at night at San Francisco Law School and became an attorney for the East Oakland Legal Aid Society. Two years later he quit his law practice to wander around the Southwest in search of a vision; after being briefly jailed in Mexico, Acosta assumed a new identity—Buffalo Z. Brown—and became a political activist in Los Angeles and a leader of the Chicano Movement. After unsuccessfully running for L.A. county sheriff (as an independent, on an anarchist platform) in 1970, Acosta befriended Hunter S. Thompson and accompanied him on the trip that would be preserved for posterity in Thompson's *Fear and Loathing in Las Vegas* (1972), with Oscar transformed into the wild Samoan attorney Dr. Gonzo.

Published in 1972, the same year as *Bless Me, Ultima*, Acosta's picaresque novel *The Autobiography of a Brown Buffalo* depicts the adventures of a Chicano/a lawyer from L.A. who drops out of his profession to embark on journey through the Southwest trying to discover the roots of his "fucked up identity," ingesting copious amounts of drugs and alcohol along the way before ending up in a jail in Ciudad Juárez. Written in a style reminiscent of Thompson's "gonzo" journalism, *Brown Buffalo* begins by confronting the reader with the physical presence of its narrator, Oscar, in a manner designed to foreshadow the interplay of ethnicity and narcissism that will mark the text as a whole:

> I stand naked before the mirror. Every morning of my life I have seen that brown belly from every angle. It has not changed that I can remember.

> I was always a fat kid. I suck it in and expand an enormous chest of two large hunks of brown tit. . . . But look, if I suck it in just a wee bit more, push the bellybutton up against the back; can you see what will surely come to pass if you but rid yourself of this extra flesh? Just think of all the broads you'll get if you trim down to a comfortable 200. . . . I enter the bathroom and struggle to the toilet. With my large, peasant hands carefully on the rim of white, I descend to my knocked knees. I stare into the repository of all that is unacceptable and wait for the green bile, my sunbaked face where my big, brown ass will soon sit.

The comma between "big" and "brown" in the description of Oscar's "ass" is emblematic: bigness and brownness emerge as the axes upon which both his identity and his narrative locate themselves. Fined and released by a Mexican judge in Ciudad Juarez who tells him to "go home and learn to speak your father's language," told by an immigration officer at the border, "You don't look like an American, you know?" Oscar finds himself at the end of the novel back where he began: "I stand naked before the mirror. I cry in sobs. My massive chest quivers and my broad shoulders sag. I am a brown buffalo lonely in a world I never made." What Oscar realizes at the end of his odyssey is that he is "neither a Mexican nor an American. I am neither a Catholic nor a Protestant. I am a Chicano by ancestry and a Brown Buffalo by choice." Refusing to build his personal identity around the ready-made template signified by "Chicano," Oscar chooses to define a new hybrid identity for himself and to build a new cultural identity around it.[25]

The individualism of this stance surfaces throughout Acosta's second novel, *The Revolt of the Cockroach People* (1973), which opens with Oscar leading a Chicano Militant demonstration at an L.A. Roman Catholic church. In the second chapter, Oscar describes the moment, lying awake in bed, in which he determined to become a radical, after thinking about a humiliating incident of racial discrimination that he suffered while in high school: "That night I get no sleep. My brain goes off like explosives and by dawn I have made innumerable resolutions. I will change my name. I will learn Spanish. I will write the greatest books ever written. I will save the world. I will show the world what is what and who the fuck is who. Me in particular." Angry at the dominant culture's mistreatment of Chicanos/as in general and himself in particular,

Oscar rechristens himself "Buffalo Z. Brown," meets César Chávez, participates in the bombing of a supermarket, runs for sheriff of L.A. County, and describes himself as a "professional revolutionary."[26]

Throughout the novel, however, Oscar's animosity shifts back and forth between the dominant culture and the Chicano Movement itself. Oscar's commitment to the movement is intermittent: after his unsuccessful run for sheriff, he decides to "drop out again," going to Acapulco to visit his brother Jesus and pursue a sybaritic existence. He returns only after the death of the Chicano journalist Roland Zanzibar, a fictionalized version of Ruben Salazar, a prominent Chicano television anchorman in Los Angeles, who was killed by the police while covering the first National Chicano Moratorium to protest the Vietnam War. While defending the demonstrators known as the Toomer Flats Seven, Oscar is accused of "directing the activities of the Chicano Liberation front," in particular "the bombings during the riots," but Oscar laughs and portrays himself not as a leader but as a victim: "Those guys wouldn't do what I told them to do if their lives depended on it. They are *vatos locos*! *Nobody* tells crazy guys what to do. . . . It is *they* who have driven me to this brink of madness. It is they who are watching and wondering and complaining about me. *I* am the sheep. *I* am the one being used" (ellipsis in original).[27] The militants are suspicious of Oscar because he has received a book offer: "That I would think to make money off the struggle for freedom of the Cockroaches has made some people whisper traitor, *vendido, tío taco,* uncle tom and a capitalist pig to boot." But Oscar sees himself filling the shoes left empty by the death of Zanzibar; echoing Walt Whitman, he writes, "I shouted it to the rooftops: we *need* writers, just like we need lawyers. Why not me? I *want* to write." Oscar's motives prove to be overdetermined at the end of *Revolt*: self-aggrandizement, revolutionary fervor, and the profit motive merge. After his successful defense of the Toomer Flats Seven, believing that he has "helped start a revolution to burn down a stinking world," Oscar opts out once again, deciding to "split with the Chicanos" in order "to carry on the species and my own Buffalo run as long as I can"—and to write his memoirs. The end of the novel promises that more of Oscar's story will soon be told, but *Revolt of the Cockroach People* would have no sequel: in June 1974 Acosta left Mazatlán, Mexico, on a friend's boat and was never heard from again.[28]

Acosta's identification with the mainstream counterculture, including his appropriation of Hunter S. Thompson's narrative stylistics, led a number of Chicano/a critics to argue that he was not an authentic Chicano/a writer: Raymund Paredes, for example, argued in an essay included in the groundbreaking Modern Language Asssociation collection *Three American Literatures* (1982) that "Chicano literature is that body of work produced by United States citizens and residents of Mexican descent for whom the portrayal of their ethnic experience is a major concern." Acosta thus becomes problematic because although he does seem to attempt "to retrieve his ethnic heritage, . . . the reader is struck by the superficiality of his quest and the flimsiness of the foundation upon which he hopes to build his ethnic identity."[29] What Paredes takes for granted here is that ethnic identity must lie at the core of a Chicano/a's personal identity if he or she is to be a true Chicano/a, for surely Acosta fulfills both criteria that Paredes designates for Chicano/a literature: Acosta's novels devote considerable space to representing the psychological damage inflicted upon a Mexican American because of his ethnicity. What makes Acosta problematic is his refusal to grant the ethnic component of his identity primacy: he writes explicitly at the end of *Brown Buffalo* that his "single mistake has been to seek an identity with any one person or nation or with any part of history." Acosta's novels finally insist on the need for individualism, and insofar as individualism is a dominant component of mainstream American ideology, this insistence places both the author and his novels at odds with Chicano/a culture. Despite its countercultural stance, therefore, Acosta's writing has far more in common with Villarreal's *Pocho* than it does with such Chicano/a *Bildungsromans* as Rivera's *Tierra* or Anaya's *Bless Me, Ultima*.

Writings by Chicano/a authors dominated discussions of late-twentieth-century fiction by Hispanic Americans, in part because of the conscious attempts to found a Chicano/a literary canon described above, and in part because Chicano/a literary scholars have been prominent participants in the development of minority discourse theory. Though centered from the outset on the work of male authors, the Chicano/a canon is already shifting to include writings by Gloria Anzaldúa, Ana Moraga, Sandra Cisneros, and Cherríe Moraga. At the end of the twentieth century, Chicano/a fiction and poetry outstripped that produced by writers of Puerto Rican, Cuban American, and Dominican American descent both in sheer volume and in critical attention, but there were signs that this situation would change before long.

Native American Renaissance

In his seminal study *Native American Renaissance* (1985), Kenneth Lincoln describes the "reemergence" of Native American literature as a "written renewal of oral traditions translated into Western literary forms."[30] The poet Simon Ortiz (Acoma Pueblo) identifies N. Scott Momaday (Kiowa), Vine Deloria, Jr. (Sioux), and James Welch (Blackfeet/Gros Ventre) as the writers who initiated a tradition of written Native American literature that did not exist before.[31] After producing a privately published study of Kiowa myths entitled *The Journey of Tai-Me* in 1967, Momaday published his novel *House Made of Dawn* the following year; in 1969, it was awarded the Pulitzer Prize. The Pulitzer jury's decision took author, publisher, and reading public by surprise: according to Momaday's biographer, Matthias Schubnell, "Momaday at first refused to believe the news, and some of the senior editors at Harper and Row could not even remember the novel."[32] James Welch describes Momaday's winning the Pulitzer as a crucial turning point: "suddenly people started to notice Indian literature, [and] the way kind of opened for Indians; . . . younger people who didn't think they had much of a chance as a writer, suddenly realized, well, an Indian can write."[33] Momaday's novel coincided with a renewal of political and social activism among Native Americans that gained national attention with the publication of Deloria's *Custer Died for Your Sins* (1969) and Dee Brown's *Bury My Heart at Wounded Knee* (1970), as well as the occupation of Alcatraz Island for nineteen months from late 1968 to 1971.

The 1960s saw the creation of a new pan-Indian consciousness exemplified by the Chicago Conference of 1961, which brought together hundreds of Native Americans from different tribes to discuss issues of common interest. Calling upon the U.S. government to respect the treaties that it had made with Indian tribes and to cease taking "our lands . . . for a declared public purpose," the Conference's "Declaration of Indian Purpose" recognized that differences among tribes are less important in the present moment than a sense of Indian solidarity: "in the beginning the people of the New World, called Indians by accident of geography, were possessed of a continent and a way of life. In the course of many lifetimes, our people had to adjust to every climate and condition from the Arctic to the torrid zones. In their livelihood and family relationships, their ceremonial observances, they reflected the diversity of the physical world they occupied." Moving here from a sense of the collective "people of the New World" to a sense of the "diversity" of Indian tribes, the "Declaration" finally described American Indians in collective terms again in recognizing "the complexities which beset a people moving toward new meaning and purpose." The goal of the document was to "ask for assistance, technical and financial, for the time needed, however, long that may be, to regain in the America of the space age some measure of the adjustment [the Indians] enjoyed as the original possessors of their native land."[34] Studying the situation of Native Americans in 1961, the United States Commission on Civil Rights concluded that they were being subjected to discrimination and infringement of opportunity in such areas as voting, employment, education, housing, and justice. In the aftermath of the Commission's report, Native Americans made slow gains throughout the 1960s in the area of civil rights, and in 1968 Congress passed the Indian Civil Rights Act, which guaranteed to Native Americans rights that white Americans had always taken for granted, such as freedom of speech, press, and religion (the sacramental use of peyote had been protected by the U.S. Supreme Court four years earlier); the rights of assembly and petition; and protection against the seizure of property without just compensation.

Dissatisfied both with the rate of improvement under federal programs that were often implemented incompletely and with the imperious attitude of the Bureau of Indian Affairs (BIA), which continued to wield a substantial amount of power over Native American programs, off-reservation and urban Native Americans formed a variety of different activist organizations to supplement the existing National Congress of American Indians and the National Indian Youth Conference. Of these new organizations, the most militant was the American Indian Movement (AIM), founded in Minneapolis in 1968 by two members of the Chippewa tribe, Dennis Banks and George Mitchell, who were later joined by a third Chippewa, Clyde Bellecourt. Originally intended simply to assist Native Americans who were moving from upper Midwest reservations to cities (particularly to protect them from selective law enforcement and unequal justice), AIM increasingly devoted itself to agitating on behalf of restoration of Native American lands illegally seized by the federal government and of bona fide application of the Indian civil rights law. The tactics used by AIM and other groups ran the gamut of political action, from peaceful demonstration to the seizure of land and buildings and occasionally armed resistance to the authorities.

The increase in Native American militancy can be measured by comparing the 1961 Chicago Conference's "Declaration of Indian Purpose" to "A Proclamation from the Indians of All Tribes, Alcatraz Island, 1969," released after Native American activists occupied Alcatraz (since 1963 no longer used as a federal prison) and claimed their right to the island (which had been declared surplus property by the federal government) under the Fort Laramie Treaty of 1868, which allowed any male Native American over eighteen whose tribe was a party to the treaty to file for a homestead on government land. Five years earlier, Sioux activists had attempted to claim Alcatraz Island under federal law, staging a sit-in (complete with lawyers) that the national media described as "wacky." "Looking back, I'm not surprised," writes the Native American activist Russell Means in his autobiography *Where White Men Fear to Tread* (1996). "White America has always trivialized Indian people. . . . Our treaty wasn't 'wacky,' it was the law of the land. . . . The lawyers filed suit to press our claim on Alcatraz, but eventually the case was thrown out. There was no legal basis for the judge's refusal to hear the suit, but in those days there was so much racism that no one cared. It would be five more years before another group of Indians took over Alcatraz—and then the white man knew we were serious."[35] The Alcatraz Proclamation addresses itself to "the Great White Father and All his People" and begins: "We, the native Americans, re-claim the land known as Alcatraz Island in the name of all American Indians by right of discovery." Designed to express dissatisfaction with the federal government's trusteeship of native lands, the document proposes to offer a "treaty" to the U.S. Government:

> We will purchase said Alcatraz Island for twenty-four dollars ($24) in
> glass beads and red cloth, a precedent set by the white man's purchase

of a similar island about 300 years ago. We know that $24 in trade goods for these 16 acres is more than was paid when Manhattan Island was sold, but we offer that land values have risen over the years. Our offer of $1.24 per acre is greater than the 47 cents per acre the white men are now paying the California Indians for their land. We will give to the inhabitants of this land a portion of the land for their own, to be held in trust by the American Indian Government—for as long as the sun shall rise and the rivers go down to the sea—to be administered by the Bureau of Caucasian Affairs. We will offer them our religion, our education, our life-ways, in order to help them achieve our level of civilization and thus raise them and all their white brothers from their savage and unhappy state. We offer this treaty in good faith and wish to be fair and honorable in our dealings with all white men.[36]

The occupation of Alcatraz Island drew wide national and international attention, and public support lasted until 1971, when federal officials found that they could remove the protesters from the island with little public outcry. Native American militancy did not end with the removal of protesters from Alcatraz: in 1972, during the so-called "Broken Treaties Caravan" to Washington, protesters occupied the Bureau of Indian Affairs building, destroying federal records and other pieces of public property. And in 1973, led by members of AIM, armed Native Americans occupied the village of Wounded Knee, made famous by Dee Brown's book, which concludes by describing the horrific massacre of Sioux men, women, and children by the Seventh Cavalry in 1890.

Momaday's *House Made of Dawn* participates in this new sense of pan-Indian consciousness by bringing together Kiowa, Navajo, and Walotowa (Jemez Pueblo) mythic and oral traditions. The novel is framed with the traditional Walotowa formula words for "opening" (*Dypaloh*) and "closing" (*Qtsedaba*), and the bulk of the novel's prologue offers an image of a Walotowa ceremony, the annual foot race of the "runners after evil." But the first paragraph of the prologue also draws from another set of beliefs and rituals:

Dypaloh. There was a house made of dawn. It was made of pollen and of rain, and the land was very old and everlasting. There were many colors on the hills, and the plain was bright with different-colored clays and sands. Red and blue and spotted horses grazed in the plain, and there was a dark wilderness on the mountains beyond. The land was still and strong. It was beautiful all around.

This first paragraph (and the novel's title) allude to a chantway—the Navajo Night Chant—a healing ritual that the novel's protagonist, Abel, will encounter after his relocation to Los Angeles, sung to him by his Navajo friend Ben Bennally:

> Tséghi.
> House made of dawn,
> House made of evening light,
> House made of dark cloud,
> House made of male rain,
> House made of dark mist,
> House made of pollen,
> House made of grasshoppers,
> Dark cloud is at the door.
> The trail out of it is dark cloud.
> The zigzag lightning stands high upon it.
> Male deity!
> Your offering I make.
> I have prepared a smoke for you.
> Restore my feet for me,
> Restore my legs for me,
> Restore my body for me,
> Restore my mind for me.
> This very day take out your spell for me.
> Your spell remove for me.
> You have taken it away for me;
> Far off it has gone.
> Happily I recover.
> Happily my interior becomes cool.
> Happily I go forth.
> My interior feeling cool, may I walk.
> No longer sore, may I walk.
> Impervious to pain, may I walk.

As it used to be long ago, may I walk.
Happily may I walk.
Happily, with abundant dark clouds, may I walk.
Happily with abundant showers, may I walk.
Happily, with abundant plants, may I walk.
Happily, on a trail of pollen, may I walk.
Happily may I walk.
Being as it used to be long ago, may I walk.
May it be beautiful before me,
May it be beautiful below me,
May it be beautiful above me,
May it be beautiful all around me.
In beauty it is finished.

According to Navajo belief, health depends on a harmonious and integrated psyche, with little distinction made between physical and mental
illness, and a state of health is conceived as a state of beauty and accord.
An individual who is isolated or alienated—from his or her tribe, from
the land—is thus a sick individual, and the rituals of healing center on
reintegrating this isolated or alienated individual into the organic unity
of the universe.

Abel is doubly isolated and alienated. He is a mixed-blood, who "did
not know who his father was. His father was a Navajo, they said, or a
Sia, or an Isleta, an outsider anyway, which made him and his mother
and [his brother] Vidal somehow foreign and strange."[37] Abel's inability
to fit into the ceremonial life of the village is exemplified and magnified
by his violation of the ritual of the Bakyush eagle hunt: feeling sorry for
the captive eagle, he strangles her. But Abel is also isolated and alienated because he is a contemporary Native American in a white-dom-
inated culture, unable to adjust to the frames of reference offered first
by the government boarding school to which he is sent and then the
U.S. Army into which he is drafted. Moreover, assimilating into white
American society, even if it were possible, would mean accepting an
ideology based in individualism that runs counter to all of his tribe's
traditional beliefs. Returning home, nearly psychotic after his experiences in World War II, Abel is sent to prison for the ritual murder of an
albino who has humiliated him during a Walotowa ceremony and then

is relocated to the urban ghetto of Los Angeles, where he encounters the Native American preacher John Big Bluff Tosamah; befriends Ben Bennally, a young urban Navajo, as well as a white social worker named Milly, who becomes his lover; and is finally beaten nearly to death by a Mexican American policeman for refusing to pay protection money. Lying near death, he begins to understand the significance of both the Navajo healing chant and the Walotowa foot race, to understand why he has "lost his place . . . and was even now reeling on the edge of the void."[38]

In the story that accompanies the Navajo Night Chant, Crippled Boy and Blind Boy—left behind when the tribe must migrate and thus all but left for dead—help each other to climb a cliff where they meet the Holy People who teach them the healing Night Chant.[39] Momaday's Abel is a combination of these two figures: not blind but mute and therefore—in his culture of storytelling and oral tradition—crippled.

Abel's inability to speak is a powerful emblem of his alienation from his tribe and from himself, and it lies at the center of the novel's consideration of the nature of human language. Commenting on the expression "white man speaks with forked tongue," Momaday once told an interviewer that the expression "seems to me to reach farther into basic perceptions than most of us would understand at first. It is, unwittingly or not, a sensitive commentary upon the way in which the Indian and the non-Indian look at language."[40] *House Made of Dawn* dramatizes the differences between Indian and non-Indian understandings of language that result from the Indian's participation in traditions of oral literature. The Indian "Priest of the Sun," the "Right Reverend John Big Bluff Tosamah," preaches a sermon on the opening line of the Gospel of St. John: *In principio erat Verbum*, "In the Beginning was the Word." The sermon quickly becomes an indictment of "the way in which the white man thinks of [language]":

> The white man takes such things as words and literatures for granted, as indeed he must, for nothing in his world is so commonplace. On every side of him there are words by the millions, an unending succession of pamphlets and papers, letters and books, bills and bulletins, commentaries and conversations. He has diluted and multiplied the Word, and words have begun to close in upon him. He is sated and insensitive; his

regard for language—for the Word itself—as an instrument of creation has diminished nearly to the point of no return. It may be that he will perish by the word.[41]

Obviously, however, the novel—first, by virtue of its simply being a novel—does not eschew "the white man['s] . . . literatures" altogether, for if the *House Made of Dawn* novel owed a formal debt to the Walotowa, Navajo, and Kiowa traditions upon which it draws, it also owed a debt to the modernist experimentalism of Faulkner, Joyce, and Lawrence, since it relies heavily on such techniques as flashbacks, interior monologue, multiple narrators, and typographical differentiation. According to Paula Gunn Allen, Joyce was one of the few Western writers whose writing could embody something like a Native American mythic space—the kind of mythic space that "make[s] you dance"— and, "if it weren't for Joyce," she suggests, "we wouldn't have Momaday." (Allen credits Gertrude Stein with playing a similar role for her.)[42] Drawing from both Native American oral traditions and high modernist written traditions, *House Made of Dawn*—both in its form and in its subject—captured both the pain and the potential power of cultural hybridity, and it would become a model for later Native American writers. According to the writer Joseph Bruchac (Abnaki), Momaday's novel "opened the eyes of a new generation of Native American writers. They read the novel and heard the deeper meanings of its powerful writing: a person caught between cultures can, despite the deepest of problems, find a way to survive, a road which circles out of the past, 'The House Made of Dawn,' and ends in understanding."[43]

Leslie Marmon Silko was one member of that new generation of Native Americans writing in the wake of *House Made of Dawn*, and in many respects her first novel, *Ceremony* (1977), seems to be a response to and even a rewriting of Momaday's novel. Both novels are set primarily in the pueblos of the Southwest, and like Momaday's Abel, Silko's protagonist, Tayo, is not a full-blooded Native American: Abel is a mixed-blood, but Tayo is even further outside the tribal norm since he is a half-breed, taken in by his aunt "to conceal the shame of her younger sister."[44]

Weaving together fragments of Laguna Pueblo and Navajo mythology, Silko tells the story of Tayo's return to the Laguna Pueblo from combat in the Pacific during World War II. He has been released from a veteran's hospital, but still suffers from a complex form of guilt: he blames himself for failing to protect his beloved half-brother, Rocky, upon whom all of his family's hopes had been placed; for causing the draught that has been afflicting the Laguna Pueblo by cursing the jungle rain while on duty in the Pacific; and finally for bringing about the death of his beloved uncle Josiah, to whom he left the task of managing an entire herd of Mexican spotted cattle, and whose face he saw in the faces of every Japanese soldier that he killed.

As in Momaday's novel, Tayo's redemption comes through his participation in a healing ceremony. When the traditional ceremonies of the tribal elders fail to mend Tayo's injured and alienated psyche, he is sent to the revisionist Navajo medicine man Betonie, whose hazel eyes and Mexican ancestry make him a hybrid figure like Tayo. Betonie is distrusted by traditionalists because he makes use of modern implements—such as phone books—in his ceremonies. Like *House Made of Dawn*, Silko's novel thus makes crucial use of Navajo ceremonial tradition, but the myth that undergirds the novel is the story of Ts'its'tsi'nako—referred to variously as Thought-Woman, Spider Woman, and Grandmother Spider—the author of all thought and all stories: "She is sitting in her room / thinking of a story now," we are told in the poetic lines that begin the novel; "I'm telling you the story / she is thinking." The life-force of the universe is thus a feminine principle, and it is contrasted in the novel with the death-force, the "witchery," that is associated with technology, white culture, and the masculine violence embodied by the veterans who return home from the war, particularly Emo, Tayo's nemesis.

Tayo's ceremony can be completed only with a quest:

"One night or nine nights won't do it any more," the medicine man said; "the ceremony isn't finished yet." He was drawing in the dirt with his finger. "Remember these stars," he said. "I've seen them and I've seen the spotted cattle; I've seen a mountain and I've seen a woman."

The woman turns out to be Ts'eh, a member of the Montaña family, who lives with her brother on Mount Taylor, the Laguna sacred mountain, and who helps Tayo to recover his lost cattle. What *Ceremony* presents that *House Made of Dawn* does not is a vision of the power of the creative and curative powers of the female principle, which is always allied with and generated by the land. Near the end of the novel, Tayo thinks to himself, "we came out of this land and we are hers," and he realizes, "They had always been loved. He thought of her then; she had always loved him, she had never left him; she had always been there."[45]

Tayo's nemesis, the war veteran Emo, who carries around a bag of teeth taken from Japanese corpses, represents a counter-myth, invented by Silko: he is the embodiment of "the witchery," the novel's mythic explanation for the genesis of white culture. Betonie tells Tayo, "That is the trickery of the witchcraft":

> They want us to believe all evil resides with white people. Then we will look no further to see what is really happening. They want us to sepa-rate ourselves from white people, to be ignorant and helpless as we watch our own destruction. But white people are only tools that the witchery manipulates; and I tell you, we can deal with white people, with their machines and their beliefs. We can because we invented white people; it was Indian witchery that made white people in the first place.

The novel then presents an account of the witchery, which takes place "Long time ago / in the beginning" when "there were no white people in this world" and "nothing European." The witch people get together for a storytelling contest, and one of them tells a story about "white skin people / like the belly of a fish / covered with hair," who "see only objects" when they look at the world, for whom "the world is a dead thing." This storyteller wins the contest, but other witches ask that the story be taken back: "what you said just now—it isn't so funny. . . . Call that story back." But words and stories have efficacy; they have creative power:

> the witch just shook its head
> at the others in their stinking animal skins, fur and feathers.
> *It's already turned loose,*
> *It's already coming,*
> *It can't be called back.*

The ideology of white culture, which the novel portrays as the tool of the witchery, is a mechanistic ideology that values technology over nature and brings violence into the world. But Emo too is a victim: white culture has made him a sociopath by recruiting him for its war and then shunning him as an outsider afterward. It is only when he can reject the temptation to kill Emo, can renounce the violence that is Emo's way of life, that Tayo is finally cured. It is, finally, the rejection of violence that proves to be the culmination of Tayo's ceremony.

Ceremony is a critique of American individualism. When he first meets Betonie, Tayo remembers what he has been told in the hospital: "That he had to think only of himself, and not about the others, that he would never get well as long as he used words like 'we' and 'us.' " But even though he wants to believe them, Tayo already knows that they are wrong, "because the world didn't work that way. His sickness was only part of something larger, and his curse would be found only in something great and inclusive of everything."[46] White culture attempts to recruit Native American culture to its individualistic conception of the world, but when he finally takes up the role of storyteller at the end of the novel, Tayo signals that he has successfully resisted and reinserted himself into the communal life of his tribe.

Unlike *House Made of Dawn* and *Ceremony*, James Welch's first two novels, *Winter in the Blood* (1974) and *The Death of Jim Loney* (1979), are set in the Northwest, and offer a far bleaker vision of Native American life. Asked to comment on the storytelling tradition in these novels, Welch says first of all that they "are written in the Western, European-American tradition," in part because they lack the moral that Welch associates with "the storytelling tradition of traditional Indians." Welch is a mixed- blood, Blackfeet on his father's side and Gros Ventre on his mother's, and in *Winter in the Blood* he draws ironically on both traditions. Standing Bear, the first husband of the narrator's grandmother, is a Blackfeet warrior who meets his doom while leading his people away from the "Long Knives"—federal soldiers—"in a futile raid on the Gros Ventres, who were also camped in the valley." The Montana Blackfeet were reputedly the fiercest tribe on the Great Plains, the last tribe to negotiate a truce with the U.S. Government, but those days of heroic resistance are long gone in Welch's novel; all that remains are memories of humiliation, as this sardonic added detail—typical of Welch's black humor—makes clear: "When the survivors [of the raid] led [Standing Bear's] horse into camp, his eldest son killed it and the family lived off the meat for many days. The horse was killed because Standing Bear would need it in the other world; they ate it because they were starving."[47]

Welch's novel seems to draw on Blackfeet and Gros Ventre traditions in other ways as well, but always ironically. The ever-unnamed narrator may represent an updating of the Blackfeet tradition that forbade one to speak one's own name to others. The fact that he is thirty-two years old may signify that he is about to embark on a vision quest: according to Gros Ventre tradition, when a man reaches thirty-two, he must go on a vision quest, look for a wife, and attempt to qualify for initiation in a Crazy Lodge via the "crying for pity ritual." At the beginning of Welch's novel, however, the narrator has seemingly found a wife, a Cree woman whom he has brought home, only to have her run away with his shotgun and his razor. The narrator does in fact set out on several trips to neighboring towns throughout the novel, ostensibly to recover her and his belongings, and the result is several absurdist encounters that seem unlikely to result in any revelation. Welch denies that he modeled the novel after a vision quest, as many critics have suggested, and he argues that a vision quest is no longer possible for a twentieth-century Native American like the narrator:

> in the real vision quest the people went to seek a vision and from that vision they would know how to conduct themselves, not only in their everyday lives but in things that really counted for them, like in battle they'd been courageous. Depending upon which power animal appeared to them, they would take the attributes of that animal, so if a raven came to them, they would probably become farseeing. . . . So, a traditional vision quest always had a particular thing it sought and then once the vision came it had almost a practical aspect; then you could use the power that the vision represented.

Winter in the Blood is a modern-day vision quest in the same way that Joyce's *Ulysses* (1922) is a modern-day epic: both genres can exist only in diminished form in the twentieth century, and heroism is to be found not in grand actions or visionary power but in the simple resilience that is signified by getting through the day.[48]

Welch's style has as much in common with the black humor of Faulkner's *As I Lay Dying* (1930) as it does with the trickster tales to which it is often compared, and the climax of the novel, in which the narrator struggles to rescue a cow caught in the mud, seems reminiscent of those moments in Faulkner's narratives—such as the flood in "Old Man"—when humans find themselves overmatched in their battle with the elements. The narrator of *Winter in the Blood* does learn something about his identity: he learns that he isn't a half-breed but is in fact a full-blood Blackfeet, but what difference this will make in his life is unclear at the end of the novel. The narrator begins the novel feeling alienated: "The distance I felt came not from country or people; it came from within me. I was as distant from myself as a hawk from the moon. And that was why I had no particular feelings toward my mother and grandmother. Or the girl who had come to live with me." The ending of the novel tells us little about whether the narrator's experiences will ultimately thaw this winter in his blood.[49]

Unrelieved by the comic moments that leaven the sardonic realism of *Winter in the Blood*, Welch's second novel, *The Death of Jim Loney*, is a bleak narrative that portrays the liminal space between white culture and Native culture as an existential no-man's land from which its protagonist cannot escape. Like the protagonists in both *House Made of Dawn* and *Ceremony*, Jim Loney is a hybrid character, in this case a half-breed who is abandoned by his parents—his white father, Ike, and his mother, Eletra Calf-Looking—and he finds that he can feel no connection to either parent or to either of their cultures. Accidentally killing his high-school rival Myron Pretty Weasel while the two are hunting, Loney lets the tribal police believe he has committed murder and allows himself to be shot in Mission Canyon, a site believed to be a gateway into the next life. The Native American scholar Kathryn W. Shanley points out that "in Gros Ventre tradition, when you've done something grievous" as Loney has done in becoming an alcoholic and bringing about the death of his friend, "then you have an obligation to mete out your own punishment in a public way." *The Death of Jim Loney* eschews the richly textured mythic substructures that undergird Momaday's *House Made of Dawn* and Silko's *Ceremony* in favor of a more stripped-down narrative style reminiscent of Hemingway. Drawing on this masculinist literary tradition allows Welch to reinforce the idea that Jim Loney is a character who achieves manhood only in death. In the course of the novel, Loney is associated with a number of stereotypes, but, as Shanley argues, by the end he has "stopped being a child of the government, or an innocent noble savage, or all the other things that he is mistaken for in the novel—at that point he becomes a man, because he takes the responsibility for what he ought to have known."[50]

In their different ways, Momaday, Silko, and Welch create hybrid novels that bring together Native American oral traditions with the powerful legacy of American and British modernist writing, as if to assert that the Native American novel will not conform to critical expectations that have linked ethnic writing to realism. Like Villarreal's *Pocho*, *House Made of Dawn* stands at the head of a novelistic tradition, but the two novels could not be more different stylistically. Inspired in part by Joyce's *Portrait of the Artist as a Young Man*, *Pocho* belongs to the tradition of autobiographical realism that is the norm for American ethnic writing in the first half of the twentieth century. *House Made of Dawn*, however, has less in common with *Pocho* than it does with Henry Roth's *Call It Sleep* (1934), long regarded as an anomaly within American ethnic writing because of its formal experimentalism. *Call It Sleep* gained national recognition only after it was rediscovered and reissued in paperback in 1964, becoming a national bestseller. Roth's novel found its audience in the mid-1960s, the same cultural moment that produced Momaday's *House Made of Dawn*, and significantly both novels are inconceivable without the prior example of Joyce—not the Joyce of *Portrait*, however, but the Joyce of *Ulysses*. What *Call It Sleep* and *House Made of Dawn* have in common with each other, as well as with Silko's *Ceremony* and Welch's *Winter in the Blood* and *The Death of Jim Loney*, is that they are revisionist novels that revise in two directions: they bring ethnic traditions to bear on modernist writing and modernist experimentalism to bear on ethnic writing.

Formal experimentation marks the work of the novelist and essayist Gerald Vizenor, who finds a natural affinity between Native American oral traditions and literary postmodernism. A mixed-blood Native American who is an enrolled member of the Anishinabe (Chippewa) tribe, Vizenor sees in the ambiguity of mixed blood an opportunity to be seized rather than a problem to be solved. Momaday, Silko, and Welch portray their mixed-blood characters as pained figures who can

avoid tragedy only by resolving the ambiguities of their identities. Vizenor's mixed-bloods, however, are tricksters who revel in ambiguity and
marginality; they are portrayed as comic rather than tragic characters.
Vizenor takes issue with the analysis of tribal tricksters presented by
anthropologists such as Paul Radin, who claims that the trickster "possesses no values, moral or social" and "knows neither good nor evil yet
is responsible for both." For Vizenor, the trickster —no matter how disruptive he or she may prove to be —is always "a compassionate and
imaginative character." In the prologue to *The Trickster of Liberty: Tribal
Heirs to a Wild Baronage* (1988), Vizenor writes:

> The Woodland trickster is a comic trope; a universal language game. The
> trickster narrative arises in agonistic imagination; a wild venture in com-
> munal discourse, an uncertain humor that denies aestheticism, trans-
> lation, and imposed representations. The most active readers become
> obverse tricksters, the waver of a coin in a tribal striptease.

Like the novels of John Hawkes, Vizenor's narratives are designed to
produce discomfort in his readers through sudden shifts in narrative
reality and through jarring depictions of graphic violence and explicit,
often perverse, sexuality.[51]

As in many traditional trickster narratives, the comedy of Vizenor's
novels is frequently dark and sardonic. His first novel, *Darkness in Saint
Louis Bearheart* (1978, republished in 1990 as *Bearheart: The Heirship
Chronicles*), is a postmodern frame tale that begins with an elliptical
account of the takeover of the Washington office of the Bureau of Indian
Affairs by radicals from the American Indian Movement. A young militant woman discovers a manuscript written by an old shaman-turned-
bureaucrat named Saint Louis Bearheart, and it is this manuscript that
will serve as the bulk of the novel that we are going to read. "What is
your book about?" she asks Bearheart, and he replies, "Sex and violence." Bearheart's manuscript is a bleakly futuristic account of a time
when the U.S. government orders the cutting of forest preserves, forcing
Proude Cedarfair to abandon the sacred grove of cedars that his family
has protected for generations. Cedarfair and his wife, Rosina, embark
on a pilgrimage, joined by a strange band of companions that includes
"thirteen weird and sensitive women" poets living in a communal

"scapehouse"; a little man named Bigfoot who possesses an enormous uncircumcised penis that the poets have nicknamed "president jackson"; a homosexual tribal lawyer and his lover; a tribal historian named Wilde Coxswain; and a woman named Lilith Mae, whose lovers are her two pet boxer dogs. The manuscript's loosely connected series of episodes are a mixture of reimagined trickster tales, such as the story of the Evil Gambler, whose defeat brought back the rains, and contemporary fables that dramatize the plight of Native Americans, such as the poisoning of Belladonna Darwin-Winter Catcher who can conceive of her "tribal identity" only as a series of inherited clichés. Such clichés are examples of what Vizenor calls "terminal creeds," belief-systems that subject the world to static definitions, and it is the goal of his novel to disrupt and transform the terminal creeds that are poisoning Native American cultures. The novel ends with a transformative moment that pays homage to N. Scott Momaday: near the Walatowa Pueblo that provides the setting for much of *House Made of Dawn*, Proude Cedarfair and his companion Inawa Biwide reach the "vision window" that allows them "to enter the fourth world as bears," like the boy in Momaday's retelling of the Kiowa legend of the origin of the Big Dipper. [52]

Vizenor's subsequent novels became increasingly abstract and elliptical, full of passages that seem more appropriate to literary theory than fiction and structured around what Vizenor (following Jean-François Lyotard) calls "wisps of narratives." In an essay entitled "Trickster Discourse," Vizenor quotes Lyotard's suggestion that "the people do not exist as a subject but as a mass of millions of insignificant and serious little stories that sometimes let themselves be collected together to constitute big stories and sometimes disperse into digressive elements." Like Proude Cedarfair, who leaves his reservation to lead a band of pilgrims and ultimately leaves the present world behind, Vizenor's writing increasingly abandons the rootedness in place and the particularity of tribal affiliation that marks so much Native American writing. Steeped in post-structuralist literary theory, Vizenor's fiction, like his critical writing, is full of puns and jargon; it is deliberately inaccessible and almost compulsively self-referential. His "novel" *The Trickster of Liberty* consists of what look like outtakes from his earlier novels, episodes that will make little sense to readers who are not already participants in Vizenor's discursive enterprise. Speaking of Bagese, a tribal woman who "became a bear last year in the city," the narrator of Vizenor's *Dead Voices: Natural Agonies in the New World* (1992) says, "I pretended to understand, but some of her stories were obscure and she never responded to my constant doubts," a sentiment no doubt echoed by many of Vizenor's readers. What Vizenor has done, however, is to push the insights of emergent literature to an extreme: his fiction accepts and welcomes the violence of cultural hybridity, and he does not shy away from depicting scenes that may leave even his most sympathetic readers feeling assaulted. His goal is to transform words into "wordarrows" that can serve as weapons in what the subtitle of Bearheart's manuscript calls "the cultural word wars."[53]

Although the Anishinabe novelist Louise Erdrich is frequently described as postmodern by literary critics, her novels bear relatively little resemblance to those of Vizenor. In comparison to Vizenor, Erdrich writes in a neo-realist mode that is firmly rooted in palpable depictions of place and character. The word "heir" occurs repeatedly in Vizenor's writing, but of the two novelists it is Erdrich who is more interested in portraying the generational histories of the Anishinabe people. The tetralogy that begins with *Love Medicine* (1984) and includes *The Beet Queen* (1986), *Tracks* (1988), and *The Bingo Palace* (1994) charts some eighty years in the life of the Turtle Mountain Reservation in North Dakota, juxtaposing different narrative voices in the manner of Faulkner's *As I Lay Dying* (1930). A word that consistently recurs in critics' descriptions of Erdrich's prose is "lyrical," and her lyricism has the effect of heightening the real without pushing it into the surreal. It gives her rendering of mythical elements the same palpability as her rendering of contemporary social problems, while allowing her to question frames of reference that her readers might otherwise take for granted. In the novel *Tracks*, for example, Erdrich's lyrical style enables her to present Catholic belief and Anishinabe legend on equal footing, with just a hint that of the two, it may be Catholicism that is the more fantastic. Erdrich, like Vizenor, seeks to challenge shibboleths of mainstream culture, but her novels are gently, rather than aggressively, subversive of readers' expectations.

Erdrich draws upon some of the same tribal traditions that inspire Vizenor, in particular the trickster figure Nanabozho, who serves as the archetype upon which such Erdrich characters as Old Nanapush,

Moses Pillager, Gerry Nanapush, and Lipsha Morrissey are patterned. Like Vizenor, she works primarily in the comic mode; in an interview with Bill Moyers, Erdrich suggested that "the one universal thing about Native Americans from tribe to tribe" may be "the survival humor," the ability to "live with what you have to live with" and "to poke fun at people who are dominating your life and your family," in part by recognizing the "dark side to humor."[54] In the episode to which the title *Love Medicine* refers, Lipsha Morrissey's ad hoc updating of an Anishinabe ritual intended to renew his grandparents' love for one another and restore his grandfather's memory has an aura of slapstick about it, yet it results in the grandfather's death by choking. Erdrich's comic irony, however, lacks the savagery of Vizenor's, and her depictions of violence rarely seemed designed to be an assault upon her reader. In Erdrich's novels, storytelling serves less as a mechanism for disruption and subversion than as a way of preserving spirituality, creating community, and ensuring survival. In her novel *Tales of Burning Love* (1996), Erdrich presents four Great Plains women who, like Scheherezade or the characters in the *Decameron*, must tell stories in order to stay alive, in this case to stay awake and keep themselves from freezing to death or suffocating in their snowbound car. As its title suggests, sexuality is a central theme in *Tales of Burning Love*, as it is in all of Erdrich's novels, yet it is not the barren sexuality portrayed by Vizenor. Among the prominent Native American novelists, Erdrich emerges as the one most interested in exploring the dynamics of love and sexuality and the extent to which relationships between men and women might serve as a basis for the renewal of culture.

Momaday, Silko, Welch, Vizenor, and Erdrich represent the core of the canon of Native American prose fiction that has arisen in the last thirty years, and their combined influence can be seen in the work of a writer like Sherman Alexie, whose novels draw liberally from the styles they pioneered: his short story collection *The Lone Ranger and Tonto Fistfight in Heaven* (1993) uses a variety of narrative personae to portray reservation life in the Northwest with the same flashes of dark comedy that mark Erdrich's novels; his first novel, *Reservation Blues* (1995), draws upon the mythical overtones seen in the novels of Momaday, Silko, and Erdrich; and his second novel, *Indian Killer* (1996), is a gritty urban work set in Seattle that seems indebted above all to Welch.

Midway through *Indian Killer*, a well-to-do white man named Daniel Smith searches among Seattle's homeless Native American population for his emotionally disturbed adopted son, John, a Native American whose tribal heritage was kept secret by the adoption agency. "He spent most of the day in downtown Seattle," Alexie writes, "but never found anybody, white or Indian, who had ever heard of an Indian named John Smith, though they all knew a dozen homeless Indian men." And then we get this list:

"Yeah, there's that Blackfeet guy, Loney."
    "Oh, yeah, enit? And that Laguna guy, what's his name? Tayo?"
    "And Abel, that Kiowa."

This reference to the protagonists of novels by Welch, Silko, and Momaday is a Native American novelist's in-joke, but it also suggests one of *Indian Killer*'s powerful insights: that all Native Americans are in some fundamental way homeless, victims of displacement, dispossession, and cultural damage. The young Native activist Marie Polatkin, one of the protagonists of Alexie's novel, believes "that homeless people were treated as Indians had always been treated. Badly. The homeless were like an Indian tribe, nomadic and powerless . . . so a homeless Indian belonged to two tribes, and was the lowest form of life in the city."[55]

The lives of the Native American protagonists of *Indian Killer* can be seen as parables of the cultural damage suffered by Native Americans as a result, first, of the European conquest of the Americas, and later of the U.S. government's attempts to assimilate Native Americans into mainstream American culture. John Smith, for example, is taken from his teenage mother and his reservation at birth, raised by two loving and liberal white parents, and baptized a Catholic. Regarded by the teachers at the St. Francis school (in which he is one of four non-white students) as "a trailblazer, a nice trophy for St. Francis, a successfully integrated Indian boy," John eventually proves himself to be quite the opposite, a schizophrenic who finds himself at home nowhere.[56] John Smith thus embodies the physical displacement of the U.S. government's policy of Indian Removal in the mid-nineteenth century and the process of detribalization through which the U.S. government sought to assimilate Native Americans by weaning them from their tribal orientation. And the fact that John is so emotionally damaged despite his liberal parents' efforts both to make him feel loved and to teach him Native American history is a signal that the cultural damage perpetrated by the U.S. government will not so easily be undone.

The title of Alexie's novel refers to a serial killer who is stalking, scalping, and otherwise mutilating white men in Seattle. The killings spawn a cycle of racially motivated violence, as whites begin to beat innocent Native Americans, and Native Americans launch unprovoked attacks on innocent and indeed sympathetic whites. As the violence escalates, the power of the so-called "Indian Killer" seems to grow:

> A full moon. A cemetery on an Indian reservation. On this reservation or that reservation. Any reservation, a particular reservation. The killer wears a carved wooden mask. Cedar, or pine, or maple. The killer sits alone on a grave. The headstone is gray, its inscription illegible. There are many graves, rows of graves, rows of rows. The killer is softly singing a new song that sounds exactly like an old one. As the killer sings, an owl silently lands on a tree branch nearby. The owl shakes its feathers clean. It listens. The killer continues to sing, and another owl perches beside the first. Birds of prey, birds of prayer. . . .
>
> The killer spins in circles and, with each revolution, another owl floats in from the darkness and takes its place in the tree. Dark blossom after dark blossom. The killer sings and dances for hours, days. Other Indians arrive and quickly learn the song. A dozen Indians, then hundreds, and more, all learning the same song, the exact dance. The killer dances and will not tire. The killer knows this dance is over five hundred years old. . . . The killer plans on dancing forever. The killer never falls. The moon never falls. The tree grows heavy with owls.

This passage is taken from the novel's concluding chapter, which is entitled "A Creation Story." Late in the novel, Marie Polatkin suggests that "maybe this Indian Killer is a product of the Ghost Dance. . . . Maybe this is how the Ghost Dance works." Later on, she tells the police, "[I]f some Indian is killing white guys, then it's a credit to us that it took over five hundred years for it to happen. And," she says, "there's more[:]Indians are dancing now, and I don't think they're going to stop." Decolonization here is, indeed, a violent phenomenon.[57]

As the twentieth-century drew to a close, the Native American novel seemed to have become darker and more pessimistic. The hopes for change that marked Native culture as a result of the revolutionary fervor of the 1960s seem to have been worn down, overtaken perhaps by the desire for entrepreneurial success that motivates Erdrich's Lyman Lamartine in *Love Medicine* and *The Bingo Palace*. While Erdrich maintains her faith in the healing powers of human love and traditional Native American beliefs, she seems increasingly to be the exception rather than the rule. The shift in Leslie Marmon Silko's work may perhaps be an indication of the direction in which the Native American novel is headed. The healing of wounds that takes place at the end of *Ceremony* with Tayo's disavowal of violence and the departure of his nemesis, Emo, is replaced in Silko's massive second novel, *Almanac of the Dead* (1991), by a sense that the evil represented by men like Emo is resilient and powerful and not so easily dismissed. In form and subject matter, *Almanac* is as difficult and jarring as any of Vizenor's novels, but it lacks Vizenor's sense of the comic. Described by Silko as a "763-page indictment for five hundred years of theft, murder, pillage, and rape," *Almanac* portrays a nightmarish world of violence, sexual perversion, and corruption at every level of society, a world in which the "witchery" has won out. None of the characters in *Almanac* are capable of love, and few of them seem capable even of hatred. The triumph of individualism has created a hierarchical, mechanistic, misogynist culture, in which the ontological norm might well be the stupor of the drug addicts who abound throughout the novel. If there is any hopefulness in *Almanac of the Dead*, it is perhaps in the novel's conviction that the Eurocentric regimes that now rule the Americas are destined to be overthrown.

Silko told an interviewer in 1992 that "*Almanac* spawned another novel about a woman who is a serial killer" whose victims are only "policemen and politicians." It was, she said, "way more radical than *Almanac*," but she set it aside because she believed that it was too soon "to serve the narrative again on something so hard." Asked by the interviewer "what happened to the nice, charming Leslie Silko who used to write poems," Silko laughed and described "what happened" as "classic," simply a matter of "development," the result of "reading, learning," and emerging from a "sheltered" life.[58] What Silko sees in her own life is the inevitability of encountering the violence that is inherent in cultural emergence, a violence that was increasingly given life in the Native American novel at the end of the twentieth century, embodied in characters like Vizenor's tricksters, Alexie's Indian Killer, and Silko's drug addicts and sadists.

Model Minority

For Asian Americans, the 1960s offered a different legacy. Considered unassimilable aliens until World War II, Asian Americans would in the aftermath of the war become cast in the role of the "model minority," in contradistinction to those minorities—particularly African Americans and Chicanos—who were growing increasingly militant in their calls for social equality. According to the literary scholar Elaine Kim, Asian Americans were portrayed by the white mainstream during the 1960s as "restrained, humble, and well-mannered, a people who respect law, love education, work hard, and have close-knit, well-disciplined families."[59]

This shift in stereotypical portrayals of Asian Americans may well have begun with the success of Earl Derr Biggers's six Charlie Chan novels, which appeared between 1925 and 1932 and were all published in novel form after being serialized in the *Saturday Evening Post*, and which provided an alternative to Sax Rohmer's sinister Fu Manchu. "Sinister and wicked Chinese are old stuff," Biggers would claim, "but an amiable Chinese on the side of law and order has never been used."[60] Charlie Chan became a phenomenon, with forty-eight Chan films produced by four different studios featuring six different non-Chinese actors as the detective who solves crimes in exotic settings both in Chinatown and abroad.

The image of Chinatown as an inviting place of mystery would become the basis for a genre of writing that might be called the "Chinatown Book," first made popular by Leong Gor Yun's *Chinatown Inside Out* (1938). In the introduction to *Aiiieeeee!* (1974), the first anthology of Asian American writing, Frank Chin, Jeffery Paul Chan, Lawson Fusao Inada, and Shawn Wong argue that "*Chinatown Inside Out* was obviously a fraud," noting that "the author's name 'Leong Gor Yun,' means "two men' in Chinese." Consisting of what the editors identify as "items cribbed and translated from the Chinese-language newspapers of Chinatown in San Francisco tied together with Charlie Chan/Fu Manchu images and the precise logic of a paranoid schizophrenic," *Chinatown Inside Out* fooled "even scholars of Chinese America," who failed to notice "the awkward changes of voice and style, the differences between the outright lies and the rare facts," and the clue contained in the author's pen name. *Chinatown Inside Out* would prove influential, nevertheless, becoming the source for the novel *Chinatown Family* (1948), written by the Chinese émigré Lin Yutang, which presents an idealized portrait of Chinese American family life that draws on the model of the Horatio Alger success story, suggesting that success can be achieved through a mixture of hard work and well-deserved good fortune.

Autobiographical accounts published by Asian Americans in the 1940s, when China was an ally of the United States against Japan, tended to reinforce the idea that Chinese people were in fact assimilable. Pardee Lowe's *Father and Glorious Descendant* (1942) belittles Chinese culture as "alien" and "strange," while presenting the United States as "God's own country"; the dust jacket presented the book as an example of why the United States should "assimilate her loyal minorities" and noted that Lowe "enlisted in the U.S. Army shortly after delivering the manuscript of the book." Jade Snow Wong's autobiography, *Fifth Chinese Daughter* (1945), adopted the alternative but complementary strategy of Orientalizing Chinatown, making it seem exotic but safe. Wong's book was a financial success, reprinted several times in paperback and translated into a variety of languages. The influence of the "Chinatown Book" would continue to be felt in the 1960s. S. W. Kung, a Chinese émigré, would cite Lin's *Chinatown Family* as an influence on his study *Chinese in American Life* (1962); Calvin Lee, a former assistant dean at Columbia University, would cite both Leong Gor Yun and S. W. Kun in describing his assimilation into white American society in *Chinatown U.S.A.* (1965). Betty Lee Sung's *Mountain of Gold: The Story of the Chinese in America* (1967) praised Chinese Americans for not being "overly bitter about prejudice," but lamented their tendency to gather in ethnic enclaves instead of dispersing themselves around the country to "reduce the degree of visibility."[61] Like both Pardee Lowe and Jade Snow Wong, Sung blames Chinese Americans themselves for adding to their hardships.

For Japanese Americans, the road to being typecast as a model minority was far more bumpy. In the years leading up to World War

II, many second-generation Japanese Americans— known as *Nisei*—
wished to distinguish themselves from what they viewed as the back-
wardness of the first generation, the *Issei*. This desire found public
expression in the policies of the Japanese American Citizens League
(JACL), a political organization that excluded Issei from membership
because they were not U.S. citizens. The goal of the JACL was to demonstrate that Japanese Americans were true blue Americans, despite
their ostensibly Japanese faces. The organization's official creed, written
in 1940 by the JACL's national secretary and field executive, Mike Masaoka, in the face of escalating tensions between the United States and
Japan, is an oath of loyalty to the United States:

> I am proud that I am an American citizen of Japanese ancestry, for my
> very background makes me appreciate more fully the wonderful advan-
> tages of this nation. I believe in her institutions, ideals and traditions; I
> glory in her heritage; I boast of her history; I trust in her future. She has
> granted me liberties and opportunities such as no individual enjoys in
> this world today. She has given me an education befitting kings. She has
> entrusted me with the responsibilities of the franchise. She has permitted
> me to build a home, to earn a livelihood, to worship, think, speak and act
> as I please—as a free man equal to every other man.
>
> Although some individuals may discriminate against me, I shall
> never become bitter or lose faith, for I know that such persons are not
> representative of the American people. True, I shall do all in my power
> to discourage such practices, but I shall do it in the American way—
> above board, in the open, through courts of law, by education, by prov-
> ing myself to be worthy of equal treatment and consideration. I am firm
> in my belief that American sportsmanship and attitude of fair play will
> judge citizenship and patriotism on the basis of action and achieve-
> ment, and not on the basis of physical characteristics. Because I believe
> in America, and I trust she believes in me, and because I have received
> innumerable benefits from her, I pledge myself to do honor to her at all
> times and all places; to support her constitution; to obey her laws; to
> respect her flag; to defend her against all enemies, foreign and domestic;
> to actively assume my duties and obligations as a citizen, cheerfully and
> without any reservations whatsoever, in the hope that I may become a
> better American in a greater America.

Deeply individualistic in its outlook, the JACL's creed denied that racism was a pervasive social phenomenon, ascribing it instead to the actions of a few ignorant individuals.

In her memoir *Nisei Daughter* (1953), Monica Sone echoes the optimism of the JACL, describing the contentment and optimism that she had just begun to feel before the attack on Pearl Harbor disrupted her life: "Father had found this marvelous big barn of a house on lovely Beacon Hill from where we could see the early morning mist rising from Lake Washington in the east, a panoramic view of Puget Sound and the city in the west. In such a setting, my future rolled out in front of me, blazing with happiness. Nothing could possibly go wrong now." This picture of tranquility disintegrates on the very next page, however, as Sone describes her reaction when a friend bursts into her living room to tell her family about the attack: "I felt as if a fist had smashed my pleasant little existence, breaking it into jigsaw puzzle pieces. An old wound opened up again, and I found myself shrinking inwardly from my Japanese blood, the blood of an enemy. I knew instinctively that the fact that I was an American by birthright was not going to help me escape the consequences of this unhappy war."[62] Toshio Mori describes a similar scene in his short story "Slant-Eyed Americans" (1949):

> Mother's last ray of hope paled and her eyes became dull. "Why did it have to happen? The common people in Japan don't want war, and we don't want war. Here the people are peace-loving. Why cannot the peoples of the earth live peacefully?"
>
> "Since Japan declared war on the United States it'll mean that you parents of American citizens have become enemy aliens," I said.
>
> "Enemy aliens," my mother whispered.[63]

The nature of the Nisei's ambivalence is also captured in the entry that Charles Kikuchi, a resident of Berkeley, California, made in his journal on December 7, 1941: "Pearl Harbor. We are at war! Jesus Christ, the Japs bombed Hawaii and the entire fleet has been sunk. I just can't believe it. I don't know what in the hell is going to happen to us, but we will all be called into the Army right away. . . . I think of the Japs coming to bomb us, but I will go and fight even if I think I am a coward and I don't believe in wars but this time it has to be. I am selfish about it."

Taken out of context, these might seem like the words of young white racist, but as his name suggests, Kikuchi was in fact a Nisei. The journal entry expresses the fears that were on the minds of many Nisei in the days that followed Japan's bombing of Pearl Harbor: "The next five years will determine the future of the Nisei. . . . If we are ever going to prove our Americanism, this is the time. . . . The Anti-Jap feeling is bound to rise to hysterical heights, and it is most likely that the Nisei will be included as Japs. . . . I don't know what to think or do."[64]

American by birth but Japanese to those inclined to judge solely by outward appearance, the Nisei had good reason to fear that they and their families would be mistreated in the aftermath of Japan's declaration of war. They had only to think about the experience of their parents, the Issei, the first generation of Japanese immigrants. Japanese immigration followed the pattern already established by the Chinese: most of the early Japanese immigrants to the United States were young men who tended to regard themselves as sojourners, exiled from Japan in order to earn money but determined to return some day to their homeland without being contaminated by their exposure to U.S. culture. This attitude is presented as one of the primary characteristics of the Issei in many of the autobiographies and novels written by Nisei after the war. For example, when Ichiro, the Nisei protagonist of John Okada's *No-No Boy* (1953), asks his father, "What made you and Ma come to America?" the answer he receives is simple: "We came to make money." Ichiro thinks to himself that the Issei "rushed to America with the single purpose of making a fortune which would enable them to return to their own country and live adequately." Despite the fact that "their sojourns were spanning decades instead of years," these Issei "continued to maintain their dreams by refusing to learn how to speak or write the language of America and by living among their own kind and by zealously avoiding long-term commitments such as the purchase of a house." Thinking about his parents' friends the Kumasakas, Ichiro remembers that, before World War II, they had "lived in cramped quarters" above their dry-cleaning shop "because, like most of the other Japanese, they planned some day to return to Japan and still felt like transients after thirty or forty years in America." When he learns that they have decided to buy a house, Ichiro is "impressed" because it "could only mean that the Kumasakas had exchanged hope for reality and, late as it was, were finally sinking roots into the land from which they had previously sought not nourishment but only gold." In contrast, Ichiro's parents are resolute in the determination to return to Japan; even after the end of the war, Ichiro's father still believes that the family will be returning to Japan—"pretty soon."[65]

Because they regarded themselves simply as sojourners, many of the early Issei had little interest in integrating themselves into American society. As a rule they spoke little English. Ichiro reflects that

> his parents, like most of the old Japanese, spoke virtually no English. On the other hand, the children, like Ichiro, spoke almost no Japanese. Thus they communicated, the old speaking Japanese with an occasionally badly mispronounced word or two of English; and the young, with the exception of a simple word or phrase of Japanese which came fairly effortlessly to the lips, resorting almost constantly to the tongue the parents avoided.

Similarly, in Hisaye Yamamoto's short story "Seventeen Syllables" (1949), the language gap between Issei and Nisei is emblematic of a larger cultural divide. The Nisei daughter Rosie pretends to appreciate the *haiku* that her mother has just composed because she is ashamed to reveal just how shaky her command of Japanese really is: "The truth was that Rosie was lazy; English lay ready on the tongue but Japanese had to be searched for and examined, and even then put forth tentatively (probably to meet with laughter). It was so much easier to say yes, yes, even when one meant no, no." Remembering a haiku written in English and French that she has seen in a magazine and that delighted her—

> It is morning, and lo!
> I lie awake, comme il faut,
> sighing for some dough.

—Rosie reflects upon the problem of translating not only from one language to another but from one culture to another: "how to reach her mother, how to communicate the melancholy song? Rosie knew formal Japanese by fits and starts, her mother had even less English, no French. It was much more possible to say yes, yes." Avoiding situations in which they would have to speak English, the Issei kept themselves isolated. In Hawai'i, they lived in the camps reserved for Japanese workers on the sugar plantations; on the mainland, they lived either on small farms in rural areas or else in ethnic enclaves like the "Lil' Yokohama" that Toshio Mori describes in his collection of short stories *Yokohama, California* (1949).[66]

As depicted in novels like Okada's *No-No Boy* or Milton Murayama's *All I Asking for Is My Body* (1975), the Issei live in a fantasy world in which Japan can do no wrong: in Okada's novel, the protagonist's mother refuses to believe that Japan has lost World War II, while the father in Murayama's novel refuses to admit that the Japanese army committed atrocities during the military operation that the rest of the world refers to as "the rape of Nanking." Not all Issei shared this perspective, however; in a secret report commissioned by the State Department as war with Japan became seemingly inevitable, Curtis B. Munson provided the following description of the Issei:

> First generation Japanese. Entire cultural background Japanese. Probably loyal romantically to Japan. They must be considered, however, as other races. They have made this their home. They have brought up children here, their wealth accumulated by hard labor is here, and many would have become American citizens had they been allowed to do so. They are for the most part simple people.

Two prominent Nisei autobiographers present portraits of their parents that fit Munson's description. Monica Sone relates that her father had "succumbed to the fever which sent many young men streaming across the Pacific to a fabulous new country rich with promise and opportunities," chief among which was the opportunity "to continue his law studies at Ann Arbor, Michigan." In *Desert Exile: The Uprooting of a Japanese Family* (1982), Yoshiko Uchida describes her father's desire "to go to Yale and eventually to become a doctor"; unlike most Issei men, Dwight Takashi Uchida was actually going to the United States to be reunited with his family, in this case with his mother and his sister.[67]

But even those Issei who, like Uchida's father, did wish to settle in the United States permanently and assimilate into U.S. culture knew that accepting the United States as their home did not mean that the United

States would accept them in turn. Prevented by the 1870 Naturalization Act from becoming citizens, the Issei were also prevented from owning land or even leasing it for more than three years by California's Alien Land Law Act of 1913 (which would remain in effect for nearly fifty years). Hisaye Yamamoto recalls that "our family and other farm families we knew moved quite frequently. . . . The availability of land to lease came down in a kind of pipeline from other Japanese, usually friends of the family who had come from the same area in Japan. So there was this kind of floating community that we belonged to, with village and prefectural picnics every year." And, she adds, "There wasn't much mingling with the white community, although there were probably some lasting contacts formed with some landlords, business people, neighbors."[68] Isolated by a white culture that accused *them* of being isolationist, the Issei realized that it was only through their children, who were U.S. citizens by birth, that they might be said to have a future in America. The Nisei, it was hoped, would be a "bridge" (*kakehashi*) between the United States and Japan, "intermediaries" who could serve as cultural interpreters and promote better understanding between the two cultures.

Many Issei parents, however, hedged their bets by registering their children as citizens of Japan. For example, 84 percent of the Nisei living in the Pacific Coast and Rocky Mountain States in 1926 were registered as Japanese citizens, and in 1940 over half of all the Nisei in the United States were registered as Japanese citizens.[69] Understanding the precariousness of their situation as unnaturalizable aliens in a country where they were constantly subjected to racial discrimination, many Issei wanted to be able to take their children with them in the event that they might be forced to return to Japan and to give their children the option of returning there on their own. While many Issei sent their children to Japanese language schools, some parents took the further step of sending their children to Japan in order to learn about Japanese culture firsthand; these so-called "Kibei" tended to live in Japan for several years before returning to the United States. In the December 7, 1941, entry of his journal Charles Kikuchi worries about "Kibei spies" perpetrating "sabotage" though a Kibei friend later assures him that "Kibei are loyal." Indeed, many Kibei returned to the United States with a renewed appreciation for the country of their birth.

As a whole, Nisei writing is marked by the tension between the perspective of those like Sone and the JACL, who sought to prove their loyalty as Americans by supporting the U.S. government's wartime policies toward American Japanese, and those who became and remained bitterly disillusioned. The English-language magazines that were produced in three of the internment camps—*Trek* (Topaz, Utah), *Tulean Dispatch* (Tule Lake, California), and *The Pen* (Rowher, Arkansas)—reflect the struggle between these perspectives, though critical points of view were blunted by government censorship. In response, the wartime poetry of Toyo Suryemoto uses a facade of natural metaphors to convey the bitterness and despair brought about by internment. For example, Suryemoto's poem "In Topaz," published in *Trek* in 1942, seems at first glance simply to be an example of nature poetry:

> Can this hard earth break wide
>> The stiff stillness of snow
> And yield me promise that
>> This is not always so?
>
> Surely, the warmth of sun
>> Can pierce the earth, ice-bound
> Until grass comes to life,
>> Outwitting the barren ground.

Suryemoto reproduces the poem in her memoir, *I Call to Remembrance: Toyo Suyemoto's Years of Internment* (2007), describing it as a response to the fact that in the Topaz camp "young and old seemed to reflect the philosophical acquiescence of the Issei in bearing the rigors of the weather." Analyzing Sureyemoto's figurative strategies in the poems that she published while interned, the literary scholar Susan Schweik argues that "once embedded in the context to which the title of the [poem "In Topaz"] pointedly refers," these poems invoke "a sense of a whole politics and mythology of agriculture in Nikkei experience: of an American promised land which kept revealing itself to immigrants from Japan as a wasteland" in which their labor was exploited.[70]

This disagreement about the necessity of internment continues in Japanese American writing after the war. In prose, it is reflected in the gap between the conciliatory rhetoric of Sone's *Nisei Daughter* (1953) and the bitter ambivalence of Okada's *No-No Boy*. Perhaps because it did not provide the ringing affirmation of the American Way that many Japanese Americans perceived to be necessary in the aftermath of World War II, Okada's novel was not a popular success. "At the time we published it," wrote Charles Tuttle, the publisher of the book's first edition, "the very people whom [sic] we thought would be enthusiastic about it, mainly the Japanese-American community in the United States, were not only disinterested but actually rejected the book." In contrast, Monica Sone's *Nisei Daughter* ends on a note of complete acceptance and forgiveness, as the narrator tells her mother, "I don't resent my Japanese blood anymore. I'm proud of it, in fact, because of you and the Issei who've struggled so much for us. It's really nice to be born into two cultures, like getting a real bargain in life, two for the price of one. The hardest part, I guess, is the growing up, but after that, it can be interesting and stimulating. I used to feel like a two-headed monstrosity, but now I find that two heads are better than one." She argues that "the war and the mental tortures we went through" have given the Nisei "a clearer understanding of America and its way of life, and we have learned to value her more." The final chapter of Sone's book is an example of the Nisei's eagerness to prove themselves American, a restatement of Mike Masaoka's JACL creed.[71]

Issei poets such as Shumpa Kiuchi and Shusei Matsui wrote poems that harked back to heroic traditions in Asian literature, while many Nisei authors, writing in the JACL's national paper, *Pacific Citizen*, and in such Japanese American newspapers as *Rafu Shimpo* (Los Angeles) and *Hokubei Mainichi* (San Francisco), devoted themselves to the projects of forgetting the miseries of internment and reintegrating themselves into U.S. culture. The poet Mitsuye Yamada, born in Japan and therefore an Issei but raised among Nisei in the United States, cuts across the grain of these generalizations. Her first collection, *Camp Notes* (1976), brings together pieces written during and after her internment at Minidoka and poems written during the 1970s. Crafted with an ironic detachment and an eye for poignant detail, her poems adopt the anti-racist and anti-patriarchal attitudes that are usually attributed to sansei (third-generation) writing about the war.

In the aftermath of the civil rights movements of the 1960s and the Vietnam War, sansei poets such as Lawson Fusao Inada and Janice

Mirikitani sought to make their poetry a vehicle for the reconstruction of Japanese American identity. In the introduction to his second volume of poetry, *Legends From Camp* (1993), Inada wrote, "More and more, artist and audience are becoming one—for the greater cause of community and mutuality. . . . I began functioning as a community poet—with new people, places, and publications to work with."[72] Sharing Inada's sense of political commitment, Mirikitani adds a strain of self-reflective meditation on the limits of what poetry and thought can accomplish. After listening to the experiences of a Vietnam veteran, the speaker of "Jungle Rot and Open Arms" asks:

> so where is my
> *political education?* my
> *rhetorical answers to everything?* my
> *theory into practice?* my
> *intensification of life in art?*

Some sansei writers have sought to ground their poetry in a new regionalism: Juliet Kono's collection *Hilo Rains* (1989) explores the ways in which three generations of her family have been shaped by the land of Hawai'i, while Garret Kaoru Hongo writes about Hawai'i and about other communities where Asian Americans live, seeking to draw connections across regional and ethnic boundaries.

Frank Chin and the editors of the *Aiiieeeee!* anthology argue that "much of Asian-American literary history is a history of a small minority being cast into the role of the good guy in order to make another American minority look bad. In World War II, the Chinese were used against the Japanese." Citing both a *Newsweek* article entitled "The Japanese-American Success Story: Outwhiting the Whites" (June 21, 1971) and the "favorable reception" accorded Sung's *Mountain of Gold* and Daniel I. Okimoto's *American in Disguise* (1970), Chin and his colleagues contend that "today, the Chinese- and Japanese-Americans are used to mouth the white racist cliches of the fifties." They note that Sung's book, which "went through two printings of 7,500 and in 1971 was issued in a paperback edition," was "the only book by a Chinese-American still in print" in 1974. An article published in *U.S. News and World Report* at the end of 1966 suggested that the Chinese could serve as a model for African Americans and other "troublesome minority groups," because they have managed to succeed "on their own" despite past "hardships" that would "shock those now complaining about the hardships endured by today's Negroes." Praising Chinatown as "the safest place" in New York City, where residents "stay out of trouble" and "overcome their handicaps quietly," the article proclaims:

> At a time when it is being proposed that hundreds of billions be spent to uplift Negroes and other minorities, the nation's 300,000 Chinese are moving ahead on their own with no help from anyone else. Still being taught in Chinatown is the old idea that people should depend on their own efforts . . . not a welfare check . . . in order to reach America's "promised land."[73]

Originally published by Howard University Press in 1974 but reprinted the following year in a paperback edition by Anchor Books, *Aiiieeeee!* set itself against the stereotype of Asian Americans as the model minority, lamenting that "seven generations of suppression under legislative racism and euphemized white racist love have left today's Asian-Americans in a state of self-contempt, self-rejection, and disintegration." As of 1975, they claim, fewer than "ten works of fiction and poetry have been published by American-born Chinese, Japanese, and Filipino writers," not because "in six generations of Asian-Americans there was no impulse to literary or artistic self-expression" but because mainstream American publishers were only interested in publishing works written by Asian Americans that were "*actively inoffensive* to white sensibilities."

Aiiieeeee! was intended to counter the accepted wisdom that a literature that could be called "Asian American" simply did not exist; in an essay describing the genesis of the anthology, the editors. wryly cite the different reasons given for this lack: "Sung says we're working too hard to write; Kung says we were too low class to write; Okimoto says we were too full of self-contempt to write and that if we could write we would have nothing to say. All three had obviously let their library cards lapse." Describing their method of "searching the past for works" as more "serendipitous" than "scientific," they write: "We found John Okada on the shelf of a grocery store; Louis Chu we found in the card catalog of the Oakland Public Library; Toshio Mori we found on the shelf of a used book store we'd gone into seeking shelter on a rainy day in Berkeley."[74] After a polemical introduction entitled "Fifty Years of Our Own Voice," *Aiiieeeee!* offered its readers selections from Carlos Bulosan's *America Is in the Heart* (1946); Diana Chang's novel *The Frontiers of Love* (1956); Louis Chu's novel *Eat a Bowl of Tea* (1961); Momoko Iko's drama *The Gold Watch*; Toshio Mori's *Yokohama, California* (1949); John Okada's *No-No Boy* (1957); as well as stories by Wallace Lin, Oscar Peñaranda, Sam Tagatac, and Hisaye Yamamoto, and writings by editors Frank Chin, Jeffery Paul Chan, and Shawn Hsu Wong. "My writer's education owes a big debt to this first *Aiiieeeee!*," writes the Filipino American writer Jessica Hagedorn:

> The energy and interest sparked by *Aiiieeeee!* in the Seventies was essential to Asian American writers because it gave us visibility and credibility as creators of our own specific literature. We could not be ignored; suddenly, we were no longer silent. Like other writers of color in America, we were beginning to challenge the long-cherished concepts of a xenophobic literary canon dominated by white heterosexual males. Obviously, there was room for more than one voice and one vision in this ever-expanding arena.[75]

In 1990, the editors of *Aiiieeeee!* produced a sequel entitled *The Big Aiiieeeee!*, which restricted itself to Chinese American and Japanese American literature, despite the fact that it contained twice as many writers as the original volume. In narrowing its focus, *The Big Aiiieeeee!* contributed to the perception that "Asian American Literature" essentially consists of literature by Chinese and Japanese Americans, with sporadic contributions by writers of Southeast Asian and Asian Indian descent.

The original *Aiiieeeee!* anthology contained fiction and drama but no poetry, and in general Asian American poetry has lagged behind the other genres in achieving prominence on the literary landscape. *The Big Aiiieeeee!*, however, brought attention to a recently recovered tradition of Chinese American poetry, written by immigrants to the San Francisco Bay area during the first two decades of the twentieth century. During this period, poetry had been appearing in two daily newspapers written in Cantonese and published in San Francisco's Chinatown:

the *Chung Sai Yat Po*, which was established in 1900 and began issuing a daily literary supplement in 1908, and the *Sai Gat Yat Po*, which was established in 1909. Chinatown had a number of literary societies, which sponsored poetry competitions, and in 1911 the prominent bookseller Tai Quong Company published an anthology of 808 vernacular poems, entitled *Jinshan ge ji* (*Songs of Gold Mountain*, after the popular name given to the United States by Chinese sojourners); a second volume, published in 1915, collected an additional 832 folk rhymes. Together, these poems present a rich account of the experience of early Chinese immigrants in the United States, and (as I noted in Chapter 3) many of them express the loneliness, despair, and frustration of discovering that American practices do not always live up to American ideals.[76] An additional set of 135 poems, which had been scribbled in Cantonese on the walls of the Angel Island Immigration Station by those detained there, were preserved when two detainees copied them down and brought them to San Francisco.

Implicit in the logic of both *Aiiieeee!* anthologies, as it was in the Quinto Sol prize project, was the desire to establish a canon of writings that would promote non-stereotypical depictions of Asian Americans, a goal that was shared by the Combined Asian Resources Project (CARP), in which Chin, Chan, and Wong all participated. The introduction to *The Big Aiiieeeee!* denounces the adoption by Asian American writers of autobiography, which they claim is a form that can only "ventriloquiz[e] the same old white Christian fantasy of little Chinese victims of 'the original sin of being born to a brutish, sadomasochistic culture of cruelty and victimization' fleeing to America in search of freedom from everything Chinese and seeking white acceptance." Arguing that "every Chinese American book ever published in the United States of America by a major publisher has been a Christian autobiography or autobiographical novel," they present a list of works that must be excluded from any Asian American canon, beginning with Yung Wing's *My Life in China* (1909), moving through Leong Gor Yun's *Chinatown Inside Out* (1936), Pardee Lowe's *Father and Glorious Descendant* (1943), and Jade Snow Wong's *Fifth Chinese Daughter* (1950), and concluding with Maxine Hong Kingston's *The Woman Warrior* (1976), *China Men* (1980), and *Tripmaster Monkey* (1989) and Amy Tan's *The Joy Luck Club* (1989)—because they "all tell the story that Will Irwin, the Christian social Darwinist practitioner of white racist love, wanted told in *Pictures of Old Chinatown* (1908) about how the 'Chinese transformed themselves from our race adversaries to our dear subject people.'" They identify only "four works by Chinese American authors" that "do not suck off the white Christian fantasy of the Chinese as a Shangri-La people": two published by "major publishing houses"—Diana Chang's *Frontiers of Love* (1956) and Louis Chu's *Eat a Bowl of Tea* (1961)—and two written by editors of the anthologies—Shawn Wong's novel *Homebase* (1979) and Frank Chin's collection of short stories, *The Chinaman Pacific & Frisco R.R. Co.* (1988).[77]

What appeals to Chin and his co-editors about a work like *Eat a Bowl of Tea* is its author's refusal to present either Chinese or Chinese American culture as exotic: Chu portrays the last vestiges of bachelor society in New York's Chinatown from the inside, from the point of view of waiters, barbers, and laundrymen who comprised it. His Chinatown is, as the editors put it, "drab, even boring." Chu was born in Toishan but emigrated at the age of nine with his family to Newark, New Jersey; he served in the U.S. Army during World War II and returned to China shortly thereafter to marry. *Eat a Bowl of Tea* chronicles the transformation of New York's Chinatown from a community of bachelors to a community of young families by telling the story of an old "bachelor" named Wah Gay and his son, Ben Loy. After decades working as a waiter, Wah Gay has established himself as the proprietor of the "Money Come club house," a dingy basement where Wah Gay and other lonely "bachelors" convene to play mahjong. Technically not a bachelor, Wah Gay has a wife in China, whom he married twenty-five years earlier during a brief return visit and whom he has not seen since: "Each time he had received a letter from his wife he began to relive the past. He knew it was not right to let the old woman stay in the village by herself. He often wondered, during lonely moments, if perhaps some day he and Lau Shee would have a joyous reunion."[78] What takes the place of actual families in the lives of these old men are memberships in clan associations and tongs, and sex with prostitutes.

When the novel opens, Wah Gay's son, born in China but now living in the United States, has also returned to his native village to marry the daughter of his father's friend Lee Gong; unlike his father, however, Ben Loy is able to bring his bride, Mei Oi, back with him due to the repeal of the Exclusion Act and a subsequent law permitting Chinese brides of American citizens to enter the United States on a non-quota basis (facts left unstated by the novel). Mei Oi's presence proves highly disruptive to Chinatown's bachelor society: Ben Loy, an experienced frequenter of prostitutes, becomes impotent in the face of what he conceives to be his wife's "purity"; Mei Oi is seduced by an unscrupulous bachelor named Ah Song, causing a scandal throughout Chinatown; Wah Gay cuts off the seducer's ear in revenge and is saved from jail only when fellow members of the Sing On tong compel Ah Song to withdraw the charges he has filed with the police; and ultimately, Wah Gay and Lee Gong leave Chinatown to spare themselves further humiliation, Ah Song is ostracized by the tong for five years, and the young couple relocate to San Francisco. Ben Loy's impotence becomes a trope for the sterility of Chinese American bachelor society, a sterility created by the racist policies of the U.S. government. What breaks the cycle of impotence is not simply the bitter bowl of tea prescribed by an herbalist he visits, but his forgiveness of his wife and his acceptance of the child she has given birth to that is not his by blood but will be his by choice. In moving from New York to San Francisco, Ben Loy and Mei Oi move to the cultural heart of Chinese America, and the conclusion of the novel promises reunion and regeneration, as the couple plan to invite their estranged fathers to the haircutting party for their second child. Realistic in its rendering of Cantonese figures of speech into English, naturalistic in its sexual frankness, *Eat a Bowl of Tea* did not achieve popular success or critical recognition during Chu's lifetime, but it has become an inspiration to Asian American artists like Chin and the director Wayne Wang, whose film version of the novel was released in 1988.

Unlike the Quinto Sol prize project, which managed to build the core of a Chicano canon around Rivera, Anaya, and Hinojosa, *The Big Aiiieeee!* failed to solidify an Asian American canon centered on the work of Chang, Chu, Okada, Wong, and Chin. Members of CARP were influential in bringing about the University of Washington Press's Asian American Studies series, which issued new editions of Bulosan's *America Is in the Heart*, Okada's *No-No Boy*, Chu's *Eat a Bowl of Tea*, and Sone's *Nisei Daughter* between 1973 and 1979. But it is Maxine Hong Kingston who is the most widely taught Asian American writer.

To render the hostility that Chin et al. feel for Kingston's writing comprehensible, we should remember that CARP devoted itself to dismantling the two, seemingly contradictory but pervasive myths about Asian Americans: either that they are temporary "sojourners" determined to remain unassimilable or that they represent a "model minority" within U.S. culture, docile and eager to assimilate. For the members of CARP and in particular for Frank Chin, both of these myths represent a threat to Asian American culture because they represent a threat to Asian American masculinity. What bothers Chin most about Charlie Chan is the fact that he walks with "the light dainty step of a woman," asexual at best, at worst feminized and emasculated. Seeing this emasculated Chinese man as the core stereotype of Asian Americans, Chin has described himself as a "Chinatown Cowboy," thus asserting both the possibility of a Chinese American masculinity and rooting that masculinity in the history of the American West. A second strand to his argument has been the desire to distinguish Chinese Americans from Chinese, as a way of dissociating Chinese Americans from what he conceives to be the mainstream American view of Chinese culture as unmanly: "The Asian culture we are supposedly preserving is uniquely without masculinity; we are characterized as lacking daring, originality, aggressiveness, assertiveness, vitality, and a living art and culture."[79]

Chin has gone so far as to argue that the comparatively large number of Asian American women writers and their commercial success also pose a threat to Asian American manhood. These beliefs result in a misogynist current that runs through the selections chosen in *The Big Aiiieeee!*. Elaine Kim has argued that "aside from Toshio Mori, few Asian American male writers have attempted multidimensional portrayals of Asian American women," while Asian American women writers like Noriko Sawada, Emily Cachapero, Wakako Yamauchi, Eleanor Wong Telemaque, and Hisaye Yamamoto have "demonstrated a profound sympathy for an understanding of their men." Not surprisingly, these writers are appreciated by Chin and his co-editors because, as Kim suggests, their efforts "complement the efforts of male writers to correct distortions and omissions about Asian American men."[80]

For Chin, however, Maxine Hong Kingston represents the enemy, a critically and commercially successful writer, whose subject is the double disenfranchisement of Chinese American women. Both Chin and

Kingston share the goal of combating the stereotypical views of Asian Americans established by mainstream U.S. culture, but in Kingston's writing this is only part of the story: she also depicts the relegation of Chinese American women to second-class status within both American *and* Chinese American culture. In Kingston's writing, the claims of ethnicity and gender occasionally conflict, and her writing does not always assign the claims of ethnicity first priority. Her writings dramatize the deleterious effects of both white American discrimination against Chinese Americans *and* of Chinese American misogyny and homophobia. From Chin's perspective, Kingston is like the sister who airs family problems in public, outside of the sanctity of the home.[81]

The Big Aiiieeeee!'s prejudices soon rendered it more useful as a historical document than as a state-of-the-art collection of Asian American writing. In 1993, that distinction went to Jessica Hagedorn's collection *Charlie Chan Is Dead*, which represented itself as "the first anthology of Asian American fiction by a commercial publisher" in the United States and includes selections from forty-eight writers—not only Chinese and Japanese, but also Filipino, Korean, and Indian American. The volume presents forty-eight writers, and like both *Aiiieeeee!* collections, it seeks to move beyond the stereotype of the model minority. "Charlie Chan is indeed dead, never to be revived," writes Elaine Kim in the preface to the anthology. "Gone for good his yellowface asexual bulk, his fortune-cookie English, his stereotypical Orientalist version of 'the [Confucian] Chinese family.'"[82] But, as if in tacit rebuke of the *Aiiieeeee!* editors, Hagedorn's introduction proclaims finally:

> For many of us, what is personal is also political, and vice versa. We are asserting and continually exploring who we are as Asians, Asian Americans, and artists and citizens of what Salman Rushdie calls "a shrinking universe." The choice is more than whether to hyphenate or not. The choice is more than gender, race, or class. First generation, second, third, fourth. Uncle Tom or Charlie Chan. And the language(s) we speak are not necessarily the language(s) in which we dream.[83]

The revised edition of *Charlie Chan Is Dead* that appeared in 2004 points to the increasing breadth of the term "Asian American." Although the term had been invented in order to promote political solidarity among

Americans of Asian descent, the idea of a unifying "Asian American" sensibility that depends on being born in North America has come to seem stifling, particularly after the sharp increase in Asian immigration that followed the 1965 Immigration and Nationality Act, which abolished the quotas that favored immigrants from northern European countries. By century's end, the label "Asian American" had been broadened to include native and naturalized Americans of not only Chinese, Japanese, and Filipino but also Bangladeshi, Burmese, Cambodian, Indian, Indonesian, Korean, Laotian, Nepalese, Thai, and Vietnamese descent.

Stonewall and Gay Liberation

On the night of Friday, June 27, 1969, New York City police raided a gay bar called the Stonewall, the sixth such raid in three weeks. This time, however, the response was different. The novelist Edmund White described the scene in a letter to his friends Ann and Alfred Corn:

> Well, the big news here is Gay Power. It's the most extraordinary thing. It all began two weeks ago on a Friday night. The cops raided the Stonewall, that mighty Bastille which you know has remained impregnable for three years, so brazen and conspicuous that one could only surmise that the Mafia was paying off the pigs handsomely. . . . A mammoth paddy wagon, as big as a school bus, pulled up to the Wall and about ten cops raided the joint. The kids were all shooed into the street; soon other gay kids and straight spectators swelled the ranks to, I'd say, about a thousand people . . . Someone shouted "Gay Power," others took up the cry—and then it dissolved into giggles. A few more prisoners—bartenders, hatcheck boys—a few more cheers, someone starts singing "We Shall Overcome" and then they started camping on it. A drag queen is shoved into the wagon; she hits the cop over the head with her purse. The cop clubs her. Angry stirring in the crowd. The cops used to the cringing and disorganization of gay crowds, snort off. But the crowd doesn't disperse. . . .
>
> Some adorable butch hustler boy pulls up a *parking meter*, mind you, out of the pavement, and uses it as a battering ram (a few cops are still inside the Wall, locked in). . . . Finally the door is broken down and the kids, as though working to a prior plan, systematically dump refuse

from waste cans into the Wall, squirting it with lighter fluid, and ignite it. Huge flashes of flame and billows of smoke.[84]

With the aid of riot police and two fire engines, the crowd was eventually dispersed, but the demonstrations would continue through the weekend. On June 29, a gay rights group called the Mattachine Action Committee issued a flier calling for organized resistance. The gay liberation movement was born.

Gay and lesbian writing has, of course, been around since at least the time of Socrates and Sappho, but the idea of a self-constituted field called "gay and lesbian literature" did not exist before the era of gay liberation that began in 1969 and could not have existed before the latter part of the nineteenth century. The labels "gay," "lesbian," and "homosexual" take for granted a relatively recent idea: namely, the idea of sexual orientation, according to which same-sex erotic attraction, if present, constitutes an abiding and defining characteristic of personal identity. "Homosexuals are essentially disagreeable people," wrote the psychoanalyst Edmund Bergler in *Homosexuality: Disease or Way of Life?* (1956), adding that "there are no healthy homosexuals."[85]

By 1956, however, American attitudes towards homosexuality were beginning to change, in large part due to the furor created by the publication of Arthur Kinsey's *Sexual Behavior in the Human Male* (1948). Trained as an entomologist, Kinsey began his research into human sexuality inadvertently, when he supervised an interdepartmental course on marriage at Indiana University in 1938 and found himself serving as an unofficial counselor to students seeking advice for sexual problems. After consulting the prevailing scientific literature on human sexuality, Kinsey discovered that "in many of the published studies of sex there were obvious confusions of moral values, philosophic theory, and scientific fact."[86] The notes that Kinsey kept on his students' problems soon proved to be more extensive than the case studies found in the sources that he had consulted in putting his course together, and they led him to conceive the project that resulted in *Sexual Behavior in the Human Male*. Although falling short of the planned one hundred thousand case histories, the study eventually drew upon in-depth interviews with more than twenty thousand individuals, interviews that lasted between ninety minutes and two hours, and covered as many as five hundred questions.

Kinsey's results, disputed by most of his contemporaries, showed a far more widespread incidence of homosexuality than anyone had suspected. Thirty-seven percent of Kinsey's male subjects had at least one post-adolescent homosexual experience leading to orgasm, with the rate climbing to 50 percent among men who remained unmarried until age thirty-five. Twelve-and-a-half percent of the men reported having periods of at least three years in which homosexual activity predominated, and 4 percent reported being exclusively homosexual throughout adulthood. Although Kinsey and his team were themselves initially skeptical about the results, Kinsey finally concluded that "persons with homosexual histories are to be found in every age group, in every social level, in every conceivable occupation, in cities and on farms, and in the most remote areas of the country."[87] Moreover, the data disputed the fixity of sexual orientation that most medical theories about homosexuality took as an article of faith. Kinsey eventually developed what became known as the "Kinsey Scale," which ranked individuals from 0 to 6 according to proportions of homosexual experience, with individuals ranked "0" being "exclusively heterosexual with no homosexual experience" and those ranked "6" being "exclusively homosexual."[88] The proportions among women, published in 1953 in *Sexual Behavior in the Human Female*, were lower, but still statistically significant: by age thirty, 25 percent of females interviewed had "recognized erotic responses to other females"; by the age of forty-five, 13 percent of women reported experiencing orgasm with another woman. Kinsey emphasized that most of the lesbians interviewed led "normal" lives: they included "many assured individuals who were happy and successful in the homosexual adjustments, economically and socially well established in their communities and, in many instances, persons of considerable significance in the social organization."[89]

Most behavioral scientists and psychiatrists dismissed Kinsey's study as methodologically flawed, often distorting Kinsey's numbers in the process. But the study provided crucial impetus for the formation of organizations devoted to the pursuit of equal rights for gays and lesbians, providing scientific evidence that they were not deviants and perverts but instead an oppressed American minority.

This is the plea made by Edward Sagarin in his landmark study *The Homosexual in America* (1951), published under the pseudonym Donald

Webster Cory. Describing twenty-five years of experience as a homo-sexual, Sagarin refers to homosexuals as "the unrecognized minority," and he makes an analogy to the situation of other oppressed marginal-ized groups:

> We are a minority, not only numerically, but also as a result of a caste-like status in society. . . . Our minority status is similar, in a variety of respects, to that of national, religious, and other ethnic groups: in the denial of civil liberties; in the legal, extra-legal and quasi-legal discrimi-nation; in the assignment of an inferior social position; in the exclusion from the mainstreams of life and culture; in the development of a special language and literature and a set of moral tenets within our group.

The Homosexual in America documents the hostility, discrimination, and persecution that gay men faced, as well as the variety of homosex-ual lifestyles and the richness of emerging gay social institutions. Saga-rin's book is a polemic addressed to the general reader, but in his final chapter, he addresses himself directly and "only" to the reader who is gay: "My story is yours, just as your story is mine, no matter how diver-gent our paths of life, no matter how sharp our disagreement on the specific aspects of life." Ultimately, the book is designed to foster gay culture's transition from a state of marginalization to a state of emer-gence: confident that "the combined efforts of many will surely effect a beneficial change," Sagarin concludes, "The future belongs to all who will have it. It is yours and mine, and it belongs to all worthy men of good will. I am confident that you, like so many others who are gay, will utilize the years ahead to good advantage, undismayed and undefeated, inspired by the knowledge that your temperament can make you a bet-ter person and this a better world."[90]

The year 1951 was marked not only by the publication of *The Homo-sexual in America*, but also by the formation of the Mattachine Soci-ety in Los Angeles by Harry Hay and Rudi Gernreich. Named after a society of court jesters in medieval Italy who presented veiled politi-cal satires, the Society sought to promote social and political change in the face of persecution brought on by the McCarthyist linking of homosexuality to communism. The previous year a Senate subcommit-tee investigating "Employment of Homosexuals and Other Sex Perverts in Government" had concluded that homosexuals were "perverts" and that "the lack of emotional stability which is found in most sex perverts and the weakness of their moral fiber, makes them susceptible to the blandishments of the foreign espionage agent." The report claimed that "one homosexual can pollute a Government office," proposing therefore that all homosexuals be purged from government. It also revealed that in the three preceding years, homosexuality had been used as the basis for turning down 1,700 applicants for government jobs, as well as for forcing the resignation or dismissal of 420 government workers and 4,380 members of the military.[91]

Ironically, three of the founding members of the Mattachine Society—Hay, Bob Hull, and Chuck Roland—had in fact been members of the Communist Party, and they used its organizational structure as a model for their new society, creating a hierarchical system of cells that emphasized secrecy. The Mattachine Society described itself as "homophile," a term coined to stress loving relations rather than sexuality, and its aim was to educate other homosexuals about their status as an oppressed minority and to affirm the validity of a homosexual identity. In their founding statement of "Missions and Purposes," the Society pledged to develop

> a highly ethical homosexual culture . . . paralleling the emerging cultures of our fellow-minorities—the Negro, Mexican, and Jewish Peoples. The Society believes homosexuals can lead well -adjusted, wholesome and socially productive lives, once ignorance, and prejudice, against them is successfully combatted [sic], and once homosexuals themselves feel they have a dignified and useful role to play in society.[92]

The historian John d'Emilio points out that while the Mattachine Society was "not the first homophile movement in the U.S.," its foundation "does mark the start of an *unbroken* history of homosexual and lesbian organizing that continues until this day."[93]

The Mattachines gained national attention when one of their members, Dale Jennings, was arrested in 1952 for "lewd and dissolute" behavior after being bullied by an undercover police officer into inviting him home.[94] Jennings's lawyer admitted that his client was indeed a homosexual, but that he was innocent of wrongdoing because he had not engaged in any actual sexual contact with the officer; simply being a homosexual, in other words, was not a crime. The jury deadlocked, leading to the dismissal of the case. The Mattachine Society's ad hoc Citizens Committee to Outlaw Entrapment proclaimed the outcome of the trial "a great victory for the homosexual minority." The first issue of *ONE*, a magazine founded by several Mattachine members and edited by Jennings, appeared in January 1953, and with a national circulation reaching two thousand in a matter of months, it helped to spread the word about the society. Later in the year, however, the Mattachine Society held its first convention, which resulted in a change of leadership, an anticommunist stance, and a new accommodationism that would define Mattachine policy for over a decade. The strategy of the new leadership was to argue that homosexuals and heterosexuals were alike in every way save for what they did in bed, and they stressed that gay sexuality was a private and relatively unimportant matter. Jennings and Rowland continued to work for *ONE*, publishing several withering attacks on the Mattachines, and although these attacks would cease once Jennings and Rowland left the magazine, *ONE*'s outlook would remain more radical than the society's, and it would eventually metamorphose into One, Inc., an organization that included both gay men and lesbians.

In 1955, Del Martin and Phyllis Lyon got together with three other lesbian couples in San Francisco to form the first lesbian political association. Named the Daughters of Bilitis (DOB) after an erotic poem by Pierre Louÿs entitled "Songs of Bilitis" (1894), the organization was founded as a social club—"a *safe* place, where we could meet other women and dance," according to Lyon—but it soon became an activist organization. Its statement of purpose described the DOB as "a women's organization for the purpose of promoting the integration of the homosexual into society"; a 1959 article from its monthly magazine, the *Ladder*, describes the prototypical Daughter of Bilitis as a "thoughtful, public spirited, responsible type" and described the DOB as "an organization for social, not anti-social, ends."[95] The Mattachine Society, the DOB, and One, Inc. would remain the dominant forces in the homophile movement through the middle of the 1960s, but their frequent in-fighting and conflicts with one another prevented the movement from transcending its grassroots origins and becoming a truly national enterprise.

In addition to the publication of *The Homosexual in America* and the foundation of the Mattachine Society, the year 1951 also saw the publication of a short story by James Baldwin entitled "Outing," his first published story devoted to a homosexual theme. The story centers on a day spent together at a church picnic by two boys, one of whom begins to realize that he has feelings for the other. The theme of an adolescent's awakening into gay sexuality is explored further in Baldwin's autobiographical first novel, *Go Tell It on the Mountain* (1953), though it is overshadowed by the novel's treatment of the roles played by family history and race relations in the formation of its protagonist's identity. Two years later, Baldwin confirmed his literary reputation and established himself as an important African American cultural commentator in his first collection of nonfictional work, *Notes of a Native Son* (1955). His second novel, *Giovanni's Room*, which appeared the following year, proved controversial because Baldwin turned his attention away from the representation of African American life, choosing instead to explore the dynamics of gay identity. Set in Paris, where Baldwin had moved in 1948 and would live on and off for the rest of his life, *Giovanni's Room* focuses on the love affair between two men, a white American named David and an Italian named Giovanni. The ambivalence that marked the story "Outing" reappears here in the form of David's guilty recollections, in which he blames himself for setting in motion the train of events leading to Giovanni's imminent execution for the accidental murder of a bar owner. In abandoning Giovanni, David shows himself to have internalized his culture's normative expectations of heterosexuality, refusing to face up to the validity of his private erotic feelings for other men. Attempting to live a lie by promising to marry his girlfriend, Hella, David cannot keep himself from seeking solace in a gay bar, where Hella discovers him and abandons him to a life of thwarted loneliness. The novel presents a gloomy picture of gay life, in which erotic relationships between men are doomed to be short and unsatisfactory, and homosexuality is portrayed as something akin to illness.

The lack of prominent African American characters in *Giovanni's Room* and its overt treatment of homosexuality disappointed many of Baldwin's previous readers, though Baldwin was generally spared harsh public criticism, perhaps because of his position as a prominent African American writer. The reception of Baldwin's novel *Another Country*

(1962) was another matter, however. A complex novel that explicitly links racial and sexual protest in an effort to show that homophobia is a form of bigotry as heinous as racism, *Another Country* is set in New York City and focuses on the interwoven lives of eight characters with diverse economic, regional, racial, and sexual backgrounds; its prescient multiculturalism suggests that this circle of characters should be read as a microcosm of contemporary American society. In the years between *Giovanni's Room* and *Another Country*, Baldwin had changed his ideas about homosexuality, no longer presenting homosexual panic as inevitable. In the later novel, homosexuality and heterosexuality exist as equally viable—and equally problematic—forms of romantic attachment. To be sure, contemporary life in *Another Country* is bleak, and the novel's gay characters in do suffer, but Baldwin suggests that this suffering can lead to self-knowledge and redemption. Although the novel became a bestseller, reviews of *Another Country* were generally negative, with favorable commentary almost exclusively reserved for its portrayal of racism. Baldwin would come under fire from writers of the Black Arts Movement, which (in the words of the theater scholar Larry Neal) "envision[ed] an art that speaks directly to the needs and aspirations of Black America" and saw itself as "the aesthetic and spiritual sister of the Black Power concept." Baldwin's analogy between racism and homophobia was anathema to them. In *Soul on Ice* (1968), the Black Panther leader Eldridge Cleaver would accuse Baldwin of "a shameful, fanatical fawning" love of whites that made him an unfit spokesperson for African Americans. Baldwin refused to capitulate to what he viewed as reverse racism, referring to himself as "an American writer" rather than "merely a Negro writer," and exploring gay themes in two subsequent novels, *Tell Me How Long the Train's Been Gone* (1968) and *Just above My Head* (1979).[96]

Nineteen-sixty-three marked a watershed of sorts for gay and lesbian fiction because of two best-selling novels that featured gay and lesbian protagonists. Mary McCarthy's *The Group* was the year's second biggest seller for fiction and would sell over 3 million copies during the next fifteen years. Although it was written by a prominent heterosexual author and left the details of lesbian sexuality largely to the reader's imagination, the novel demonstrated that lesbianism could be an acceptable subject for mainstream fiction. Its central character, Lakey, a woman who dresses in violet suits and has an affair with a baroness, is a strong-minded romantic heroine who cannot be dismissed either by "the Group" of Vassar graduates to which she belongs or by McCarthy's reader. Lakey's career represents a glamorous rejection of the idea— dramatized by Radclyffe Hall's landmark lesbian novel *The Well of Loneliness* (1928)—that homosexuality is a form of perversion or sickness.

The same cannot be said of John Rechy's *City of Night* (1963), which reached number one on bestseller lists in New York and California and number three nationally, despite savage reviews from publications like the *New York Times*, *The New Republic*, and *The New Yorker*. The novel originated in a letter intended for a friend in Evanston, Illinois, describing a stay in New Orleans during Mardi Gras; Rechy rescued the unmailed letter from the trash, reworked it into a story called "Mardi Gras," and sent it to the *Evergreen Review*. Don Allen, one of the *Review*'s editors, wrote back, admiring the story and asking whether it was part of a novel. "I had never intended to write about the world I had first seen on Times Square," Rechy writes in the introduction to a 1984 reprinting of the novel. "'Mardi Gras' for me remained a letter. But thinking this might assure publication of the story, I answered, oh, yes, indeed, it was part of a novel and 'close to half' finished." The story appeared in the sixth issue of *Evergreen*, the first of several pieces that appeared in the journal and attracted the notice of such writers as Norman Mailer and James Baldwin. Allen helped Rechy to procure a contract for the novel from Grove Press, which appealed to Rechy because it was "publishing the best of the modern authors—and battling literary censorship." (At the time that Rechy was writing *City of Night*, Grove was involved in defending its edition of Henry Miller's *Tropic of Cancer* [1934], with its scenes of graphic heterosexual sex, from obscenity charges.)

At first, Rechy resisted the call of his novel, returning to what he called his "streetworld," until a friend and patron urged him to return to El Paso "where it had begun." And so, Rechy writes,

> I returned to my mother's small house and wrote every day on a rented Underwood typewriter. My mother kept the house quiet while I worked. After dinner, I would translate into Spanish and read to her (she never learned English) certain passages I considered appropriate. "You're writing a beautiful book, my son," she told me.[97]

Rechy's "beautiful book" presented a frank depiction of life as a hustler in the gay underworlds of New York, Los Angeles, and New Orleans. Its first chapter suggests a Freudian explanation for its unnamed Mexican American narrator's homosexuality: a childhood marked by a "father's inexplicable hatred" and a "mother's blind carnivorous love." The novel alternates between two types of narrative: chapters labeled "City of Night" that detail the unnamed Mexican American narrator's wanderings, and vivid character sketches that introduce us to the narrator's friends and customers. As soon as we get to know one of these characters, a "City of Night" chapter moves us away and forward. The effect of this alternation is to put the reader in the position of the hustler, whose acquaintances are brief and whose life is marked by rootlessness. The hustlers' lives are depicted as joyless and alienated, in part because they construct their identities around the idea that they aren't really queer if they engage in homosexual relations only for the money. The novel's penultimate chapter, a portrait entitled "Jeremy: White Sheets" that introduces us to a character who offers the narrator true love and affection, ends with the narrator compelling Jeremy to have sex with him, in order to create distance rather than closeness: "The orgasms have made us strangers again. All the words between us are somehow lost, as if, at least for this moment, they have never been spoken." The narrator thinks to himself, "Yes, maybe youre right. Maybe I could love you. But I wont," and he returns to "the grinding streets."[98]

Many of the themes of City of Night would resurface in Rechy's later writings. If the first novel depicts the lives of men who hustle at least in part in order to avoid coming to terms with their identities as homosexuals, Rechy's less pessimistic second novel, Numbers (1967), depicts an ex-hustler named Johnny Rio who now indulges only in casual sex, but still finds himself constrained by a conventional view of masculinity, in which he must assert his manhood by dominating others: the "numbers" whom he seduces in Griffith Park must perform fellatio on him with no reciprocation. Unlike the earlier novel, however, Numbers suggests that Rio's inability to exist in a loving relationship arises from his particular view of masculinity rather than from his identity as a homosexual. The suffocating mother returns in This Day's Death (1969), which depicts the arrest of a Texas man during a vice raid in Griffith Park, a man whose life is defined by his role as the dutiful son of a dying mother. *The Sexual Outlaw: A Documentary* (1977) features a bifurcated narrative that alternates between realistic and often nearly pornographic passages describing the adventures of a hustler named Jim, and expository passages that ruminate upon society's negative constructions of homosexuality. Rechy's critique of heteronormative discourses in the meditative sections of the book is reinforced by its juxtaposition with the erotic gay narrative centered on Jim, even as it depicts the ways in which homosexuality depends upon heterosexuality: gay culture as depicted in *The Sexual Outlaw* is a truly emergent culture, one that defines and structures itself through its antagonistic relationship to a dominant mainstream heterosexual culture. *The Sexual Outlaw* is Rechy's most overtly political book, and it is characteristic of the militant stance that began to characterize gay and lesbian culture in the aftermath of the Stonewall Rebellion in 1969.

For lesbian fiction writers in the years surrounding the Stonewall Rebellion, liberation meant rejecting Radclyffe Hall's portrayal of lesbianism as a sickness. Many lesbian writers depicted what amount to lesbian utopias that provide an alternative to the pathologies generated within mainstream, patriarchal culture. For example, the year 1972 saw the publication by a commercial press of *Patience and Sarah* by Isabel Miller (pseudonym for Alma Routsong), which had been published privately three years earlier as *A Place for Us*. The novel imagines two nineteenth-century women who leave patriarchal culture behind to build a farm in upstate New York. The protagonist of Elana Nachman's *Riverfinger Women* (1974) fantasizes about making a movie with her lover that will demistify lesbianism for heterosexuals, "so that people would see that lesbians are beautiful," that "there is nothing, nothing at all unnatural about them," that "they too can have weddings and be in the movies."[99] Both novels epitomize the kind of communitarian feeling that marks the lesbian novel after Stonewall.

An exception to this rule is the novel that is still the most famous fictional treatment of lesbianism since *The Well of Loneliness*, Rita Mae Brown's *Rubyfruit Jungle* (1973), which makes use of both picaresque and *Bildungsroman* conventions to tell the story of Molly Bolt, a self-described "bastard" adopted by a German American family. Molly's name suggests both the rootless freedom of Twain's Huckleberry Finn and the ironic appropriation of a male world of building and construction. Molly's intelligence and ambition set her apart from the rest of her working-class family, while her lesbianism places her on the margins of U.S. culture, kept at arm's length even by the radicals of the 1960s: "My bitterness was reflected in the news, full of stories about people my own age raging down the streets in protest," she tells us at the end of the novel. "But somehow I knew my rage wasn't their rage and they'd have run me out of their movement for being a lesbian anyway." The novel's title refers to one of Molly's sexual fantasies: "When I make love to women," she says late in the novel, "I think of their genitals as a, as a ruby fruit jungle, [because] women are thick and rich and full of hidden treasures, and besides that, they taste good." Even when her bigoted mother disowns her and calls her "a stinking queer," Molly refuses to fall into the self-loathing that marked protagonists of earlier lesbian novels. Traveling to New York, Molly earns a degree in filmmaking from NYU, graduating *summa cum laude* as a result of the unfashionable but brilliant senior project that she chooses to present, "a twenty-minute documentary of one woman's life"—her mother's life, as it turns out. Molly's lesbianism becomes both a source of personal pride and the wellspring of her artistic vision. "I wish the world would let me just be myself," she tells us finally, "but I knew better on all counts. I wish I could make my films. That wish I can work for. One way or another I'll make those movies and I don't feel like having to fight until I'm fifty. But if it takes that long then watch out world because I am going to be the hottest fifty-year-old this side of the Mississippi."[100] Molly's story thus embodies the Emersonian values of self-reliance and self-making, but it also serves as a parable of the transformation of marginalization into emergence.

Liberation is also a central theme in fictions about male homosexuality produced in the aftermath of the Stonewall Rebellion. Some novelists, like Patricia Nell Warren and Armistead Maupin, take up the project embodied by Christopher Isherwood's *A Single Man* (1964), which depicted the life of a middle-aged, middle-class man, a life that in its very ordinariness implicitly attacked the idea that gay men were effeminate, deviant, and predatory. Warren's novels *The Front Runner* (1974), *The Fancy Dancer* (1976), and *The Beauty Queen* (1978) seek to demystify homosexuality by presenting stories of self-discovery in a resolutely realistic and conventional narrative style. In its depiction of the relationship between a track coach and one of his athletes, *The Front Runner* challenges the idea that gay relationships are necessarily ephemeral and dominated by an obsession with sexual experience. The unhappiness of Warren's gay characters arises not from some inner sickness but from social persecution. Indeed, Tom Meeker, the gay Roman Catholic priest who is the protagonist of *The Fancy Dancer*, comes to understand that the alienation and suffering that gay people endure gives them a special and valuable perspective: "In spite of the pressures on them, or maybe because of the pressures, gay people had found the ability to explore and express a richness of inner human experience that straight people had somehow missed. The Church would impoverish herself to the degree that She refused to tap this richness."[101] Maupin's *Tales of the City* (1978), which was successful enough to generate six sequels and to be adapted for television, presents the intertwined homosexual and heterosexual lives of San Francisco's elite society in a way that demonstrates the existence of a shared culture with idiosyncrasies and foibles that make it a target for satire. Maupin treats homosexuality as simply one aspect of personality, and often it is not the most important or defining aspect.

Occasionally in Maupin's fiction, the quest for a meaningful relationship leads only to sex, an idea that links his work to the strain of post-Stonewall gay fiction that takes its cue from Rechy's *City of Night* and seeks literary liberation through the exploration of gay sexuality. Two prominent books that chronicle the promiscuity of life in the urban gay fast lane are Larry Kramer's *Faggots* and Andrew Holleran's *Dancer from the Dance*, both published in 1978. Narrating the attempts of a New York screenwriter named Fred Lemish to find a love relationship in the three days before his fortieth birthday, *Faggots* depicts a milieu of gay men who lead successful professional lives, but whose personal lives are desperate and lonely. Many of the men whom Fred encounters during his weekend-long search are single, dreaming of an ideal lover; some are so traumatized by their homosexuality that they can manage only brief, anonymous encounters, followed by bouts of guilt and self-loathing; and those few in relationships are dissatisfied and generally unfaithful. "Of all the 2,639,857 faggots in the New York City area," Kramer writes, "2,639,857 think primarily with their cocks."[102] The response to Kramer's novel within the gay community was largely negative: "Everyone hates it," wrote the novelist Felice Picano in his journal. "Not only because it's politically retrograde or repulsive (which it is), not only because it's slanderous, self-hating, homophobic (which it is), but also because it's poorly written, even after four years of writing and one of editing."[103] Holleran's novel offered a similarly bleak view of the way in which promiscuity thwarts gay men's ability to have meaningful relationships, but his novel was celebrated by the gay press, because its depiction of glamorous, self-destructive lives seemed to evoke both the lyricism of F. Scott Fitzgerald and the acerbic wit of Evelyn Waugh. Holleran's narrator describes the men who come to dance at the Twelfth Floor club as "the romantic creatures in the city. . . . If their days were spent in banks and office buildings, no matter: Their true lives began when they walked through this door—and were baptized into a deeper faith, as if brought to life by miraculous immersion. They lived only for the night." The novel is profoundly ambivalent about the lives it depicts, both drawn to and repulsed by the "doomed queens" that populate its pages. Several years later, at the height of what has come to be known as "the Reagan era," the adjective "doomed" would take on a meaning that neither Holleran nor any of his peers could have imagined in 1978.[104]

5

Multiculturalism and Beyond

In April 1988, Ronald Reagan's secretary of education, William J. Bennett, publicly excoriated Stanford University for transforming its course on "Western Culture" into a course called "Cultures, Ideas and Values" that would include "works by women, minorities and persons of color."[1] More specifically, the plan set the modest requirement that each student study "at least one work each quarter addressing issues of race, sex or class." Four years earlier, as head of the National Endowment for the Humanities, Bennett had written a special report entitled "To Reclaim a Legacy" in which he argued on behalf of a panel of "31 nationally prominent teachers, scholars, administrators and authorities on higher education" that "the past twenty years have seen a steady erosion in the place of the humanities in the undergraduate curriculum." The report contended that "the nation's colleges and universities must reshape their undergraduate curricula based on a clear vision of what constitutes an educated person, regardless of major, and on the study of history, philosophy, languages and literature."[2] Stanford's curricular changes, however, were not what Bennett had in mind because they veered away from the teaching of the so-called "Western canon." Bennett complained that the new course represented capitulation to the demands of a vocal minority: "a great university was brought low by the very forces which modern universities came into being to oppose: ignorance, irrationality and intimidation. . . . The loudest voices have won, not through force of argument but through bullying, threatening and name-calling."[3] The feminist literary scholar Nina Baym responded to a *New York Times* article about Bennett's commentary by pointing out the courses "on Western culture and the 'great books,'" rather than being an abiding part of a college education as Bennett had suggested, were instead "a curricular invention of the early 20th century, designed to counter the growing professional and technical orientation of the modern university." Moreover, Baym argued that

> scrutiny of the reading lists of such [great books] courses over time shows they are constantly changing, and are full of johnny-come-latelies like Herman Melville and William Faulkner, who obviously could not have been taught for centuries. If one responds that it is not a masterpiece's duration but its particular values that make a work valuable, then it becomes clear that "'great books" courses are as political as Stanford's alternative course.[4]

Some months earlier, Christopher Clausen, the chair of the English Department at Pennsylvania State University, had published a piece in the *Chronicle of Higher Education* entitled "It Is Not Elitist to Place Major Literature at the Center of the English Curriculum" in which he wrote that he was willing to "bet that [Alice Walker's] *The Color Purple* is taught in more English courses today than all of Shakespeare's plays combined."[5] This ill-advised bit of hyperbole sparked a tumult of commentary and was taken as gospel by such conservative commentators as Dinesh D'Souza (author of *Illiberal Education*) and David Brooks, who wrote an opinion piece in the *Wall Street Journal* called "From Western Lit to Westerns as Lit." Meanwhile, Allan Bloom's book *The Closing of the American Mind* was a national bestseller.[6]

Welcome to the so-called "culture wars" of the late 1980s and early 1990s.

The Culture Wars

The roots of the culture wars lie in the unrest that was created by the combination of the civil rights movement and immigration reform. In 1965, the Hart-Celler Act reformed U.S. immigration policy, abolishing the quota system based on national origins that had been in place since the 1920s and had been upheld in 1952 by the McCarran-Walter Act. The new system put in place worldwide per-country limits of 20,000 visas per year, with an overall annual ceiling of 290,000 immigrant visas. These were divided between 170,000 for the Eastern Hemisphere and 120,000 for the Western Hemisphere, the first time that any limits had been placed on immigration from the Western Hemisphere.[7]

The combination of these new immigration policies, sentiment against the Vietnam War, and the rise of the Black Power movement created a powerful tide of ambivalence about the idea of "America" in the late 1960s. The melting pot and assimilation became synonymous with racial and ethnic oppression, and "affirmative action" as a governmental mechanism for remedial antidiscrimination came into being. Immigration historian Reed Ueda argues that "unlike the political climate that absorbed immigrants of the early twentieth century according to individual identities, the reorganization of the political system based on ethnic identity led to the absorption of immigrants not as individuals but as members of official groups."[8] Four groups were deemed to be qualified for remediation on the basis of historical and ongoing discrimination: African Americans, Asian and Pacific Island Americans, Hispanic Americans, and Native Americans.

In 1972, the American Association of Colleges and Teacher Education published a policy statement entitled "No American: A Statement on Multicultural Education" that rejected the idea of the melting pot in favor of the promotion of "cultural pluralism":

> Multicultural education is education which values cultural pluralism. Multicultural education rejects the view that schools should seek to melt away cultural differences or the view that schools should merely tolerate cultural pluralism. Instead, multicultural education affirms that schools should be oriented toward the cultural enrichment of all children and youth through programs rooted to the preservation and extension of cultural alternatives. Multicultural education recognizes cultural diversity as a fact of life in American society, and it affirms that this cultural diversity is a valuable resource that should be preserved and extended. It affirms that major education institutions should strive to preserve and enhance cultural pluralism.

Declaring that "to endorse cultural pluralism is to endorse the principle that there is no one model American" and "to understand and appreciate the differences that exist among the nation's citizens," the statement connects multicultural education not to the empowerment of groups but rather to the tradition of liberal individualism by arguing that seeing "differences as a positive force in the continuing development of a society which professes a wholesome respect for the intrinsic worth of every individual."[9] Describing "cultural pluralism" as "a basic quality of our culture" rather than "a temporary accomodation to placate racial and ethnic minorities," the statement advocates a four-pronged program designed to promote cultural pluralism "at every level":

> (1) the teaching of values which support cultural diversity and individual uniqueness; (2) the encouragement of the qualitative expansion of existing ethnic cultures and their incorporation into the mainstream of American socioeconomic and political life; (3) the support of explorations in alternative and emerging life styles; and (4) the encouragement of multiculturalism, multilingualism, and multidialectism.

By the 1990s, this view of education seemed to have carried the day throughout the U.S. secondary school education system. The American history syllabus adopted by the public school system in New York City in 1990 announced, "In the final analysis, all education should be multicultural education."[10]

A fitting emblem of the triumph of multiculturalism came in the same year when the U.S. government offered restitution to Japanese American families that had suffered the ordeal of internment. In the aftermath of Michi Weglyn's revisionist history of internment, *Years of Infamy: The Untold Story of America's Concentration Camps* (1976), late twentieth-century Nisei writing had become less willing to forgive the injustice perpetrated against them by their own government. "Instead of directing anger at the society that excluded and diminished us," writes Yoshiko Uchida, "such was the climate of the times and so low our self-esteem that many of us Nisei tried to reject our own Japaneseness and the Japanese ways of our parents." In the preface to the 1979 reissue of her autobiography, Monica Sone took a far more activist stand, praising President Gerald Ford for rescinding Executive Order

9066 in 1976, charging the Supreme Court with "overlook[ing] the vital American principle that consideration of guilt and punishment is to be carried out on an individual basis and is not to be related to the wrong-doing of others," and urging Japanese Americans to pursue the issue of redress.[11]

In 1979, Congress enacted legislation creating the Commission on Wartime Relocation and Internment of Civilians, which was appointed in the last days of the Carter administration. Its report, *Personal Justice Denied*, was released early in 1983 and contained this summary of its findings:

> The promulgation of Executive Order 9066 was not justified by military necessity, and the decisions which followed from it—detention, ending detention and ending exclusion—were not driven by analysis of military conditions. The broad historical causes which shaped these decisions were race prejudice, war hysteria and a failure of political leadership. Widespread ignorance of Japanese Americans contributed to a policy conceived in haste and executed in an atmosphere of fear and anger at Japan. A grave injustice was done to Americans and resident aliens of Japanese ancestry who, without individual review or any probative evidence against them, were excluded, removed, and detained by the United States during World War II.

Shortly before the expiration of its legislative mandate, the Commission issued five recommendations to Congress on the subject of redress: 1) a joint resolution of Congress signed by the president apologizing for the injustices committed by the U.S. government as a result of its policy of evacuation and internment; 2) presidential pardons for those who were convicted of violating statutes related to the evacuation; 3) the recommendation that the executive branch look generously upon applications by Japanese Americans for the restitution of benefits and entitlements taken away during the war on the basis of ethnicity; 4) the appropriation of money to establish a special foundation to "sponsor research and public educational activities" in order to promote better understanding of the history of internment; and 5) an appropriation of $1.5 billion to cover the cost of funding the fouth recommendation and of making one-time redress payments of $20,000 to those who were excluded.[12] After five years of debate over the issue of whether monetary compensation was appropriate and if so in what amount, a bill enacting the redress provisions was passed in 1988. The first payments—to the oldest of the camp survivors—were made in 1990.

Hybridity and the New American Studies

By the late 1980s, multiculturalism was reverberating throughout the U.S. education system. Given the importance, as we have seen, of the academy in shaping and reshaping emergent literatures, it is important to sketch out some of the parameters of this shift to multiculturalism as it occurred in higher education, using literary scholarship as a case study. Multiculturalism initially seemed to be the cure for what ailed U.S. literary studies, but it proved in the event to be another obstacle to the realization of cross-cultural conversation.

In 1988, the literary critic Carolyn Porter published a widely read essay in the journal *American Literary History*, entitled "What We Know That We Don't Know: Remapping American Literary Studies." Porter reported with a mixture of anxiety and excitement that the lines and boundaries that had long structured the field were being "remapped." The anxiety in her review essay arose from the realization that the erosion of boundaries meant that "Americanists these days" find themselves in the disorienting position of "trying to keep up with developments in a field bearing an increasingly remote resemblance to the one in which many of them were trained." These developments were, according to Porter, the result of a series of scholarly endeavors energized by identity politics: "Once compartmentalized by historical periods, American literature has been remapped first by African-Americanist and feminist critics and then by the flourishing scholarship on Asian-American, Native American, and Chicano literatures." What made this remapping exciting if unnerving was the fact that "these emerging fields" within American studies promised to produce new vantage points from which to survey the "American" scene, vantage points that are gained in part by severing the commonly accepted synecdochic identification of "America" with "the United States." What was wrong with the old compartmentalization was its unstated reliance upon "frames . . . dictated by the national, and nationalist, narrative of the U.S." According to Porter, a work such as José David Saldívar's *The Dialectics of Our America* (1991) made manifest the possibilities of a new American studies because it sees American identities as plural and seeks to provide alternative histories of the Americas, thus producing a new history that is far better than the old. Saldívar dares to ask what the literary and cultural history of the Americas would look like if we were to locate its "political and artistic capital" not anywhere in the U.S. but in Havana, Cuba. For Porter, such a reorientation "goes a long way toward overcoming the parochialism of traditional, and even not so traditional, American literary studies."[13]

Porter was right to assign a leading role in the remapping of the field to scholars working in areas related to minority discourse. In the introduction to *Ideology and Classic American Literature* (1986), an anthology to which Porter was a contributor, Myra Jehlen wrote that the collection was "inspired" by "an increasing recognition that the political categories of race, gender, and class enter into the formal making of American literature such that they underlie not only its themes, not only its characters and events, but its very language." In his afterword to the volume, Sacvan Bercovitch traced the "adversarial stance" adopted by most of its essays to the work being done in "Black Studies and Women's Studies." Scholars working in these fields, Bercovitch argued, "have contributed in many ways to American literary scholarship," but their "most important contribution has been ideological." Never again, according to Bercovitch, will we "be able to feel so pure about our acts of canonization, or so innocently to claim that our models of literary development embody the American spirit."[14] *Ideology and Classic American Literature* was among the texts that led the critic Frederick Crews to coin the term "New Americanism" in an essay published in *The New York Review of Books* in 1988. Crews's essay made it clear that the "adversarial" stance to which Bercovitch refers had already spread well outside the disciplines of "Black Studies and Women's Studies" by the mid-1980s. Of the eight books reviewed in Crews's essay, only one—Jane Tompkins's *Sensational Designs* (1987)—was typically included under the rubric of feminist criticism, and the essay included no books by African Americanists or other scholars working in minority discourse.[15]

Writing when the debates over the "Western canon" were just beginning to heat up, Crews suggested that such goals as "the need to 'uphold tradition,' to 'honor aesthetic standards,' and to expose our students to time-tested 'great thoughts' "— goals commonly enunciated by the traditionalist side of the debate over the canon—were seen by the New Americanists as "sheer ideology, false consciousness that calls for the exposure of its historical determinants. . . . Where do 'aesthetic standards' come from if not from the cliques whose dominance is no longer to be acquiesced in without debate?"[16] Here Crews pointed to the attempt by certain critics—most prominently those associated with New Historicism—to contextualize commonly accepted aesthetic standards within the history of taste and to understand the cultural biases that mark supposedly objective aesthetic judgments and indeed all appeals to universal standards in matters of culture and art.

The triumph of the New Americanism that Crews predicted at the end of his essay did indeed come to pass by the end of the 1990s, but proved ultimately to create an equally oppressive set of boundaries, which were in turn challenged by the need to create what Gregory Jay called a "multicultural and dialogical model for the study of writing in the United States."[17] Jay himself described the shift to multiculturalism in his work as a seeming inevitability: "I remember the somewhat guilty pleasure I felt in coming up with the title 'The End of "American" Literature.' . . . The appearance of [that] essay . . . changed my career to a degree I had not anticipated. Although I had written two previous books and edited others, nothing I had done earned me the notoriety of this piece. Obviously I was on to something."[18]

Like many critics who were then seeking to revise the academy's conception of "American Literature" in the light of multiculturalism, Jay found a useful conceptual tool in the idea of the "borderlands," which has replaced the "frontier" as the dominant site within American studies. In the introduction to the collection *Cultures of United States Imperialism* (1993), Amy Kaplan called for a "multicultural critique of American ethnocentrism" that links the "internal categories of gender, race, and ethnicity to the global dynamics of empire-building." The goal of this critique is to deconstruct "the binary opposition of the foreign and the domestic," an opposition reinforced within American studies by the field's early obsession with the idea of "the Frontier" in the aftermath of Henry Nash Smith's landmark study, *Virgin Land: The American West as Symbol and Myth* (1950). Describing "the Frontier" as "a major conceptual site in American studies," Kaplan noted that it has "undergone revision from the vacant space of the wilderness to a bloody battlefield of conflict and conquest, and more recently to a site of contacts, encounters, and collisions that produce new hybrid cultures." In Kaplan's view, all of these accounts were limited by their reliance upon "a model of center and periphery, which confront one another most often in a one-way imposition of power." Kaplan found an alternative model in the field of Chicano studies, which "has begun to redress the conceptual limits of the frontier, by displacing it with the site of 'the borderlands.'" What appealed to Kaplan about the model of the borderlands is its emphasis upon the "multidimensional and transterritorial"; for Chicano theorists, the borderlands "not only lie at the geographic and political margins of national identity but as often traverse the center of the metropolis. . . . The borderlands thus transform the traditional notion of the frontier from the primitive margins of civilization to a decentered cosmopolitanism."[19]

Part of the appeal of the influential "frontier hypothesis" that Frederick Jackson Turner presented to the American Historical Association during the Chicago Exposition of 1893 was its ability to account for the prevalence of ontological individualism within U.S. political philosophy and for the pervasiveness of rugged individualism within U.S. cultural mythology. Turner contended that "American social development has been continually beginning over again on the frontier" and that "this perennial rebirth, this fluidity of American life, this expansion westward with its new opportunities, its continuous touch with the simplicity of primitive society, furnish the forces dominating the American character." Among the "traits called out . . . because of the existence of the frontier" were what Turner described as "that coarseness and strength combined with acuteness and inquisitiveness; that practical, inventive turn of mind, quick to find expedients; that masterful grasp of material things, lacking in the artistic but powerful to effect great ends; that restless, nervous energy; that dominant individualism, working for good and for evil, and withal that buoyancy and exuberance which comes with freedom."[20] Turner's hypothesis planted the seeds of the celebrated "myth-and-symbol" school of American studies, but his vision of the American character probably helped to create an intellectual climate in which individualistic accounts of literary creation such as Harold Bloom's "anxiety of influence" theory of literary history and Richard Poirier's Emersonian neopragmatism would eventually grow and flourish. Compare, for example, Bloom's defense of Emersonianism to Turner's account of the American character: in a piece entitled "Mr. America" written for the *New York Review of Books*, Bloom predicted that it would be Emerson rather than Nietzsche who would turn out to be the guiding spirit of American criticism at century's end, and he proclaimed that "individualism, whatever damages its American ruggedness continues to inflict on our politics and social economy, is more than ever the only hope for our imaginative lives."[21]

Scholars who were drawn to the insights of New Americanism and multiculturalism were far less tolerant than Bloom of the "damages" inflicted by U.S. culture's fascination with individualism, and the movement away from a frontier hypothesis to a borderlands hypothesis about "American social development" is linked to the critique of U.S. individualism that seemed implicit everywhere within New Americanist scholarship. For example, the historian Lester D. Langley argued in his study *The Americas in the Age of Revolution, 1750–1850* (1996) that the contradictions inherent in liberal ideology had a profound effect on each of the three revolutionary situations that he investigates. Because it "presumed a universality in human aspirations for a better life," liberal ideology "invigorated the revolutionary cause." In the aftermath of revolution, however, liberalism "embraced individual freedom," thus eroding "the democratic ideal and its inherent faith in community and tradition." Moreover, translated into the realm of political economy, liberalism "required continuing rule of the few over a non-slave but subservient labor force of the many." It required the creation of what Langley called the "leviathan state," which the United States achieved in the aftermath of the Civil War with the victory of the federal government over the renegade Southern states. "Within a generation," Langley wrote, "Latin American leaders would be pointing to the noticeable economic progress and material achievements of the United States to justify their sometimes brutal use of power in the crafting of the modern nation-state, and their defilement of community and folk culture in the name of progress."[22] Along with community and folk culture, liberal individualism also downplays the importance of such categories as race, ethnicity, class, gender, or sexuality, which it conceives as contingent, incidental, and ultimately irrelevant aspects of individual identity.

The borderlands scholarship that Porter identified as the cutting edge of American studies scholarship in the 1990s positioned itself against this claim; it sought to take advantage of the theoretical spaces opened up by such categories as race, ethnicity, class, gender, sexuality, and in particular the concept of cultural hybridity. For example, in a contribution to a volume entitled *Poetics of the Americas* (1997), Mireille Rosello argued that when borders are conceived as "frontiers," they "continue to reproduce the binary fight between the colonizer and the colonized even if the opposition has become anachronistic." Too often "the principle of the border" serves to police essentialist conceptions of identity and "successfully pretends that hybridity is an exception to the rule of national homogeneity."[23] Historically, the concept of hybridity was a conceptual leap forward for theorists of minority discourse, postcoloniality, and emergent literatures, opening up what Homi Bhabha has called "the Third Space of enunciation." In his study *The Location of Culture* (1994), which was the most influential account of cultural hybridity to appear during the 1990s, Bhabha himself points to the link between hybridity and the idea of the border by beginning with a section entitled "Border Lives" and pointing to "in-between" spaces that "provide the terrain for elaborating new strategies of selfhood . . . that initiate new signs of identity, and innovative sites of collaboration, and contestation."[24] Bhabha uses Mikhail Bakhtin's conception of hybridization as "a mixture of *two* social languages within the limits of a single utterance" to redescribe a binary relationship in which the two opposed terms are unequal in force: the colonial situation.[25] The concept of hybridity allows us to see that what appeared to be an either/or situation is in reality a situation of both/and. Hybridity shifts the balance of power between colonizer and colonized—at least partially. It allows the empire, as it were, to write back, by demonstrating that the colonizer is always changed by the fact of colonization, existing in a Hegelian master-slave relationship of co-dependence with those who have been colonized. The inequality between the positions of colonizer and colonized is not fully redressed by the mobilization of "hybridity," but it is at least *addressed*.

Hybridity opens the door for cultural emergence by breaking the impasse of the binary logic of hyphenation. As a matter of literary practice, hybridity sometimes takes the form of a reversal of the polarity of an oppressive opposition, rendering positive what the culture typically portrayed as negative, powerful what the cultural typically designated as weak. This strategy can be found in nineteenth-century domestic and sentimental novels like *Uncle Tom's Cabin*, in which gentleness, docility, and love of family—traits portrayed as characteristic of both women and blacks—prove to be sources of power because they make those who possess them better Christians. Similarly, a novel like Silko's *Ceremony* finds transformative strength in what it takes to be non-Western tribal traditions, shifting the balance of power away from individualism toward a holistic communitarianism, away from male aggression toward female non-violence.

Another approach to the dismantling of binary oppositions is to deny the validity of a particular opposition. Frank Chin devotes his writing to refuting the idea that Asian Americans are necessarily the victims of an "identity crisis" in which they are forced to choose between two opposed and incompatible identities—the Asian and the American. Chin's stories and plays depict a Chinatown that is dying because it provides no models of "manhood" for its younger generation: Tam Lum, the protagonist of Chin's play *Chickencoop Chinaman* (1972), says, "I'm a Chickencoop Chinaman. My punch won't crack an egg, but I'll never fall down." Chin's dramas of beset Asian American manhood look back to a more heroic era in which Chinese men were men: in an essay entitled "Confessions of a Chinatown Cowboy" (1972), he writes wistfully about Ben Fee, "a word of mouth legend, a bare knuckled unmasked man, a Chinaman loner out of the old West, a character out of Chinese sword-slingers, a fighter," now "forgotten" in "his hometown, Chinatown San Francisco." Asserting that the cultural mythologies of China, with its "sword-slingers," and the United States, with its gunslinging loners, are fundamentally alike, Chin claims a place for Asian American men within the archetype of the American rugged individualist.[26] In thus denying the opposition between American and Asian forms of masculinity, Chin moves away from the necessity to choose implicit in the idea of an "identity crisis" toward a conception of cultural hybridity in which the Asian and the American fuse into a seamless whole.

Chin's account of identity proved problematic, however, because it was, in fact, a dramatic oversimplification. For Chin, the only identities that matter are the "American" and the "Asian," and he vilifies those Asian Americans who try to assert the primacy of other categories such as gender or sexuality. Chin's aim is not to reconceptualize American identity but simply to reconfigure it, to enable it to accommodate his vision of Asian masculinity. Not only has Chin thus accepted the general premise of binary thinking, but he has also accepted some of the particular premises of the opposition he is seeking to refute—namely, its misogyny and homophobia. It comes as no surprise, therefore, that Chin must necessarily attack the writings of Amy Tan, David Henry Hwang, and Maxine Hong Kingston, which refuse to give primacy to the vicissitudes of Asian American masculinity in their depictions of Asian American identity. Chin's depiction of hybridity is, in fact, symptomatic of one of the major limitations of hybridity as a concept: the fact that it remains rooted in binary thinking.

The limitations of the concept of hybridity begin to appear when we take a closer look at Gloria Anzaldúa's *Borderlands/La Frontera* (1987) and realize that to account fully for the complexities of Anzaldúa's identity, we need to move beyond the available models of hybrid identity to a more complex model of heterogeneous identity. Let us return to Anzaldúa's description of herself as a "border woman": "I grew up between two cultures, the Mexican (with a heavy Indian influence) and the Anglo (as a member of a colonized people in our own territory). I have been straddling that *tejas*-Mexican border, and others, all my life." The phrase "and others" is suggestive here, for though the border is a powerful metaphor for Anzaldúa and other Chicana/o writers, it is still a metaphor that describes crossing from one cultural space into another: it is still a binary system. Anzaldúa describes herself as "*mestiza, mulata, half-breed*," yet these terms do not do justice even to Anzaldúa's ethnic background, let alone her sexuality: elsewhere, she calls herself "a Chicana *tejana* lesbian-feminist poet and fiction-writer." Anzaldúa's landmark text uses the model of the borderlands to powerful metaphorical effect, even as it strains against the inherent limitations of that model.

Borderlands/La Frontera suggests that to understand emergence in U.S. culture, we must move beyond the duality implicit in late-twentieth-century theorizations of hybridity. We need to ask ourselves what happens when two or more emergent categories are located in a single identity or text. To understand hybridity fully, imaginative writers and scholars had to make a transition from an understanding based on "either/or" to an understanding based on "both/and." The next stage, however, in the conceptualization of U.S. emergent literatures, is to move beyond the duality implicit in the hybrid model of "both/and" to a model that captures the interplay of multiple hybrid states. It should come as no surprise that it was Kingston's and not Chin's work that captured the imaginations of the vast majority of scholars and students of Asian American literature. While Chin's work remains rooted in the vagaries of binary thinking, Kingston's work dramatizes the limitations of the available models of hybrid identity and seeks to move beyond hybridity to a more complex model of heterogeneous identity that can account for the dynamics of cosmopolitan contamination.[27]

What It Means to Be "Nuyorican"

The genesis and transformation of the term "Nuyorican" offers a case study in the dynamics of cultural contamination and way in which literary and artistic cultures can unsettle categories of identity. Its genesis lies in Paris in 1898, where commissioners from both the United States and Spain met at the beginning of October to seek a treaty that would end the Spanish-American War. Although the main issue on the table was the disposition of the Philippines, which ultimately became an American territory for which the United States paid Spain $20 million, the treaty that was signed on December 10, 1898, also gave the United States control of Puerto Rico and Guam and required Spain to relinquish its claims to Cuba. On April 2, 1900, President McKinley signed the Foraker Act into law. Officially known as the Organic Act of 1900, the legislation established a civil government in Puerto Rico and free trade between the island and the United States. The new government inaugurated on May 1 was led by an American governor, Charles H. Allen, and five Puerto Rican cabinet members. Fifteen years later, the Jones Act of 1917 amended the Foraker Act: it transformed Puerto Rico into a U.S. "territory"; created a bill of rights; required elections to be held every four years; declared English the official language of the island; and granted U.S. citizenship to all citizens of Puerto Rico.[28]

The Jones Act enabled Puerto Ricans to move between the island and the mainland without restriction. Immigration scholars generally identify a first wave of pioneer immigrants arriving from Puerto Rico before 1945 and a "great migration" between 1945 and 1964; after 1965, there is a greater back-and-forth flow between the United States and Puerto Rico that immigration scholars have described variously as "circular," "commuting," "returning," and "revolving."[29] In the middle of the twentieth century, the great majority of migrating Puerto Ricans settled in New York City, reaching a high of 81.3 percent in 1950, then declining as the century continued to 62 percent in 1970 and 40 percent in 1989.[30] Mainland Puerto Ricans often refer to themselves as "Boricuas" to stress their connection to the island's native inhabitants, the Taino: the term is adapted from the Taino word *borike'n*, which means "great land of the valiant and noble lord."[31] In contrast, Puerto Ricans on the mainland coined the term "Nuyorican" to describe Puerto Ricans living or born in the United States. Many Puerto Ricans disdained the Nuyoricans as non-Boricua, who were likely to contaminate Puerto Rican culture with influences from the mainland.[32]

The Nuyorican writer Esmeralda Santiago, who moved to the United States with her family in 1961, attempted to capture "that feeling of Puertoricanness I had before I came here" in her first book, the acclaimed memoir *When I Was Puerto Rican* (1993). Santiago has described the experience of being identified as "Nuyorican" rather than "Boricua":

> I felt as Puerto Rican as when I left the island, but to those who had never left, I was contaminated by Americanisms, and therefore, had become less than Puerto Rican. Yet, in the United States, my darkness, my accented speech, my frequent lapses into the confused silence between English and Spanish identified me as foreign, non-American.

Santiago realizes that the double bind she describes is an experience shared by many immigrants, who discover that "once they've lived in the U.S. their 'cultural purity' has been compromised."[33] In the case of Puerto Rican immigrants and their children, a complicating factor is race, both because of the island's mixed heritage and because of the blending of African American and Puerto Rican cultures in New York as a result of shared neighborhoods and intermarriage.

The link between African American and Puerto Rican cultures marked the book that became the first classic of Nuyorican literature, Piri Thomas's autobiography, *Down These Mean Streets* (1967), which reviewers have likened to the writings of Malcolm X, James Baldwin, and Eldridge Cleaver. Born Juan Pedro Tomás in 1928 to Puerto Rican and Cuban parents, Thomas was described in a 1967 *New York Times* interview as "a Puerto Rican Negro who grew up in Spanish Harlem."[34] *Down These Mean Streets* is an account of his fall into drugs and gang life, his incarceration for armed robbery, and his eventual redemption. The book was immediately recognized as a landmark text when it was first published in 1967. Daniel Stern, writing on the first page of the *New York Times Book Review*, described the book as a "linguistic event" because of the way in which it blends "gutter language, Spanish imagery and personal poetics."[35] The poetic prologue, which Thomas claims to have written in a moment of inspiration—"I sat down and wrote that out, scratched it out, in five minutes"—begins with a "rooftop" echo of Whitman's "barbaric yawp" in "Song of Myself," but ends by conveying the hatred that arises from living in the shadows of poverty and racism—and of being born dark, the only "black" child in a mixed race family: "when I look down at the streets below, I can't help thinking / It's like a great big dirty Christmas tree with lights but no fuckin' presents."[36] The gritty, no-holds-barred approach of Thomas's book led to its being banned in 1971 by a school district in Flushing, Queens, because of its use of obscenities and its description of heterosexual and homosexual acts. (The ban was reversed in 1975).[37]

Not all of the writing about *el barrio* is fueled by the sense of rage that marks Thomas's *Mean Streets*. For example, Nicholasa Mohr's first novel, *Nilda* (1973), describes life in the Bronx as seen by a ten-year-old girl and is written in a simple style appropriate to a child's point of view. The daughter of parents who came to the United States from Puerto Rico during World War II, Mohr grew up in the Bronx and attended the Art Students League, the Brooklyn Museum Art School, and the Pratt Center for Contemporary Printmaking, eventually becoming a prominent graphic artist. She became a writer after she was asked by her art agent to write about the experience of growing up Puerto Rican and female in the Bronx. *Nilda* was listed by the *New York Times* as one of its Outstanding Books of the Year, and three of Mohr's later works— *Felita*

(1979), *Going Home* (1986), and *All for the Better* (1993), a biography of Evelina Antonetty—are in fact intended for an adolescent audience. The stories in *El Bronx Remembered* (1986) and *In Nueva York* (1988) all emphasize the everyday dilemmas faced by their central characters in order to counter the sensationalistic stereotypes of Puerto Ricans as criminals and gang-members that arose in the aftermath of Thomas's success.

In part, the story of redemption told both by *Down These Mean Streets* and Thomas's subsequent career as a writer of both prose and poetry turns on learning not only to accept but also to celebrate his identity as a mixed-race person. Stern, the *Times* reviewer, perceptively noted: "The American Negro has, of course, developed his own argot, partly to put the white man off, partly to put him down. The Puerto Rican living in New York faces an even more complex fate and linguistic adjustment. He shares with the Negro the neologisms of the street, but the Puerto Rican's are mixed with a heavy complement of Spanish."[38] In the interview that accompanied Stern's review, Thomas cited Harlem as "a whole example for the world to follow": "Harlem is like the whole world rolled into one, with every type of human being that you can find: American Indians, Indians from India, Chinese, Japanese, black men, Polynesians, West Indians, Puerto Ricans, Filipinos, the whole bit."[39] The "contamination" and loss of "cultural purity" that Esmeralda Santiago describes is, for Thomas, a source of hope and redemption.

Marked from the start by the dynamics of cultural contamination, Nuyorican culture quickly became a site for the promotion of multi-culturalism. In the aftermath of the success of Thomas's book, Nuyorican writing gained a significant measure of cultural standing. Miguel Piñero's play *Short Eyes* premiered off-Broadway at the Public Theater in February 1974 and moved to the Vivian Beaumont Theatre on Broadway three months later. The play, whose title is prison slang for a pedophile, was written as part of a prisoners' writing workshop during the author's incarceration for armed robbery and explores the racial dynamics and ideas of justice that mark prison life. *Short Eyes* won the Obie Award and the New York Drama Critics Circle Award for Best Play and was nominated for six Tony Awards. Meanwhile, Piñero and Miguel Algarín, a professor of English at Rutgers University, co-edited an anthology enti-tled *Nuyorican Poetry* that was published in 1974 by William Morrow, a mainstream press. And the following year, Algarín founded the Nuyorican Poets Cafe along with Piñero and the poet Pedro Pietri.

The poetry salon that Algarín had been convening for the previous two years had begun to outgrow his living room, so he rented the Sunshine Cafe, an Irish bar on East 6th Street. By then the term "Nuyorican," originally used disparagingly by Boricuas to denigrate the Puerto Rican diaspora, had become a badge of honor. In the anthology *Aloud: Voices from the Nuyorican Poets Cafe* (1994), Algarín offers a definition-cum-manifesto:

> **Nuyorican** (nü yòr ˋē kən) (New York + Puerto Rican) 1. Originally Puerto Rican epithet for those of Puerto Rican heritage born in New York: their Spanish was different (Spanglish), their way of dress and look were different. They were a stateless people (like most U.S. poets) until the Cafe became their homeland. 2. After Algarín and Piñero, a proud poet speaking New York Puerto Rican. 3. A denizen of the Nuyorican Poets Cafe. 4. New York's riches.[40]

In 1980, Algarín purchased an "in rem" building at 236 East 3rd Street in order to accommodate the cafe's growing audiences and expand its programs. Two years, later, however, the cafe shut down for renovations and didn't reopen until 1990, when Bob Holman, a Kentucky native and veteran of the Chicago poetry slam scene, approached Algarín after the death of Miguel Piñero, and said, "Miguel, it's time to reopen the Cafe. This is the moment, you know, and Miky [Piñero] is insisting on it, and we are ready."[41]

When the cafe reopened, the *New York Times* noted that there were a few changes. For one thing, it "has been virtually packed from its small stage to out the door." Perhaps more significantly, "the new Nuyoricans are not necessarily young, angry, or Puerto Rican." According to Holman, "New York Puerto Rican" is "the narrow definition of Nuyorican. . . . Anyone who calls himself or herself Nuyorican is a Nuyorican."[42] Holman infused the cafe with new ideas, designed to attract attention and audiences, including the weekly poetry slam, an idea developed by construction worker and poet Marc Smith in 1984. Each Friday night, poets would compete against one another for the grand prize—the princely sum of $10—reciting poems less than three minutes in length and judged by a panel of three usually drawn from the audience. Holman acted as host and always served up his signature line: "The best poet always loses."[43]

If Chicago was the birthplace of slam poetry, New York became the place where it came of age and became a national phenomenon, thanks in large part to Holman's showmanship. Holman founded Mouth Almighty, the first record label devoted to poetry; the label sponsored the team that won the 1997 National Poetry Slam, a group of "all-stars" from the Nuyorican Poets café—Regie Cabico, Evert Eden, Taylor Mali, and Beau Sia—coached by Holman. Sia was one of the members of the "novice team" from New York City that had won the previous year's national competition, the subject of the documentary film *SlamNation* (1998), which also featured performances by Holman, Mali, and Marc Smith himself. In 2002, hip-hop entrepreneur Russell Simmons produced the HBO series *Def Poetry Jam,* a spin-off of the successful series *Def Comedy Jam.* The new show, which ran for six seasons, featured a range of spoken-word poets, including established poets, national slam winners, neophytes, and even well- known actors and musicians with a taste for poetry. *Def Poetry* did not adopt the slam format, but was influenced by the slam sensibility. According to the poet John S. Hall, a critic of the slam format,

> *Def Poetry* is still extremely slam-informed, and I think it will probably always be. What they say about *Def Poetry* is that it wants to bring an urban feel. And to me, they don't mean black or Latino, or non-white. What they really mean is, a rhythm of poetry that comes out of the Nuyorican Poets Cafe that came out of the slams.

In November 2002, a version of the show called *Russell Simmons Def Poetry Jam* opened on Broadway and won a 2003 Tony Award for Best Special Theatrical Event.[44]

Five years later, the life of *el barrio* was the subject of the Broadway musical *In the Heights,* which dramatizes a significant day in the life of a neighborhood in Washington Heights. Conceived by Lin-Manuel Miranda while he was a sophomore at Wesleyan University, *In the Heights* is a cultural hybrid: it is bilingual, with dialogue in both English and Spanish, and it blends a number of musical forms, mixing traditional Broadway show tunes with hip-hop and salsa. As is often the case with cultural hybrids, one side dominates a little bit: the bilingualism is tilted toward English, so a non-Spanish-speaking viewer will never feel ill at ease, though there are Spanish puns and in-jokes for those who get them. Most of the verbal hip-hop is delivered by Usnavi, a bodega-owner who is played by Manuel himself, and the show features a surprisingly large number of traditional Broadway ballads delivered by characters singing alone in the spotlight. The show was designed to build on, rather than challenge, the conventions of the Broadway musical. *In the Heights* demonstrates that a neighborhood like Washington Heights is in fact a confluence of different cultural traditions: Puerto Rican, Dominican, Cuban, even Mexican. In contrast to the Bedford-Stuyvesant of Spike Lee's movie *Do the Right Thing*(1989), this Washington Heights is quite civil: there's a little bit of interethnic tension, but not much, and a little more interracial tension, which in the end is not fully resolved, but the residents of this neighborhood have learned how to talk—and sing—to one another. Sad things happen during *In the Heights*, but they are part of the bittersweetness of change. The show, in the end, is all about the idea of home: where it is, what it means, what it owes you, what you owe to it. Asked about the genesis of the musical, Miranda recalled:

> I always tell people Washington Heights is full of music, and they sort of think it's just a line I use to plug the show. But I swear to God when I was writing the first draft I was walking around and I saw a Chinese delivery guy riding his bike with a boom box strapped to the front of his bike. It wasn't a little radio; it was a two speaker boom box blasting music. It was like Pimp My Ride but with a two wheeler. I always thought that was a classic New York thing: of course the Chinese delivery guy has got a subwoofer on his bike![45]

This anecdote captures one of the crucial facts about emergent literatures: that they value cultural contamination over cultural purity and find inspiration in the country's often contentious, sometimes violent, but always vibrant confluence of cultures.

The New Immigrant Literature

Scholars have suggested that after World War II, the "immigrant literature" exemplified by the work of writers like Mary Antin, Carlos

Bulosan, Abraham Cahan, Mike Gold, or O. E. Rølvaag gave way to "ethnic literature," which was less interested in dramatizing either the experience of immigration or life in newly formed immigrant communities, and more interested in depicting the dynamics of marginalization and otherness in the United States.[46] The Hart-Celler Act, however, brought about a new renaissance of immigrant writing, which like its counterpart from the early part of the twentieth-century, dramatizes the cultural marginalization, the economic challenges, and the generational conflicts that inevitably accompany the experience of immigration. The post-1965 immigration is different than the waves of immigration that preceded it because 80 percent of the people who enter the United States legally are people of color.[47] Many of the new immigrants come from countries that have been scarred by the racism that accompanies colonialism and other forms of imperialism. As a result, the new literature of immigration is more marked by U.S. racial politics than earlier immigrant literatures and thus tends to be more skeptical about American values and the process of "Americanization."[48] Literary and cultural scholars writing in the wake of this new literature of immigration have tended to share its general skepticism, focusing on the contradictions that have marked the idea of citizenship in the United States. Much of this scholarship takes up the cue offered by Lisa Lowe's landmark study *Immigrant Acts: On Asian American Cultural Politics* (1996), which analyzed the ways in which "the U.S. state has constructed different national 'emergencies' around the 'immigrant,' which have, over time, generated emergent political formations." Her study put "the specific history of Asian American racialization in relation to other forms of racialization, those of African Americans, Chicanos/Latinos, Native Americans and 'white' Americans, in order to open possibilities of cross-race and cross-national projects."[49]

Some writers who belong to immigrant communities, like Richard Rodriguez, endorse Americanization despite whatever pain it might entail; others depict a seemingly permanent state of alienation. Bharati Mukherjee's novel *Jasmine* (1989) does both, inventing a protagonist who constantly reinvents herself in ways that defy binary thinking: from Jyoti, the Hindu girl from provincial India, she transforms herself into Jasmine, the wife of a progressive thinker who teaches her to shun traditional Hindu ways; the widowed Jase, au pair to Duff and lover of

Taylor, an urban academic from whom she learns about Americanization; and Jane, the wife of a middle-aged banker in rural Iowa, whose child she is carrying as she continues her journey west at the end of the novel. Jasmine describes her own transformations as "genetic" and those of her adopted Vietnamese son, Du, as "hyphenated," by which she means that he has had more freedom to make life choices than she. Susan Koshy argues that "*Jasmine* offers a multicultural vision of a hybrid America embodied in the union of upwardly mobile Asian new immigrants and white liberals." But while it "also celebrates the transformation of America by the presence of Hmong refugees, Mexican undocumented workers, Jamaican nannies, and Afghani cabdrivers," Koshy points out that Jasmine herself "clearly distances herself from these other New Americans, who live in ethnic ghettos or seem dissatisfied with their immigrant lot."[50] Mukherjee's celebration of a "hybrid America" thus acknowledges that there are nevertheless "subtle discriminations" and "hierarchies . . . established between different forms of hybridity." *Jasmine* depicts successful Americanization—or, rather, the successful hybridization of the United States—in a context that also includes immigrants who remain alienated from the promise of America.[51]

Other writers adopt the strategy of insisting that Americanization is beside the point because the characters they depict are *already* American. Frank Chin, as we have seen, appeals to the mythology of rugged individualism to argue that Chinese men have always been a vital part of the history of the American West, having played a crucial role in the building of the transcontinental railroad. Chang-rae Lee has also characterized the different between the old and the new immigrant literature as a difference between *becoming* and *being*: "The old immigrant would say, 'I'm becoming an American.' . . . The new person is now starting out saying, 'I *am* American.'"[52]

Lee belongs to that class of immigrants who gain access to U.S. higher education after they immigrate. Lee came to the United States with his family from Korea at the age of three, attended Philips Exeter Academy and Yale University before receiving an M.F.A. in writing from the University of Oregon and eventually become a professor and director of the Creative Writing program at Princeton University. In similar fashion, the novelist Cristina García, who was born in Havana to a Guatemalan father and Cuban mother, emigrated to the United States in 1961 at the age of two, when her family fled Cuba in the wake of Fidel Castro's rise to power. She was raised in New York City, living in "ethnic" neighborhoods—Irish, Italian, and Jewish—in Queens, Brooklyn Heights, and Manhattan, all the while considering herself Cuban and speaking Spanish at home. After receiving a B.A. in Political Science from Barnard College, she earned an M.A. in International Relations from the Johns Hopkins University School of Advanced International Studies in 1981. The Korean American poet Theresa Cha immigrated to the United States with her family when she was seven years old and studied French critical theory as an art student in the 1970s, eventually producing videos, installations, and texts that sought to deconstruct hierarchies of power. Emigrating at a young age gave these writers the kind of proficiency with the English language that Richard Rodriguez describes as a necessity for the attainment of "public individuality" in the United States.[53]

Other immigrant writers who achieved prominence in the late twentieth century began their writing careers abroad before coming to the United States; many came to the United States to take advanced degrees and quite a few now teach in creative writing programs. Several South Asian writers can serve as representative examples. Zulfikar Ghose, born in pre-Partition India and Pakistan, was well published before moving to Texas in 1969. Meena Alexander, who was born in India and raised in the Sudan, published her first three books of poetry—*The Bird's Bright Ring* (1976), *I Root My Name* (1977), and *Without Place* (1978)—while living in India; she moved to New York in 1979 to take up a professorship at Fordham University. Amitav Ghosh was born in Calcutta in 1956; in 1999 he joined the Comparative Literature department at Queens College, City University of New York, as Distinguished Professor. In with what would prove to be a transnational career, Ghosh's first novel first novel, *The Circle of Reason* (1986), a picaresque story about a young weaver wrongly accused of being a terrorist, won a prestigious French literary award, the *Prix Médicis stranger*, which recognizes a book published in translation. Chitra Banerjee Divakaruni was born in India and emigrated to the United States in 1976, where she received an M.A. in English from Wright State University and a Ph.D. from the University of California, Berkeley, before becoming a member of the prestigious Creative Writing faculty at the University of Houston. Indu Sundaresan was born and raised in India, coming to the United States to earn two degrees, an M.S. in operations research and an M.A. in economics, from the University of Delaware.

Divakaruni and Sundaresan, however, transmute the immigrant experience in different ways, reminding of us of the power of literature to promote a rich variety of perspectives, even in the depiction of paradigmatic experiences. Much of Divakaruni's poetry and prose focuses on the experience of immigrant women. According to the personal statement that appears on her website, Divakaruni "earn[ed] money for her education [by holding] many odd jobs, including babysitting, selling merchandise in an Indian boutique, slicing bread in a bakery, and washing instruments in a science lab. At Berkeley, she lived in the International House and worked in the dining hall." An early collection of short stories, *Arranged Marriage* (1975), arose out of the experience of working with battered women at a center in Berkeley and then co-founding the non-profit Maitri, which works with South Asian families facing problems like domestic violence, emotional abuse, discrimination, or human trafficking. Her celebrated novel *The Mistress of Spices* (1997) uses a magical realist style to tell the story of the proprietress of a spice bazaar in Oakland, California, who is actually a mystical being who uses the power of the magic spices from her homeland to improve the lot of her customers, mostly first- and second-generation immigrants. *Queen of Dreams* (2004) tells the story of Rakhi, a divorced Indian American painter, who struggles to maintain her tea shop after a Starbucks-like cafe opens up near by, to find her artistic voice, and to make sense of the discovery that her mother was a dream teller, who could share and interpret the dreams of others. Rakhi's situation is further complicated in the aftermath of 9/11 by racist attacks on her family and friends. Divakaruni thus uses a magical realist style to dramatize the struggles of contemporary immigrant life in the United States[54]

In contrast, while Sundaresan's novels arise from her experience as an immigrant, they are historical novels that do not depict contemporary U.S. life. Reading through books about India as an antidote to homesickness, Sundaresan became fascinated by a story about Mughal harems, which led her to write a trilogy of novels ("The Taj Trilogy") set in the era of the Mughal emperors Akhbar and Shah Jahan: *The*

Twentieth Wife (2002), *The Feast of Roses* (2003), and *Shadow Princess* (2010). *The Splendor of Silence* is also a historical novel, though it is set in the more recent past and draws on Sundaresan's perspectives on U.S. culture, as it dramatizes the love story between a twenty-five-year-old U.S. Army captain who arrives in 1942 in a fictional desert kingdom called Rudrakot, where he falls in love with the daughter of the local political agent. (Her collection of stories *In the Convent of Little Flowers* [2008] is a change of pace, because it is set in twenty-first century India.) Amitav Ghosh's career is marked by a similar interest in the genre of historical fiction. *The Shadow Lines* (1988) is set against the backdrop of the nationalist Swadeshi movement of the early twentieth century and moves forward in time to the communal riots that took place in Dhaka and Calcutta in the 1960s. The first two books of his *Ibis* trilogy—*Sea of Poppies* (2008) and *River of Smoke* (2011)—are set in nineteenth-century India and China.

What Seung Hye Suh and Robert Ji-Song Ku write about Asian American literature after 1965 is a common dilemma for many late-twentieth-century emergent writers regardless of ethnic background:

> Post-1965, we see a schism between the "Asian American" narrative or poetic voice and the immigrant experiences represented in the litera-ture. Asian American writers often pen literary characters who, though sharing the ethnic or racial identities of the writers, reside nonetheless in worlds that are culturally, epistemologically, linguistically, and often also economically distant and separate.[55]

As Suh and Ku point out, Asian American writers who came of age dur-ing the 1960s and 1970s were born before World War II, at a moment when the number of Asian Americans who had been born in the United States was greater than the number who were foreign-born. In the after-math of the 1965 law, however, the demographics of the Asian Ameri-can population shifted once again toward the foreign-born. As a result, their writings often dramatize a tension between sophisticated Asian American characters or narrators who have a command of English and more recent immigrants with whom they do not identify because of dif-ferences in language, socioeconomic status, and even legal status. Max-ine Hong Kingston, for example, shows Wittman Ah Sing disparaging "fresh-off-the-boat" immigrants: "The F.O.B. stepped aside. Following, straggling, came the poor guy's wife. She was coaxing their kid with sunflower seeds. . . . You wouldn't mislike them on sight if their pants weren't so highwater, gym socks white and noticeable. *FOB* fashions."[56] A similar tension runs through Richard Rodriguez's first book, *Hunger of Memory* (1982), with its insistence that the crucial shaping factor in the formation of Rodriguez's identity is class rather than ethnicity.

Although Rodriguez's conservative politics made him wary of the apparent triumph of multiculturalism because it overemphasized the importance of ethnicity and race in the formation of American identities, other new immigrant writers feared that multiculturalism would have the effect of trivializing ethnicity and race. The Dominican American writer Julia Alvarez, whose novel *In the Time of the Butterflies* (1994) was a finalist for the National Book Critics Circle Award, fears that American "consumer culture" will simply "consume its latest ethnicity: literature and music and food. Then make a chain store out of it. And soon it'll go to the next one. You know, disposable culture." And thus she predicts that once again "the doors will close on people who are the wrong color, come from the wrong place. Those battles will still have to be fought."[57] One way in which writers from these younger emergent literatures have sought to make their texts less simply consumable has been to lace their English texts with words and linguistic structures taken from other languages. For example, Ricardo Ortíz points to

> young Cuban-American poets, novelists, and critics who, as the children of the great wave of Cuban immigration to the United States that followed Castro's revolution, write technically in English, but with an ear for the polyvalent richness of language as such, a richness, however, uniquely problematized for them by the complex positionings available to them in their language.

He offers the example of the poet and scholar Gustavo Pérez Firmat, who writes in the introduction to his monograph *The Cuban Condition* (1989), "As a 'native' Cuban who has spent all of his adult life away from the island, the notion of a 'Cuban' voice is for me as alluring as it is problematic. A Cuban voice is what I wish I had, and what I may never have." The dilemma to which Pérez Firmat refers is similar to the linguistic problem that drives Stephen Daedalus in Joyce's *Portrait of the Artist as a Young Man*: how do I use literature to create "the conscience of my race" when the language I must use is English, the language of the oppressor? For Ortíz "writing in Cuban is 'impossible' to the extent that it may never coalesce into one voice, one language," but for many Cuban American writers "it is precisely this condition of impossibility that challenges, indeed obligates, them to write."[58]

One of the landmarks of Korean American literature, Theresa Hak Kyung Cha's *Dictée* (1982), mixes prose and poetry with a variety of different visual forms including pictures of Cha's mother and Joan of Arc, representations of Chinese ideograms, and photographs of ruins. Cha's text is multilingual, juxtaposing English, Korean, Chinese, and French, and rife with wordplay. The title puns on the French word for "inspired" as well as the idea of dictation, suggesting that the author is both an active creator of representation and a passive receptacle for memory, that selves and identities are created through speech. Influenced by Cha's work, the poet Myung Mi Kim, a Korean who came to the United States at the age of nine, portrays the fragmentation of Korean American subjectivities as the result of the loss of language and homeland and the corrosiveness of U.S. racism in her collection *Under Flag* (1991).[59] Kim characterizes her use of language as "an English that behaves like Korean, an English shaped by a Korean," a kind of third language "beyond what is systematically Korean and English—a language that necessarily sets in motion questions around resemblance, contamination, boundary."[60]

Some writers have avoided this problem by turning their writerly gaze away from the most recent immigrants, finding inspiration in the struggles of their parents' generation. In this context, one of the foremost chroniclers of twentieth-century immigrant experience in the United States, the Cuban-American Oscar Hijuelos, who was born in New York in 1951 to Cuban immigrant parents, seems like a throwback. Inspired by Henry Roth's *Call It Sleep* (1934), Hijuelos generally adopts a realist style reminiscent of the early chapters of that novel. His abiding subject is the experience of Cuban-born immigrants and their descendants in cities along the eastern seaboard of the United States which he dramatizes in historical novels largely set in the first half of the twentieth century. His first novel, *Our House in the Last World* (1983), is set in

Spanish Harlem in the 1940s; his Pulitzer Prize-winning second novel, *The Mambo Kings Play Songs of Love* (1989), tells the story of two brothers, Cesar and Nestor Castillo, who move to New York in the early 1950s, forming a mambo orchestra and touring the East Coast in a "flamingo-pink" bus. Hijuelos's novel includes historical figures, most prominently the Cuban bandleader and television personality Desi Arnaz: at the height of their fame, the fictional brothers appear on Arnaz's real-life *I Love Lucy* show.

In his first two novels of the early 1990s, Hijuelos broadened his purview beyond the urban immigrant genre. Thus, *The Fourteen Sisters of Emilio Montez O'Brien* (1993) dramatizes the life of a large family (headed by an Irish father and Cuban mother) in a small town in Pennsylvania from the early 1900s to the 1980s, while *Mr Ives' Christmas* (1995) is a novel of grief and redemption inspired by Charles Dickens's *A Christmas Carol* (1843). In his subsequent novels, Hijuelos returned to his more familiar novelistic terrain: *Empress of the Splendid Season* (1999) recounts the life of a former "Queen of the Conga Line" who becomes a cleaning woman after moving to New York in the late 1940s; *A Simple Havana Melody (from when the world was good)* (2002), which blends a portrayal of Havana in the 1920s and 1930s with a Holocaust story, as it recounts the life of a Cuban musician who is interned at Buchenwald; and *Beautiful Maria of My Soul* (2010), which focuses on a character from *Mambo Kings*. *Dark Dude*, a young adult novel that draws on Hijuelos's own boyhood experiences, was published in 2008. Talking about *Mambo Kings* shortly after its publication, Hijuelos that the book was "not an immigrant novel, though it might seem like it." Arguing that "the immigrant novel implies a desperate need," Hijuelos suggests that the brothers' movement from Cuba to New York is a narrative device rather than the focus of the narrative: "I had to get characters from A to B, Cuba to New York, but the brothers' spirits were neither desperate nor needy. They would have done well if they stayed in Cuba." Hijuelos's protests to the contrary, *Mambo Kings* was routinely hailed as a "new immigrant classic."[61]

For many Cuban American writers, however, it was not the immigrant experience but rather the experience of exile that structures their literary perspectives. Cristina García's celebrated first novel, *Dreaming in Cuban* (1992), dramatizes the lives of three generations of women in the del Pino family, some of whom have remained in Cuba while others immigrated to New York City. Written in prose that shifts between a realist style that is almost journalistic and a lyrical style that recalls the writing of Toni Morrison or the Latin American magical realists, the novel moves backward and forward in time from the 1930s to the 1990s. The novel opens with the matriarch, Celia del Pino, "equipped with binoculars and wearing her best housedress and drop pearl earrings . . . guarding the north coast of Cuba. . . . From her porch, Celia could spot another Bay of Pigs invasion before it happened."[62] As she watches, Celia muses that "Pilar, her first grandchild, writes to her from Brooklyn in a Spanish that is no longer hers." Celia worries that "Pilar's eyes . . . are no longer used to the compacted light of the tropics," and indeed late in the novel, when a twenty-one-year-old Pilar visits her grandmother in 1980, she thinks, "I'm afraid to lose all this, to lose Abuela Celia again. But sooner or later I'd have to return to New York. I know it's where I belong—not *instead* of here, but *more* than here. How can I tell my grandmother this?" Meanwhile, Pilar's mother Lourdes, who is militantly opposed to Castro, finds herself at a demonstration at which Castro—El Lider—appears, and she "realizes that she is close enough to kill him. She imagines seizing El Lider's pistol, pressing it to his temple, squeezing the trigger until he hears the decisive click."[63] In the lives of these women and their relatives, García encapsulates the complex dynamics of Cuban exile.

García explored the dynamics of exile further in her second novel, *The Agüero Sisters* (1997), which interweaves the stories of two Cuban-born sisters, Constancia and Reina, who haven't spoken for thirty years, since Constancia left Cuba for the United States and remade herself as a New Yorker. García herself needed to create her own experience of exile: she once described the feeling that she doesn't belong in the Cuban community in Miami with which she has a "love-hate relationship." Criticized after a reading in Puerto Rico for claiming to be "Cuban" but writing in English, García responded by invoking the heterogeneity of "what it means to be Cuban": "The point for me," she has said, "is that there is no one Cuban exile. I am out here in California and may not fit in anywhere, but I am Cuban too."[64]

If, as Ricardo Ortíz suggests, late-twentieth-century Cuban American literature has an abiding "obsession" with the idea of "exile and return and their attendant symbolism," it resembled other emergent post-1965 literatures that are marked by traumatic relationships with their homelands or by traumas suffered there.[65] In contrast, the early stages of Native American, Chinese American, Japanese American, and Chicano/a literatures were marked by cultural traumas suffered on American soil: racism, detribalization, internment. For example, early examples of Vietnamese American literature were haunted by the Vietnam War. The novelist Monique Truong argues that because Vietnamese American literature emerges "out of a social and historical moment of military conflict," it therefore "speaks of death and other irreconcilable losses and longs always for peace—peace of mind." Truong argues that Vietnamese American literature is built on "layers upon layers of contradictions," the most fundamental of which is the contradiction, not between "death and peace," but between "life and peace: one does not guarantee the other."[66] One of the first works of Vietnamese American literature to receive national attention was Le Ly Hayslip's memoir *When Heaven and Earth Changed Places* (1989, co-written with Jay Wurts), which uses a non-linear structure to describe her childhood during the war, her escape to the United States, and her return to Vietnam sixteen years later. Hayslip continued the narrative in a more linear fashion in *Child of War, Woman of Peace* (1993), co-written with her son James, which describes her struggles in the United States as a result of loveless marriages and financial hardship. The two books served as the basis for Oliver Stone's film *Heaven & Earth* (1993). Truong's first novel, *The Book of Salt* (2004), dramatizes the pain of exile in a story that finds its seed not in the Vietnam War, but in a brief reference in the *Alice B. Toklas Cook Book* (1954) to two "Indo-Chinese" men, Trac and Nguyen, who once cooked for Toklas and her partner, Gertrude Stein.[67] Truong's novel imagines a character named Binh who ends up with Stein and Toklas after being banished from his home by his father because of a homosexual relationship. As the novel opens, Binh has accompanied Stein and Toklas to Gare du Nord; their ultimate destination is the United States, but Binh, who describes himself as "man unused to choices," will spend the novel deciding whether to follow his employers, stay in Paris, or return to Vietnam.[68] The novel is a meditation on what it means to be transcultural, a theme that is explored by many of the Vietnamese American writers collected in the Asian American Writers

Workshop anthology *Watermark* (1998), who, like Truong, choose to leave behind the experience of the war to focus instead on the immigrant experience.

For Dominican American writers like Julia Alvarez and Junot Díaz, it was the dictatorship of Rafael Trujillo that is the source of trauma. Alvarez's autobiographically inflected first novel, *How the García Girls Lost Their Accents* (1991), depicts, in reverse chronological order, the struggles of the García family to make a life in the United States after being forced to flee the Dominican Republic to avoid persecution by Trujillo's agents. (Alvarez's family did emigrate to the United States because her father had become involved in the resistance to Trujillo, but ultimately returned to the Dominican Republic, preferring Trujillo's dictatorship to the problems that they faced in the United States.) Her second novel, *In the Time of the Butterflies* (1994), which was nominated for the 1994 National Books Critics Circle Award, recounts the history of the Trujillo regime by presenting a fictionalized account of the story of the Mirabal sisters, three of whom were murdered on orders from Trujillo. In his novel *The Brief Wondrous Life of Oscar Wao* (2007), Junot Díaz makes reference to *In the Time of the Butterflies* and describes the sisters in a footnote written by the novel's narrator, Yunior:

> The Mirabal Sisters were the Great Martyrs of that period. Patria Mercedes, Minerva Argentina, and Antonia Maria—three beautiful sisters from Salcedo who resisted Trujillo and were murdered for it. (One of the main reasons why the women from Salcedo have reputations for being so incredibly fierce, don't take shit from nobody, not even a Trujillo.) Their murders and the subsequent public outcry are believed by many to have signaled the official beginning of the end of the Trujillato, the "tipping point," when folks finally decided enough was enough.

Díaz begins the novel by describing the *"Fukú Americanus"*:

> the Curse and the Doom of the New World, also called the fukú of the Admiral [Columbus] because the Admiral was both its midwife and one of its great European victims; despite "discovering" the New World, the Admiral died miserable and syphilitic, hearing (dique) divine voices. In Santo Domingo, the Land He Loved Best (what Oscar, at the end would

call the Ground Zero of the New World), the Admiral's very name has
become synonymous with both kinds of fukú, little and large; to say his
name aloud or even to hear it is to invite calamity on the heads of you
and yours.

Written in a vigorous narrative voice that mixes Spanish, Dominican,
Dominican American slang, and nerdspeak into its English prose, the
novel traces the history of the fukú that was brought down by Trujillo
on the family of Oscar, who grows up in New Jersey—an overweight
science-fiction-and-fantasy–obsessed nerd who is seemingly the antith-
esis of Dominican machismo—but ends up becoming a martyr back in
the Dominican Republic.[69]

The depredations of dictatorship fuel the most prominent work by
a late twentieth-century Filipino American author, Jessica Hagedorn,
whose *Dogeaters* (1990) dramatizes life in the Philippines during the
rule of Ferdinand and Imelda Marcos. Although it is set in the Philippines, one of the major themes of *Dogeaters* is the colonization of the
Filipino mind by American pop cultural forms. This idea proves to be
an abiding interest for many late-twentieth-century Filipino American writers, who set themselves against the description of Filipinos as
an "invisible minority," because the majority of Filipino immigrants
have seemed to take pride in their Americanization. Carlos Bulosan
chronicles his struggles against racist attitudes in his autobiography,
America Is in the Heart (1946), but he wrote poems that continued his
exploration of what it means to be an outsider in U.S. culture while still
believing in the nation's ideals. In the aftermath of the 1960s, however,
Filipino American poets began to explore the contours of U.S. racial
discrimination with a more jaundiced eye. Serafin Syquia writes paeans
to solidarity among U.S. ethnic minorities in poems like "i can relate to
tonto" (1972), while Sam Tagatac's "A Chance Meeting between Huts"
(1975) focuses on an "act / of recognition" between two Asian Americans who learn to see outside of U.S. stereotypes. In "Rapping with One
Million Carabaos in the Dark" (1974), Alfred Robles tells his fellow Filipino Americans to "put down your white mind / . . . / & burn up all that
white shit / that's keeping your people down."[70] The success of *Dogeaters*
sparked new interest in Filipino American literature and was followed
by the publication in 1996 of two anthologies—*Returning a Borrowed*

Tongue: An Anthology of Contemporary Filipino Poetry in English and *Flippin': Filipinos on America*—that contain a richly diverse set of Filipino and Filipino American poets.

Early Korean American writing was haunted by the tragic history of Korea in the twentieth century: its occupation by the Japanese from 1905 to 1945, the partitioning of the nation in the aftermath of World War II, and the Korean War that soon resulted.[71] Korean American literature was pioneered by Younghill Kang (1903–1972), who arrived in the United States in 1921, three years before the Second Quota Act of 1924 declared immigrants from Asia to be inadmissible to the United States because they were aliens ineligible for citizenship.[72] Kang's two autobiographical novels, *The Grass Roof* (1931) and *East Goes West* (1937), foreshadow the dynamics of the Korean American literature that began to take shape after the Hart-Celler Act made Koreans eligible once again for immigration to the United States.[73] *The Grass Roof* depicts a young man's life in Korea during the Japanese occupation before his emigration to the United States; the narrator depicts Korea as "a planet of death" whose former glory is fading into an "infernal twilight" as a result of the country's inability to modernize. Two landmarks of Korean American literature published in the 1980s, Theresa Hak Kyung Cha's *Dictée* (1982) and Ronyoung Kim's *Clay Walls* (1986), are also haunted by the Japanese occupation. *Dictée*, as we have seen, uses postmodern formal experimentalism to explore the after-effects of the Japanese colonization of Korea, while taking aim at U.S. national narratives of assimilation.

In the more conventionally written *Clay Walls*, Ronyoung Kim (the pen name of Gloria Hahn, who was born to immigrant Korean parents in Southern California) dramatizes the struggles of a Korean family who have fled to the United States to escape the Japanese occupation. Like *The Grass Roof*, the title of Kim's novel evokes the traditional houses of the Korean countryside and also the different dreams that the father and mother hold: the father, Chun, seeks to construct clay walls around his family's home in Los Angeles, while the mother, Haesu, yearns to return to Korea and to live there in a clay-walled house. The image of the clay wall becomes a metaphor for what the family has lost that can never be recreated: "[Chun's] country had fought for its seclusion, struggling against the penetration of eastern invasions and western ideology. A futile struggle. . . . Korean walls were made of clay, crumbling under repeated blows, leaving nothing as it was before."[74]

A similar metaphor animates Gary Pak's novel *A Ricepaper Airplane* (1998), in which Kim Sung Wha figures as a Korean patriot who has fled to a plantation on Hawai'i to escape the Japanese occupation during the 1920s. Dying in a hospital in 1979, he talks to his American-born nephew about his dream of building an airplane that can carry him back to his wife and children in Korea, an airplane made of parts from a bicycle, bamboo, and ricepaper. It is a dream, in other words, that can never be realized. Early in the novel, Wha urges his nephew to be mindful of history:

> No forget what I telling you, Yong Gil. Dis is history. Dis is what happen in da past. No forget all dis. Even when I *maké* [die], you remember what I telling you. No can forget how things was befo'. No make forget, like how da haoles [whites] trying make us forget everything what was like befo'.[75]

Pak's novel urges its readers to remember two histories of oppression: by the Japanese in Korea, by whites in Hawai'i.

Although Younghill Kang considered his *East Goes West* (1937) to be the better of his two novels, reviewers preferred *The Grass Roof*, in part because of its evocation of the seemingly exotic culture of Korea and in part because *East Goes West* depicts a racist U.S. culture that denies opportunity at every turn to the novel's often naively optimistic protagonist, Chungpa Han. Exiled as a result of the Japanese occupation, Han is a man in search of a country, stripped of his nationality by the Japanese, but unable to find a place in the United States. None of the novel's major characters manage to realize their American dreams, and the novel ends with a literal dream in which Han imagines himself trapped with some African Americans in the basement of a house that is about to be burned down by whites with torches. He interprets the dream with his typical optimism: "I have remembered this dream, because, according to Oriental interpretation, it is a dream of good omen. To be killed in a dream means success, and in particular death by fire augurs good fortune."[76]

There is something of Kang's optimism in Chang-rae Lee's novel, *Native Speaker* (1995), which finds inspiration in the cosmopolitan visions of Walt Whitman. The novel's epigraph comes from Whitman's poem "The Sleepers" (1881): "I turn but do not extricate myself, / Confused, a past-reading, another, but with darkness yet." The lines are drawn from a passage in which the poem's narrator has just imagined "a beautiful gigantic swimmer swimming naked through the eddies of the sea," a swimmer who is ultimately dashed to death against the rocks: "Swiftly and out of sight is borne the brave corpse."[77] Lee's novel, like Whitman's poem, is marked by loss: it occurs in the aftermath of the death of the narrator's son, Mitt, who is inadvertently suffocated at the bottom of a "dog pile" of neighborhood boys. Despite the bitter memories that they evoke, the streets of Flushing, Queens, remain a source of hope and promise for Henry Park:

> I love these streets lined with big American sedans and livery cars and vans. I love the early morning storefronts opening up one by one, shopkeepers talking as they crank their awnings down. I love how the Spanish disco thumps out from windows, and how the people propped halfway out still jiggle and dance in the sill and frame. I follow the strolling Saturday families of brightly wrapped Hindus and then the black-clad Hasidim, and step into all the old churches that were once German and then Korean and are now Vietnamese. And I love the brief Queens sunlight at the end of the day, the warm lamp always reaching through the westward tops of that magnificent city.

Lee's novel finds this promise in the constant influx of new immigrants to the city. "They were of all kinds, these streaming and working and dealing, these various platoons of Koreans, Indians, Vietnamese, Haitians, Columbians, Nigerians, these brown and yellow whatevers, whoevers, countless unheard nobodies." This passage echoes Whitman's "Salut au monde!" (1856): "You whoever you are! . . . All you continentals of Asia, Africa, Europe, Australia, indifferent of place! . . . Health to you! Good will to you all—from me and America sent." Whitman saw in the new arrivals the ongoing revitalization of American democracy, and *Native Speaker* dramatizes one immigrant's attempt to realize Whitman's cosmopolitan, democratic dream: the novel's plot revolves around a mayoral bid by City Councilman John Kwang, who represents the "brown and yellow whatevers [and] whoevers" of Flushing. Kwang's rise and fall, seen through the eyes of Henry Park, encapsulates the continual promise of New York cosmopolitanism, a promise that remains unfulfilled at the novel's end but is no less alluring.[78]

Jonathan Arac points out that the story of Henry's family mirrors many of the distinctive features of the post-1965 Korean immigration: Henry's father settles in New York, which, along with Los Angeles, was one of the two major areas to which Koreans migrated; he finds opportunity not in the field of engineering in which he was trained but as the owner of a grocery store; and he sends his son to a selective private college. At the same time, Arac argues, "*Native Speaker* is in many respects a highly typical American novel of the late twentieth century. It is the first-person narrative of a man nearing his midthirties, focusing on the resolution of a crisis within his marriage, which provides a new basis for going on."[79] In this respect, *Native Speaker* resembles Min Jin Lee's debut novel, *Free Food for Millionaires* (2007), which follows the post-Princeton career of a second-generation Korean American woman who struggles to attain the yuppie lifestyle that she has grown to expect as a result of her college experience: in both novels, the specificity of the novel's ethnic content is less important than the fact that the main protagonist *has* an ethnic identity. Ultimately, both novels meditate on the ways in which higher education produces the subjects of American democratic liberalism.

The immigration historian Roger Daniels reminds us that "the whole notion of 'Asian Americans' was originally a government construct, and a racist one at that. Bangladeshi and Chinese, say, have as much—or as little—in common as do Belgians and Bulgarians." He notes, however, that the category soon became "real" in "American ethnic identity politics" and that "since the 1960s campus groups and others have worked to set up coalitions of Asian Americans," pushing for "Asian American courses, programs, and, in a few institutions, departments," taking their cue from the success of African American studies programs around the country.[80] These programs (and the academic study of Asian American cultures) were dominated by attention to Chinese Americans and Japanese Americans. Likewise, in its early stages, the category Hispanic American literature meant first and foremost Chicano/a literature and then came to include the literature of *puertorriqueños* and Nuyoricans. In the wake of the post-1965 immigrations, the increasing heterogeneity of both the Hispanic and Asian American populations has led scholars to question the validity of lumping together different ethnic under these rubrics.

A number of scholars have pointed out that this heterogeneity should be extended to the category of language if we are to give a full account of emergent writing. From the start, Hispanic American writers have explored the creative possibilities of their bilingualism: some of the central works of Chicano/a literature—for example, Tomás Rivera's . . . *y no se lo trago la tierra* and Rolando Hinojosa's *Estampas del valle y otras obras*—were written in Spanish, and Hinojosa has continued to move freely between Spanish and English in his fiction. Several of the essayists in King-Kok Cheung's anthology *An Interethnic Companion to Asian American Literature* (1997) felt bound to comment that their accounts are partial and incomplete because they are limited to texts written in English.

As the twentieth century came to a close, this linguistic gap in the field of American studies was beginning to be addressed by scholarly efforts like the "Recovering the U.S. Hispanic Literary Heritage Project" and those of Harvard University's Longfellow Institute, which (according to its mission statement) "has set itself the task to identify, and to bring back as the subject of study, the multitudes of culturally fascinating, historically important, or aesthetically interesting texts that were written in languages other than English," texts that range "from works in indigenous Amerindian languages, Portuguese, Spanish, French, Dutch, German, Yiddish, Russian, Chinese, and Japanese, to Arabic and French texts by African Americans."[81] The first fruits of their labors can be found in the *Multilingual Anthology of American Literature* (2000), edited by Marc Shell and Werner Sollors. The availability of such resources may lead scholars to seek out *contemporary* emergent texts written in other languages, such as Pan Xiujuan's Chinese-language story "Abortion" (1979), in which a group of sweatshop workers in San Francisco openly discusses the economic reasons to terminate a pregnancy; or the work of GUMIL (*Gunglo Dagiti Mannurat nga Ilokano iti Hawaii*), the Association of Ilokano Writers in Hawai'i, who choose to cultivate writing in the Ilokano language of the Philippines. These writers examine the conflict between mainstream and margin that is the hallmark of emergent literature, but they write for the margin, with little regard for whether the mainstream is watching. And even if the recovery of earlier non-English U.S. ethnic texts does not encourage contemporary emergent writers to produce texts in languages other than English, it is still likely to have an effect on their future writings since many of them supplement their childhood knowledge of ethnic traditions with knowledge gained from reading and research: how could a writer like Maxine Hong Kingston resist making use of a tradition of American Chinese–language sources if such a tradition suddenly became available?

From Gay to Post-Gay

Although it paved the way for immigration to the United States by groups that had formerly been excluded by law, the Hart-Celler Act created other kinds of exclusion: it emended Section 212 of the 1952 Immigration and Nationality Act (known popularly as the "McCarran-Walter Act"), which stipulated "classes of aliens . . . ineligible to receive visas and . . . excluded from admission into the United States." Section 212.a.4 excluded "aliens afflicted with psychopathic personality, epilepsy, or a mental defect." The Hart-Celler Act offered the following amendment:

> Paragraph (4) of section 212(a.) of the Immigration and Nationality Act (66 Stat. 182; 8 U.S.C. 1182(a) (4)) is amended by deleting the word "epilepsy" and substituting the words "or sexual deviation."

"Sexual deviation" was understood to include homosexuality, and the Hart-Celler was intended to clarify the intent of the McCarran-Walter Act. Indeed, when Surgeon General Julius B. Richmond declared in August 1979 that government physicians would no longer consider homosexuality "a mental disease or defect" and advised immigration officials to cease requiring that suspected homosexuals be examined by the Public Health Service, the Justice Department issued a ruling in December reinstating the policy of exclusion. The department argued that it had been the intent of Congress, when passing the McCarran-Walter, to consider homosexuality a disease and to exclude immigrants on that basis.[82] Not until 1990, when Congress passed another

Immigration and Nationality Act, was the exclusion on the basis of homosexuality repealed.

Stonewall may have initiated gay America's emergence from its cultural closet, but it took the AIDS epidemic to make "homosexual" a household word. In 1980 the U.S. medical community was puzzled by the unusually high number of men in their thirties and forties who had contracted what were thought to be rare diseases: Kaposi's sarcoma, a form of cancer generally seen only in elderly patients; toxoplasmosis, a brain disease transmitted by an animal parasite; and a form of pneumonia caused by *Pneumocystis carinii.* Two things linked most of these men together: their immune systems were malfunctioning, and they were gay. Researchers believed that these illnesses were the result of a single syndrome, which they called "gay-related immune disorder" (GRID); it was referred to frequently as "the gay plague." Because it was perceived to be something that affected only homosexuals, the syndrome was all but ignored by the U.S. media; it would take the death in 1985 of Rock Hudson, a prominent actor whose homosexuality had been hidden from the general public, to alert the U.S. public to the severity of the problem. By then it had a new name, "acquired immune deficiency syndrome" (AIDS), and it was known to be caused by virus, dubbed the "human immunodeficiency virus" (HIV), which could infect any individual, regardless of his or her sexual orientation because it was spread through the exchange of bodily fluids or through the use of infected needles. A year before Hudson's death, the truly catastrophic proportions of the epidemic had begun to emerge with the introduction of a blood test for HIV.

Promiscuous gay men were reluctant to change their lifestyles, many feeling that their identities as gay men were dependent on the free expression of their sexuality. An article in the *New York Native* in 1982 entitled, "We Know Who We Are: Two Gay Men Declare War on Promiscuity," began with the declaration that

> Those of us who have lived a life of excessive promiscuity on the urban gay circuit of bathhouses, backrooms, balconies, sex clubs, meat racks, and tearooms know who we are. We could continue to deny overwhelming evidence that the present health crisis is a direct result of the unprecedented promiscuity that has occurred since Stonewall, but such denial

is killing us. Denial will continue to kill us until we begin the difficult task of changing the ways in which we have sex.

The pamphlet's authors, Richard Berkowitz and Michael Cullen, concluded with a plea: "The 13 years since Stonewall have demonstrated tremendous change. So must the next 13 years."[83] The following year they published the first safe-sex manual, "How to Have Sex in an Epidemic."

The question of whether or not to celebrate gay sexuality despite the AIDS epidemic remains a charged one for male homosexual writers. AIDS novels like Paul Monette's *Afterlife* (1990) and *Halfway Home* (1991) implicitly reject the "excessive promiscuity" of novels like Rechy's *City of Night* and *Numbers,* or Holleran's *Dancer from the Dance* and *The Beauty of Men* (1996). According to the novelist Edmund White, AIDS produced "a new prudishness about sex" among some gay novelists and critics, as if "gay erotic literature is somehow *unworthy* of the gay community, which should now be ready to produce its world-class geniuses of the stature of Tolstoy or Flaubert." White, however, argues that gay novelists have an obligation to write about gay sexuality, not only because "every male thinks about sex once every 30 seconds, a frequency seriously underrepresented in serious fiction," but also because sexuality—promiscuous sexuality—is so intimately bound to a gay man's emotional life. In White's novel *The Farewell Symphony* (1997), the narrator reflects that

the phrase "anonymous sex" might suggest unfeeling sex, devoid of emotion. And yet, as I can attest, to hole up in a room at the baths with a body after having opened it up and wrung it dry, to lie, head propped on a guy's stomach just where the tan line bisects it, smoke a cigarette and talk to him late into the night and early into the morning about your childhood, his unhappiness in love, your money worries, his plans for the future—well nothing is more personal, more emotional.[84]

White is the most prominent of the writers who belonged to the gay literary circle that called itself "The Violet Quill," a group whose career encapsulates the history of gay culture from Stonewall through the AIDS epidemic. In addition to White, the Violet Quill consisted of Andrew Holleran, Felice Picano, Michael Grumley, Robert Ferro,

Christopher Cox, and George Whitmore, who saw each other often at gay literary and social functions and met several times during 1980–1981 to read and critique each other's work. White remembers the impetus for the meetings coming from Ferro and Grumley, lovers who had met one another at the University of Iowa Writer's Workshop. Holleran had been a classmate of theirs, and the Violet Quill was an attempt to create a reading group that could provide the kind of practical and stylistic advice that straight writers and editors seemed unable to offer. The group fell apart after Ferro took exception to Whitmore's story "Getting Rid of Robert" (1981), which Ferro regarded as an attack upon his relationship with Grumley (although the particulars of the story seem to have closer parallels to White's break-up with Cox).

In many respects, the lives of the group's members embody the dynamics of era of gay liberation. White and Cox were both present at Stonewall. Picano's journal (excerpted in David Bergman's collection *The Violet Quill Reader* [1994]) offers a glimpse of the liberated lifestyles of New York and Fire Island, while Whitmore's autobiographical novel *The Confessions of Danny Slocum* (1980; rev. ed. 1985) offers an account of the trials of gay sexuality. Ferro and Grumley's relationship lasted for twenty years; each eventually succumbed to AIDS, which has also claimed the lives of Whitmore and Cox. White, who is HIV-positive, has transformed the tetralogy that was to have begun with the autobiographical novels *A Boy's Own Story* (1982) and *The Beautiful Room is Empty* (1988) into a trilogy that concludes with *The Farewell Symphony* (1997). *The Beautiful Room* ended with an account of the Stonewall Rebellion, which would have served as the midpoint in the story of gay liberation, "the most important event in our lives." Now, however, it serves as the close of the second act of a tragedy that chronicles, according to White, how gay men "were oppressed in one generation, liberated in the next, and wiped out in the next."[85]

AIDS forced mainstream America to discuss homosexuality openly; it forced gay America to leave the relative safety of gay neighborhoods and gay bars to demonstrate and pursue political action. ACT UP, the political action group devoted to AIDS issues, adopted the slogan, "Silence = Death." In "Out of the Closet, Onto the Bookshelf," an essay written for *The New York Times Magazine* in 1991, White remembered returning to the United States the previous year from Paris to find that his "literary map had been erased," because so many distinguished gay writers had fallen victim to AIDS. "The paradox," he wrote, "is that AIDS, which destroyed so many of these distinguished writers, has also, as a phenomenon, made homosexuality a much more familiar part of the American landscape."[86] Eleven years earlier, the same *New York Times* was loathe to review works by gay writers and seemed to pan them whenever it did. In March 1980, Felice Picano wrote in his journal that "gay literature is still a hotly disputed subject—*The New York Times*, for example, doesn't seem to believe it exists," and he reflected upon the fact Edmund White, whose first novel, *Forgetting Elena* (1973) had been "highly praised, extolled even in *The New York Times*," had been "reviled in reviews since he came out [of the closet]."[87] By 1991, gay literature had made its way onto the literary map. "The grotesque irony," wrote White,

> is that at the very moment so many writers are threatened with extinction gay literature is healthy and flourishing as never before. Perhaps the two contradictory things are connected, since the tragedy of AIDS has made gay men more reflective on the great questions of love, death, morality and identity, the very preoccupations that have always animated serious fiction and poetry. Or perhaps AIDS has simply made gay life more visible. As a result even straight readers are curious to read books about this emerging troubled world that throws into relief so many of the tensions of American culture.[88]

White's prognostications were borne out by the following year's National Book Awards: Dorothy Allison's *Bastard out of Carolina* was a finalist in the fiction competition, while Paul Monette's *Becoming a Man* won the award for nonfiction.

Despite its increased visibility, however, gay and lesbian literature remains the least assimilated and most oppositional of America's emergent literatures. Gays and lesbians are, after all, the only one of the groups discussed here whose rights are not fully protected; indeed, the practice of homosexuality was still a criminal offense in areas of the United States until 2003. But the Stonewall Rebellion marked a watershed moment in U.S. culture, bringing an end to what Jill Johnston describes in her book *Lesbian Nation* (1973) as "that awful life of having to choose between being a criminal or going straight." As Johnston puts it, "We were going to legitimize ourselves as criminals!"[89] Over a quarter-century later, the project of gay emergence remains incomplete, and gay and lesbian literature retains an oppositional edge, remaining like Rita Mae Brown's Molly Bolt, unbowed and fiercely determined.

In a 2006 roundup of gay fiction for the *Village Voice*, White described Michael Cunningham's novel *The Hours* (2002) and Alan Hollinghurst's Booker Prize-winning novel *The Line of Beauty* (2004) as "post-gay" novels, because "the action of both of these books, to be sure, takes place outside the gay ghetto and includes many important straight characters." White describes "post-gay fiction" as "a subgenre that David Leavitt may have invented in his first collection of stories, *Family Dancing* [1984]."[90] Cunningham's novel, which won both the Pulitzer Prize and the PEN/Faulkner Award, takes its inspiration from Virginia Woolf's novel *Mrs. Dalloway*, as it tells three interwoven stories: the "Mrs. Woolf" sections of the novel tell the story of Woolf's final days; the "Mrs. Brown" sections tell the story of a housewife living in Los Angeles in 1949, who will ultimately leave her family, which includes a son who will grow up to be Richard, a celebrated gay poet suffering from AIDS who is one of the two main characters in the "Mrs. Dalloway" sections of the novel. These sections recapitulate elements from Woolf's novel as they focus on the preparations that Richard's friend Clarissa is making for a party in his honor. In the "Mrs. Dalloway" sections, Clarissa has a daughter, but she lives with her partner, a book editor named Sally. *The Hours* is a great middlebrow novel: it is literary but not nearly as challenging a reading experience as Woolf's formally experimental novel. Cunningham uses the middlebrow in the way that Stowe uses sentimentality: as a way of luring readers to a set of insights that they might not be otherwise willing to confront. In the case of *The Hours,* these insights center on the ordinariness of gay experience, which is omnipresent in the novel but never the novel's central subject.

The post-gay strategy of representing gay experience as "ordinary," however, is sometimes aligned with the conservative political discourse that Jasbir Puar has called "homonationalism." Puar calls attention to a set of circumstances that suggest the increasing acceptability of gay experience as a part of U.S. culture:

the decriminalization of sodomy in the United States; the global (albeit uneven) incorporation of various versions of legalized gay marriage and domestic partnership; the rise of global gay marriage and domestic partnership; the rise of a global gay right wing anchored in Europe and attaining credibility very pointedly through Islamophobic rhetoric; flourishing gay and lesbian representation (in the U.S. mainstream) such as *The L Word* and *Queer Eye for the Straight Guy*; normativizing gay and lesbian human rights frames, which produce (in tandem with gay tourism) gay-friendly and not-gay-friendly nations; the queer "market virility" that can simulate heteronormative paternity through the purchase of reproductive technology; the return to kinship and family norms implicit in the new lesbian "global family," complete with transnational adoptee babies; and market accommodation that has fostered multibillion-dollar industries in gay tourism, weddings, investment opportunities, and retirement.

Puar argues that such ostensible gains have often come at the cost of the demonization of racialized others, in particular Muslims. Puar describes "homonationalism" as a "dual movement in which certain homosexual constituencies have embraced U.S. nationalist agendas and have also been embraced by nationalist agendas." Puar builds on Lisa Duggan's analysis of a "new neo-liberal sexual politics," a "privatized, depoliticized gay culture anchored in domesticity and consumption," a politics "that does not contest dominant heteronormative forms but upholds and sustains them."[91] Duggan's work describes the assimilation of parts of U.S. gay culture into the cultural logic of Reaganism, dominant in the 1980s; Puar's work describes its recruitment by the logic of the nationalism fostered by George W. Bush in the aftermath of 9/11. In both cases, what Puar detects is a post-gay rhetoric that seeks to eradicate the distinctions between heterosexual and gay cultures rather than bridging them. This post-gay perspective is universalist in its attempt to solve the problem of gay difference by embracing the idea of sameness. The logic of comparative racism that we examined in relation to the Chinese Exclusion Act still, it would seem, continues to bedevil U.S. culture at the start of the twenty-first century.

In contrast, one of the great pieces of late-twentieth-century U.S. emergent writing, Tony Kushner's two-part play, *Angels in America*

(1992–1995), is animated by a post-gay perspective that might be called cosmopolitan in the way that it explores the interplay of sameness and differences as it explores what it means to be gay during the Reagan era at the height of the AIDS crisis. The play brings together an unlikely set of elements including Jewish humor and Mormon mythology to create a vision of cultural redemption in the face of intolerance and indifference to those in need. Late in *Perestroika*, the second part of the play, Prior Walter, who is dying of AIDS, is examined by his nurse in a scene that captures some of the play's central dynamics:

Night. Prior, Emily (Prior's nurse-practitioner) and Hannah in an examination room in St. Vincent's emergency room. Emily is listening to his breathing, while Hannah sits in a nearby chair.

EMILY: You've lost eight pounds. Eight pounds! I know people who would kill to be in the shape you were in, you were recovering, and you threw it away.
PRIOR: This isn't about WEIGHT, it's about LUNGS, UM . . . PNEUMONIA.
EMILY: We don't know yet.
PRIOR: THE FUCK WE DON'T ASSHOLE YOU MAY NOT BUT I CAN'T BREATHE.
HANNAH: You'd breathe better if you didn't holler like that.
PRIOR (LOOKS AT HANNAH, THEN): This is my ex-lover's lover's Mormon mother.
(Little pause.)
EMILY: Even in New York in the eighties, *that* is strange.

The scene is an example of the play's humor, but it also reinforces an important idea that runs throughout the play: the idea of cosmopolitanism. New York emerges in Kushner's play as a cosmopolitan space of transformation, a place that's all about learning to embrace difference and change in contrast to Heaven, depicted in *Perestroika* as a place of stasis. Most of the play's characters resist being typecast by U.S. culture—even the play's villain, a fictionalized version of the historical Roy Cohn, an attorney whose anti-Communism brought him to national prominence during the Army-McCarthy hearings and then the trial of

Julius and Ethel Rosenberg . Told by his doctor that he has AIDS, Roy counters that he has liver cancer: "AIDS is what homosexuals have. I have liver cancer." Roy's refusal to accept the label of "homosexual" is a refusal to accept the logic that his sexual preferences are in any way a determinant of his identity. He tells his doctor:

> This is not sophistry. And this is not hypocrisy. This is reality. I have sex with men. But unlike nearly every other man of whom this is true, I bring the guy I'm screwing to the White House and President Reagan smiles at us and shakes his hand. Because *what* I am is defined entirely by *who* I am. Roy Cohn is not a homosexual. Roy Cohn is a heterosexual man, Henry, who fucks around with guys.[92]

In this moment, Roy sets himself against the logic of U.S. identity politics—and of the pluralist multiculturalism that grows out of it. And in this moment, the play's sympathies are with its villain.

Angels in America is a play that recognizes, and is committed to, the transformative power of language. The play bears out Kwame Anthony Appiah's suggestion that cultural change is

> a gradual transformation from one mixture to a new mixture, a process that usually takes place at some distance from rules and rulers, in the conversations that occur across cultural boundaries. Such conversations are not so much about arguments and values as about the exchange of perspectives. I don't say that we can't change minds, but the reasons we offer in our conversation will seldom do much to persuade others who do not share our fundamental evaluative judgments already. When we make judgments, after all, it's rarely because we have applied well-thought-out principles to a set of facts and deduced an answer. Our efforts to justify what we have done—or what we plan to do—are typically made up after the event, rationalizations of what we have decided intuitively to do. And a good deal of what we intuitively take to be right, we take to be right just because it is what we are used to. That does not mean, however, that we cannot become accustomed to doing things differently.[93]

Angels in America is all about how people can learn to do things differently by learning from one another, and the play ends with a conversation—or rather two. The first conversation takes place among four friends who have come together against all odds: Prior, the AIDS survivor; Louis, his ex-lover; Hannah, his ex-lover's lover's Mormon mother; and Belize, a gay African American male nurse who serves as the moral compass of the play. The second conversation is between Prior and us, the audience, and it ends with a blessing: "More life."

It's important the Prior uses the word "citizens" in the moments before he utters that blessing: "We won't die secret deaths anymore. The world only spins forward. We will be citizens. The time has come." What Prior is evoking is the idea of the world-citizen, a fundamental concept for cosmopolitan theory. It's the idea that each of us has a fundamental obligation to humanity as a whole. The time has come, Prior is telling us, to step up and be cosmopolitan, to be citizens of the world, to take responsibility for the way in which the world spins forward. That is what the play's final line—"The Great Work Begins."—ultimately signifies. To my mind, that's a powerful way of understanding the project of emergent U.S. literatures.[94]

Conclusion

Emergent Literatures and Cosmopolitan Conversation

In the course of this study, I have argued that Raymond Williams's model of culture as the interplay of dominant, residual, and emergent forms offers us a productive way of thinking about the dynamics of both literary cultures and cosmopolitan conversation. Williams's analysis suggests that human culture has always been the product of conflict and has always depended for its coherence on the identification of certain peoples, ideas, and practices as Other. Whether we believe that this is an abiding and eternal feature of human culture, or instead look forward to the day when human cultures will no longer achieve consensus through the demonization of difference, we must recognize that U.S. culture thus far has given no sign that it is about to render Williams's model obsolete; moreover, if we have reason to be hopeful that marginalization on the basis of gender is a practice that will soon wither away, we have far less reason to hope that ethnicity, race, and sexuality will cease to be reasons for discrimination against individuals. The recognition that one's "identity" has been constructed as "other" by the surrounding culture is one of the insights that fuels emergent writing.

To study emergent literatures in the comparative way that I have promoted here is humbling, because we are constantly reminded of the limits of our knowledge. Most of the time, close reading proves inadequate unless it is set in multiple interpretive contexts, some of which are bound to prove unfamiliar to any given reader. The writers that we have been considering are interested in forming new interpretive communities with different ground rules, and shifting from one interpretive community to another is always a difficult, sometimes bewildering, experience. It helps, therefore, to embrace the doctrine that philosophers call *fallibilism*—the sense, as Kwame Anthony Appiah puts it, "that our knowledge is imperfect, provisional, subject to revision in the face of new evidence."[1] Fallibilism lies at the heart of contemporary theories of cosmopolitanism, providing one of the primary rationales for stressing the importance of conversations in which we are willing to make cherished values the subject of debate.

The logic goes like this: human beings are imperfect; we make mistakes; we commit errors of judgment; and we often fail to do what we set out to do. Because we are fallible, we can never be assured that we have either the whole truth or the best account of the way that the world works. So it's important to be intellectually curious and to listen to what others have to say. When reading emergent literatures, it's crucial to come to a text with an awareness of our own assumptions about reading and literary traditions and to be prepared to adjust those assumptions as we encounter the ideas that animate the emergent text.

The unwillingness to question and possibly adjust basic assumptions is a hallmark of what Appiah calls "counter-cosmopolitanism," which is often linked with calls for cultural purity and a resistance to foreign ideas. The hostility toward multiculturalism voiced by conservative educators and politicians in the United States during the 1980s, and the accompanying assertion that "American Literature" should be taught as a set of classic, canonical texts centered on the writers of the so-called American Renaissance, may be seen as a call for a kind of cultural purity in which the United States is seen to be, above all, a white Protestant nation that tolerates immigrants from other cultural backgrounds.

"Counter-cosmopolitanism" is often linked to fundamentalisms of various kinds. Rather than embracing cultural difference and recognizing multiple points of view, fundamentalists insist on cultural purity and believe that there is one true way of being in the world to which they hold the key.[2] Fundamentalists are counter-cosmopolitan because they refuse to put their beliefs on the line. They believe that they have a special purchase on truth, and nothing anyone can say will persuade them to alter their beliefs. For example, Puritans like William Bradford and John Winthrop, who left England for North America in the early seventeenth century, believed they were practicing the one true religion, which was their form of Calvinist Christianity. They believed that they were God's chosen people, that they alone were "elect"—chosen by God for salvation. Ironically, the idea that human beings are fallible was one of the Puritans' foundational beliefs, but unlike cosmopolitans, they didn't believe in human perfectibility. Sin was the result of the grievous error known as the Fall of Man, and nothing that human beings could do could repair this error. Salvation occurred only because God was merciful, not because human beings deserved it. In Appiah's terms, what they practiced was "universalism without toleration."[3]

This kind of fundamentalism represents a challenge for cosmopolitanism: if cosmopolitanism is predicated on conversation, what do you do with people who refuse to talk? Left to their own devices, cultures tend toward mixing rather than purity, but cosmopolitan thinkers remain acutely aware that "counter-cosmopolitanism" can be found at every level of culture and therefore recognize that the natural tendency of cultures toward cosmopolitan mixing is not enough to guarantee that a cosmopolitan perspective will prevail.

I believe that reading, studying, and teaching emergent literatures is one way to promote that cosmopolitan perspective. In examining the respective histories of Native American, Asian American, Hispanic American, and gay and lesbian writing after 1968, we've seen that the moments of real contact between these histories were few and far between until very recently. In large part, these histories were shaped as separate but equal trajectories, parallel to one another rather than in conversation with one another, because of the cultural attitudes that would eventually coalesce into the multiculturalism of the 1980s. For example, when Abdul JanMohammed and David Lloyd applied in 1986 to the National Endowment of the Humanities for a conference on "The Nature and Context of Minority Discourse," their application was rejected largely on the basis of one reviewer's argument that "the proposed conference would almost certainly devolve into an academic tower of Babel. It is not clear that a specialist on Native-American literature, for example, will have much to say to someone specializing in African literature." In recommending against funding a conference designed to provoke scholarly conversation among scholars of ethnic literatures, the reviewer both identified and perpetuated the problem with strongly pluralist constructions of multiculturalism. (Fortunately, the conference was held anyway, albeit without NEH funding.)[4]

Emergent writing demonstrates that this kind of multiculturalism, enshrined in many corners of the U.S. academy during and after the "culture wars," is untenable. Arab Americans are perhaps the latest group to be constructed as "other" by U.S. culture, and Arab American literature is emerging as a subject of scholarly inquiry and as a field that marketing departments at publishing houses recognize. Like the other emergent literatures that I have discussed in detail in this book, we will need to understand "Arab American literature" as an artificial construction, a coalition that can be empowering, but also potentially limiting, for writers who work within it. As with "Asian American literature," the broad category of "Arab American literature" indicates a confederation of writings that have their roots in different cultural traditions, even as it risks flattening a rich set of cultural identities into a uniform stereotype. But, perhaps more quickly than other emergent U.S. literatures, Arab American literature seems likely to become interested in the radical transformation of identities and the merging of traditions that U.S. culture makes possible. Alia Yunis's novel *The Night Counter* (2009), which dramatizes the lives of characters who embody a rich mixture of ethnic, racial, and sexual identities, may be a harbinger of things to come. Yunis may be ahead of the curve for emergent Arab American literature, but her novel resonates with the interest in multiplicity that is energizing writers across the spectrum of U.S. emergent literatures, so that, for example, poetry like that written by Cathy Song seems likely to become paradigmatic: Song's work crosses ethnic boundaries, deeply rooted in the Hawai'ian landscape of her birth and the dual Asian heritage that comes with having a Chinese mother and a Korean father. Fictional examples of this sort of multiplicity might include Chitra Banerjee Divakaruni's 2010 novel, *One Amazing Thing*, which tells the story of nine people of various ethnic and racial backgrounds who struggle together to survive in the aftermath of an earthquake, or Cristina García's novel *The Lady Matador's Hotel* (2010), in which the title character is a Californian woman of Mexican and Japanese descent. These writers and their texts are less in interested in the dynamics of hybridity as they were first conceived than they are in the dynamics of multiple, overlapping hybridities. It may well be that as the "late twentieth-century" recedes more firmly into "history," we will soon be asking each of the literatures that I have explored here the question that Kenneth Warren first posed about African American literature in 2002: what *was* it?[5]

*   *   *

I have meant the account presented in this book to be suggestive rather than exhaustive, to provide a sense of the general sweep of the histories of Native American, Asian American, Hispanic American, and gay and lesbian writing during the period 1968 to 2001. More importantly, I have sought to offer ways of reading these texts that highlight the structural similarities to be found in their textual strategies and contextual engagements, while not losing sight of the salient differences among them as a result of their different cultural roots. Above all, I hope that I have shown why it is more productive to understand these literatures as "emergent" rather than "multicultural." The idea of "emergent literature" is in the end a structure into which different kinds of content can be poured. It's useful both to have an understanding of the way the structure works and to be prepared for the many different forms that the structure can accommodate and enable.

Finally, because of their overt engagement with the idea of difference, emergent literatures may serve to remind us of something about the literary experience that we may tend to take for granted. The promise of literature is that it takes us out of our own subjectivities and into the subjectivity of another. When we read a novel, poem, or play, we open our consciousnesses to the consciousness of someone else. Literature enables us to experience different ways of thinking, different ways of being in the world, than those to which we are accustomed. Because they are oriented around the idea of the "new," emergent literatures often push us more obviously than other traditions to new modes of thinking, thereby promoting the perspective that I have called a "cosmopolitan." That perspective, with its embrace of difference, is ultimately, I firmly believe, what lies at the heart of any worthwhile literary experience.

NOTES

NOTES TO THE INTRODUCTION

1. In lieu of the term "Latino," I use the term "Hispanic American" throughout this book because it was the first of the two to be adopted by the U.S. Census. When referring to Mexican American writing after 1959, I use the term "Chicano/a."

2. Kenneth Warren has argued persuasively for the historicization of the idea of "African American Literature" in his study *What Was African American Literature?* (Cambridge: Harvard University Press, 2011). Warren writes that "African American literature is not a transhistorical entity within which the kinds of changes described here have occurred but that African American literature itself constitutes a representational and rhetorical strategy within the domain of a literary practice responsive to conditions that, by and large, no longer obtain" (9). Warren's analysis of the fate of African American literature is consonant with the argument that I will make here about "emergent literatures" in this period: that "African American literature as a distinct entity would seem to be at an end, and that the turn to diasporic, transatlantic, global and other frames indicates a dim awareness that the boundary creating this distinctiveness has ended" (8).

3. This way of delineating the late twentieth century means that I do not focus on careers or emergent literatures that took shape after 9/11. So, for example, I limit myself to a few suggestive comments about Arab American literature and do not deal with disability studies. I hope, however, that the book provides a productive template for thinking about the dynamics of these and other newly emergent literatures.

4. For example, Lisa Lowe's influential study *Immigrant Acts: On Asian American Cultural Politics* (Durham: Duke University Press, 1996), describes the "making of Asian American culture" in terms that are strikingly reminiscent of Williams's model: "The making of Asian American culture includes practices that are partly inherited, partly modified, as well as partly invented; Asian American culture also includes the practices that emerge in relation to the dominant representations that deny or subordinate Asian and Asian American cultures as 'other'" (65).

5. Williams alternately describes this mainstream as an "effective dominant culture" and, following Gramsci, a "hegemony." See "Base and Superstructure in

Marxist Cultural Theory" *New Left Review* 82 (1973): 3–15; *Marxism and Literature* (Oxford: Oxford University Press, 1977), 108–14, 121–27.

6. Joel Porte, *Emerson in His Journals* (Cambridge, MA: Harvard University Press), 236. Porte dates the letter "April 7? 1840."

7. Williams, *Marxism and Literature*, 123.

8. Hans Robert Jauss, "Literary History as a Challenge to Literary Theory" in *Toward an Aesthetic of Reception*, trans. Timothy Bahti (Minneapolis: University of Minnesota Press, 1982), 26, 23.

9. William Cain, *F. O. Matthiessen and the Politics of Criticism* (Madison: University of Wisconsin Press, 1998), 136.

10. Jauss, "Literary History," 25.

11. For accounts of this process of canonization, see, for example, Paul Lauter, "Melville Climbs the Canon," *American Literature* 66 (1994): 1–24; Donald Pease, *Visionary Compacts: American Renaissance Writings in Cultural Context* (Madison: University of Wisconsin Press), 1987.

12. Mark Twain, *Following the Equator* (1897) in *A Tramp Abroad, Following the Equator, and Other Travels*, ed. Roy Blount, Jr. (New York: Library of America, 2010), 567. The quotation is an epigraph to Chapter 25 and is attributed to Twain's character Pudd'nhead Wilson. The more famous quotation attributes to Twain the idea that a classic "is something that everybody wants to have read and nobody wants to read." The quotation comes from a speech subsequently titled "The Disappearance of Literature: Address at the Dinner of the Nineteenth Century Club at Sherry's, New York," given on November 20, 1900. In that case, however, Twain is quoting Caleb Winchester, Professor of Rhetoric and English Literature at Connecticut Wesleyan University. The full quotation is: "Professor Winchester also said something about there being no modern epics like *Paradise Lost*. I guess he's right. He talked as if he was pretty familiar with that piece of literary work, and nobody would suppose that he never had read it. I don't believe any of you have ever read Paradise Lost, and you don't want to. That's something that you just want to take on trust. It's a classic, just as Professor Winchester says, and it meets his definition of a classic—something that everybody wants to have read and nobody wants to read" (Twain, *Great Speeches*, ed. Bob Blaisdell [Mineola, NY: Dover Thrift, 2013], 68–69).

13. Thomas F. Gossett, *Uncle Tom's Cabin and American Culture* (Dallas, TX: Southern Methodist University Press, 1985), 99.

14. Another example might be the pared-down style of Ernest Hemingway, once thought to be revolutionary and new, which is so influential, so widely copied, that it now seems to be banal.

15. Mark Chiang's *The Cultural Capital of Asian American Studies* (New York: New York University Press, 2009) offers a detailed case study of the processes of institutionalization that lead to the creation of an emergent literature. According to Chiang, "'Asian American literature' as such can come into being only when there is a socially recognized category of identity and an institutionally defined

literary field. . . . In the dominant field, autonomy comes through a liberation from, or refusal of, the burden of representation, but in the field of Asian
American literature it can be achieved only through the *assumption* of representation" (139–40). Although Chiang draws on the work of Pierre Bourdieu and
John Guillory rather than Raymond Williams for his theoretical framework, his
account of the rise of Asian American studies demonstrates the ways in which
a dominant literary culture sets the terms of engagement for emergent literary
cultures. The volume *Multiethnic Literature and Canon Debates*, ed. Mary Jo Bona
and Irma Maini (Albany: State University of New York Press, 2006), contains
three useful essays about the dynamics of anthologizing and canon formation:
Veronica Makowsky, "From the Road Not Taken to the Multi-Lane Highway:
MELUS, The Journal," 23–40; Aureliana Maria DeSoto, "On the Trail of the
Chicana/o Subject: Literary Texts and Contexts in the Formation of Chicana/o
Studies," 41–60; and Kristin Czarnecki, "'A House Made with Stones Full of Sto-
ries': Anthologizing Native American Literature," 61–84.

16. Laura Coltelli, *Winged Words: American Indian Writers Speak* (Lincoln: University of Nebraska Press, 1990), 197.

17. Juan Bruce-Novoa, "Canonical and Noncanonical Texts: A Chicano Case Study,"
in *Redefining American Literary History*, ed. A. LaVonne Brown Ruoff and Jerry
W. Ward, Jr. (New York: Modern Language Association of America, 1990), 202.

18. Héctor Calderón, "Rereading Rivera's *y no se lo tragó la tierra*," in *Criticism in
the Borderlands: Studies in Chicano Literature, Culture, and Ideology*, ed. Héctor
Calderón and José David Saldívar (Durham, NC: Duke University Press, 1991),
99.

19. M. M. Bakhtin, *The Dialogic Imagination: Four Essays*, ed. Michael Holquist,
trans. Caryl Emerson and Michael Holquist (Austin: University of Texas Press,
1982), 358. Bakhtin further elaborates: "Such mixing of two languages within a
single utterance is, in the novel, an artistic device (or, more accurately, a system
of devices) that is deliberate. But unintentional, unconscious hybridization is
one of the most important modes in the historical life of all languages. We may
even say that language and languages change historically primarily by means
of hybridization, by means of mixing various 'languages' co-existing within
the boundaries of a single dialect, a single national language, a single branch,
a single group of different branches or different groups of such branches, in
the historical as well as paleontological past of languages—but the crucible for
this mixing always remains the utterance" (358). This conception of linguistic
hybridization is a crucial component of the model of emergent literatures that I
am developing here.

20. See for example, Charles L. Woodard, *Ancestral Voice: Conversations with N.
Scott Momaday*, (Lincoln: University of Nebraska Press, 1991), 99–96, 106, 111,
133–35, 137, 146, 148–49, 194.

21. Wittman's fascination with LeRoi Jones recalls Tam Lum, the protagonist of
Frank Chin's play *The Chickencoop Chinaman* (1972), who is fascinated by

African American culture. As I will discuss in Chapter 5, Chin has been a harsh critic of Kingston's work. The critic Amy Ling has argued that "it is immediately clear to anyone who knows him and his work that Wittman Ah Sing is modeled after the playwright Frank Chin. In a personal conversation with me, Kingston admitted that Frank Chin was 'an inspiration' for Wittman, but, as if to dilute this confession, she added that her husband (an actor), her son (a musician), and her brother were also models." See Ling's discussion in *Between Worlds: Women Writers of Chinese Ancestry* (New York: Pergamon, 1900), 149–55.

22. This is the approach taken by Morris Dickstein and Wendy Steiner in their contributions to the seventh volume of *The Cambridge History of American Literature: Prose Writing, 1940–1990*, ed. Sacvan Bercovitch (Cambridge: Cambridge University Press, 1999).

23. Arthur Schlesinger, Jr., *The Disuniting of America* (1991; revised and enlarged ed. New York: Norton, 1998), 63; Nathan Glazer, *We Are All Multiculturalists Now* (Cambridge: Harvard University Press, 1997), 94, 14.

24. Glazer, *We Are All Multiculturalists Now*, 14.

25. Paul Monette, *Becoming a Man: Half a Life Story* (New York: Houghton Mifflin Harcourt, 1992), 3.

26. Schlesinger, *The Disuniting of America*, 16–18.

27. Glazer, *We Are All Multiculturalists Now*, 96.

28. This quotation comes from an "Address to the Knights of Columbus," given at Carnegie Hall in New York, NY, on October 12, 1915 and subsequently printed under the title "Americanism" (*Works of Theodore Roosevelt, Memorial Edition*, vol. 20 [New York: Charles Scribner and Sons, 1923], 457–58).

29. Roosevelt continued:

> The one absolutely certain way of bringing this nation to ruin, of preventing all possibility of its continuing to be a nation at all, would be to permit it to become a tangle of squabbling nationalities, an intricate knot of German-Americans, Irish-Americans, English-Americans, French-Americans, Scandinavian-Americans or Italian-Americans, each preserving its separate nationality, each at heart feeling more sympathy with Europeans of that nationality, than with the other citizens of the American Republic. The men who do not become Americans and nothing else are hyphenated Americans; and there ought to be no room for them in this country. The man who calls himself an American citizen and who yet shows by his actions that he is primarily the citizen of a foreign land, plays a thoroughly mischievous part in the life of our body politic. He has no place here; and the sooner he returns to the land to which he feels his real heart-allegiance, the better it will be for every good American. There is no such thing as a hyphenated American who is a good American. The only man who is a good American is the man who is an American and nothing else. (458)

30. Chin's formulation is indebted to the famous concept of the "double consciousness" articulated by W. E. B. Du Bois in *The Souls of Black Folk* (1903) and is one

example of the ways in which an earlier emergent literature can serve as a point of departure for another. Du Bois wrote:

> After the Egyptian and Indian, the Greek and Roman, the Teuton and Mongolian, the Negro is a sort of seventh son, born with a veil, and gifted with second-sight in this American world, —a world which yields him no true self-consciousness, but only lets him see himself through the revelation of the other world. It is a peculiar sensation, this double-consciousness, this sense of always looking at one's self through the eyes of others, of measuring one's soul by the tape of a world that looks on in amused contempt and pity. One ever feels his two-ness, —an American, a Negro; two souls, two thoughts, two unreconciled strivings; two warring ideals in one dark body, whose dogged strength alone keeps it from being torn asunder. (*The Souls of Black Folk*, in W. E. B. Du Bois, *Writings*, ed. Nathan Huggins [New York: Library of America, 1986], 364–65)

31. The political philosopher George Kateb has made a powerful argument about the ways in which Emersonianism represents the fruition of both liberal individualism and American democracy. Arguing that "individualism is not always seen in its fullness and thus is disparaged unfairly or at least prematurely," Kateb distinguishes between two types of individualism, which he calls "historically related." The first is "the individualism of personal and political rights, profoundly present in Rawls, Dworkin, and Nozick, but, as we know, the creation of the English Protestant seventeenth century." The second type of individualism is what Kateb has called "democratic individuality," which he describes as "an idealism imagined and theorized initially by Emerson, Thoreau, and Whitman, and with a force that has not been equaled since then, much less surpassed." It is this second form that represents for Kateb both the "fullness" of individualism and the fruition of democracy. According to Kateb, the connection "between the two types of individualism is that democratic individuality is perhaps not the only but probably the best actuality and aspiration that grows or can grow out of a culture in which individual personal and political rights are systematically recognized and appreciated" (George Kateb, "Democratic Individuality and the Meaning of Rights," in *Liberalism and the Moral Life*, ed. Nancy L. Rosenblum [Cambridge, MA: Harvard University Press, 1989], 184–85). Kateb's conception of "democratic individuality" is developed further in *The Inner Ocean: Individualism and Democratic Culture* (Ithaca, NY: Cornell University Press, 1992); his conception of Emersonianism receives its most extensive treatment in *Emerson and Self-Reliance* (Lanham, MD: Rowand & Littlefield, 2002). See also my essay "Emersonian Strategies: Negative Liberty, Self-Reliance, and Democratic Individuality," *Nineteenth-Century Literature* 48 (1994): 440–79, for a discussion of the ways in which Kateb idealizes not only the Emersonian but also the Rawlsian tradition of individualism.

32. For an introductory account of the key concepts in Rawlsian political theory, see John Rawls, *Justice as Fairness: A Restatement* (Cambridge, MA: Harvard

University Press, 2001), especially 14–18 and 80–134 on the original position of equality and the veil of ignorance.

33. David A. Hollinger, *Postethnic America: Beyond Multiculturalism, Tenth Anniversary Edition* (New York: Basic Books, 2000), 84.

34. Hollinger, *Postethnic America*, 85.

35. Hollinger suggests that "pluralism and cosmopolitanism have often been united in the common cause of promoting tolerance and diversity" and therefore "have not always been distinguished as sharply as I believe today's circumstances demand" (*Postethnic America*, 85). In recent years, advocates of multiculturalism have begun to shift towards more cosmopolitan approaches. For example, the philosopher Richard Rorty left behind the support for ethnocentrism that characterized his writings during the 1980s to embrace a cosmopolitanism that might one day bring about a "planetary community" bound by its respect for "human rights." In "Justice as a Larger Loyalty," Rorty's contribution to the volume *Cosmopolitics*, Rorty argues that in order to construct a "global moral community" based on a respect for human rights, we must "peel apart Enlightenment liberalism from Enlightenment rationalism" (*Cosmopolitics: Thinking and Feeling beyond the Nation*, ed. Pheng Cheah and Bruce Robbins [Minneapolis: University of Minnesota Press, 1998], 57). Suggesting that "the rhetoric we Westerners use in trying to get everybody to be more like us would be improved if we were more frankly ethnocentric and less professedly universalist" (56), Rorty concludes "that getting rid of rationalistic rhetoric would permit the West to approach the non-West in the role of someone with an instructive story to tell, rather than in the role of someone purporting to be making better use of a universal human capacity" (57). The cosmopolitan implications of multiculturalism are explored by other contributors to *Cosmopolitics*: Bruce Robbins writes that "our elaboration of the term *cosmopolitics* represents one effort to describe, from within multiculturalism, a name for the genuine striving toward common norms and mutual translatability that is also part of multiculturalism" (Introduction, 12–13). The aim of the volume, as James Clifford puts it, is to explore the "promise" of cosmopolitanism "viewed without universalist nostalgia" ("Mixed Feelings," 362) but instead through the lens of "discrepant cosmopolitanisms" (365). According to Robbins, this perspective makes the term *cosmopolitanism* "available again for general use. Instead of renouncing cosmopolitanism as a false universal, one can embrace it as an impulse to knowledge that is shared with others, a striving to transcend partiality that is itself partial, but no more so than the similar cognitive strivings of many diverse peoples. The world's particulars can now be recoded, in part at least, as the world's *discrepant cosmopolitanisms*" ("Comparative Cosmopolitanisms," 259).

36. Kwame Anthony Appiah, "The Case for Contamination," *New York Times Magazine*, January 1, 2006: 52.

37. Kwame Anthony Appiah, *Cosmopolitanism: Ethics in a World of Strangers* (New York: Norton, 2006), xxi.

NOTES TO CHAPTER 1

1. Maxine Hong Kingston, *Tripmaster Monkey: His Fake Book* (New York: Knopf, 1989), 21.

2. Williams, *Marxism and Literature*, 123.

3. See, for example, Michel Foucault, *The Use of Pleasure: The History of Sexuality, Volume 2*, trans. Robert Hurley (New York: Penguin, 1998); Thomas K. Hubbard, *Homosexuality in Greece and Rome: A Sourcebook of Basic Documents* (Berkeley and Los Angeles: University of California Press, 2003); Marilyn B. Skinner, *Sexuality in Greek and Roman Culture* (New York: Wiley-Blackwell, 2005); J. W. Wright and Everett K. Rowson, eds., *Homoeroticism in Classical Arabic Literature* (New York: Columbia University Press, 1997).

4. Sodomy laws in the United States were invalidated in 2003 by the U.S. Supreme Court decision *Lawrence v. Texas*. For a good overview of the history of the debate over gay marriage in the United States through spring of 2013, see David Von Drehle, "How Gay Marriage Won," *Time*, April 8, 2013, available online at http://swampland.time.com/2013/03/28/how-gay-marriage-won/.

5. Monette, *Becoming a Man*, 25.

6. Leslie Marmon Silko, *Ceremony* (New York: Viking, 1977), 68.

7. Abdul JanMohammed and David Lloyd, *The Nature and Context of Minority Discourse* (New York: Oxford University Press, 1991), 1.

8. JanMohammed and Lloyd, *The Nature and Context of Minority Discourse*, 4. See Frantz Fanon, *The Wretched of the Earth* (1961), trans. Constance Farrington (New York: Grove, 1963). For further discussion of Fanon, cultural damage, and the relation between culture and imperialism, see also Donald Pease and Amy Kaplan, eds., *Cultures of U.S. Imperialism* (Durham: Duke University Press, 1993); John Carlos Rowe, *Literary Culture and U.S Imperialism: From the Revolution to World War II* (New York: Oxford University Press, 2000); Amritjit Singh and Peter Schmidt, eds., *Postcolonial Theory and the United States: Race, Ethnicity, and Literature* (Jackson: University Press of Mississippi, 2000).

9. Silko, *Ceremony*, 68; Ngugi wa Thiong'o, *Decolonising the Mind: The Politics of Language in African Literature* (London: James Currey, 1986), 9, 16, 26.

10. Jessica Hagedorn, ed., *Charlie Chan Is Dead: An Anthology of Contemporary Asian American Fiction* (New York: Penguin, 1993), xxiii

11. Jessica Hagedorn, *Dogeaters* (1990; rpt. New York: Penguin , 1991), 3–4.

12. Hagedorn, *Dogeaters*, 224.

13. Hagedorn, *Dogeaters*, 12.

14. Monette, *Becoming a Man*, 2–3.

15. Silko, *Ceremony*, 125; Kingston, *Tripmaster Monkey*, 246.

16. Richard Rodriguez, *Hunger of Memory: The Education of Richard Rodriguez, An Autobiography* (New York: Godine, 1982), 22–23.

17. Rodriguez, *Hunger*, 26–28.

18. Rodriguez, "An American Writer," in *The Invention of Ethnicity*, ed. Werner Sollors (New York: Oxford University Press, 1989), 4.

19. John Okada, *No-No Boy* (1957; rpt. Seattle: University of Washington Press, 1977). The novel's title refers to a questionnaire produced by the U.S. Army in the aftermath of the bombing of Pearl Harbor. Initially, all young Japanese men, including Nisei, were classified 4-C—enemy aliens—but in October 1942, the director of the Office of War Information recommended to President Roosevelt that Nisei be recruited for the war effort in order to help combat "Japanese propaganda" characterizing the war as "a racial war." In February 1943, not quite a year after signing Executive Order 9066, President Roosevelt issued a public statement in support of the army's plan to recruit an all-Nisei combat unit of approximately 5,000 men drawn from Hawaii and mainland. "No loyal citizen of the United States," Roosevelt proclaimed, "should be denied the democratic right to exercise the responsibilities of his citizenship, regardless of his ancestry. . . . Americanism is not, and never was, a matter of race or ancestry" (qtd. in Roger Daniels, *Asian America: Chinese and Japanese in the United States since 1850* [Seattle: University of Washington Press, 1988], 250).

For the Nisei internees, the announcement that Nisei volunteers were being recruited by the U.S. Army was the ultimate irony. In *Nisei Daughter* (1953), Sone describes a friend's reaction to the news: "What do they take us for? Saps? First, they change my army status to 4-C because of my ancestry, run me out of town, and now they want me to volunteer for a suicide squad so I could get killed for this damn democracy. That's going some, for sheer brass!" Asked how he can justify looking for volunteers from among those whose rights as citizens have been violated, the army recruiter who visits Sone's camp can only say, "The evacuation occurred, right or wrong, it's past. Now we're interested in your future. The War Department is offering you a chance to volunteer and to distinguish yourselves as Japanese-American citizens in the service of your country" (Sone, *Nisei Daughter* [1953; rpt. Seattle: University of Washington Press, 1979], 198–200).

Adapting an existing questionnaire designed for aliens, the army produced a form to be given to male draft-age Nisei, at the heart of which were these two questions:

27. Are you willing to serve in the armed forces of the United States on combat duty, wherever ordered?

28. Will you swear unqualified allegiance to the United States of American and faithfully defend the United States from any or all attack by foreign and domestic forces, and forswear any form of allegiance to the Japanese emperor, to any other foreign government, power or organization?

Of the 21,000 Nisei males who were eligible for the draft, 22 percent (4,600) would be known as "no-no boys" because they answered these two questions with a "no," a qualified "yes," or a blank. Only a relatively small number of the Nisei who answered "yes" to questions 27 and 28 actually volunteered—1,208 out of approximately 10,000 eligible—and in January 1944, the Selective Service reclassified Nisei who had answered "yes" from 4-C to 1-A and began issuing draft registration notices.

20. Okada, *No-No Boy*, 16.

21. N. Scott Momaday, *House Made of Dawn* (New York: Harper & Row, 1968), 116–17, 68–84, 101–103; Monette, *Becoming a Man*, 34.

22. Fanon, *The Wretched of the Earth,* 35; Dana Takagi, "Maiden Voyage: Excursion into Sexuality and Identity Politics in Asian America," in *Asian American Sexualities: Dimensions of the Gay and Lesbian Experience,* ed. Russell Leong (New York: Routledge, 1996), 26–27; Kingston, *Tripmaster Moneky,* 34.

23. Kingston, *Tripmaster Monkey,* 34; on Melville, see, for example, James Creech, *Closet Writing/Gay Reading: The Case of Melville's Pierre* (Chicago: University of Chicago Press, 1994) or Elizabeth Hardwick, *Herman Melville* (New York: Viking, 2000).

24. See Eve Kosofsky Sedgwick, *Epistemology of the Closet* (Berkeley and Los Angeles: University of California Press, 1990; rev. ed. 2008). Creech's study of Melville is an example of this strategy; other examples include Eric Haralson, *Henry James and Queer Modernity* (Cambridge: Cambridge University Press, 2003), which includes Cather, Stein, and Hemingway as examples of "queer modernity," and Marilee Lindemann, *Willa Cather: Queering America* (New York: Columbia University Press, 1999).

25. Judith Fetterley, "*My Ántonia*, Jim Burden, and the Dilemma of the Lesbian Writer," in *Lesbian Texts and Contexts: Radical Revisions,* ed. Karla Jay and Joanne Glasgow (New York: New York University Press, 1990), 161.

26. See, for example, John P. Ander's discussions of Whitman in *Willa Cather's Sexual Aesthetics and the Male Homosexual Literary Tradition* (Lincoln: University of Nebraska Press, 1999) and Gary Schmidgall, *Walt Whitman: A Gay Life* (New York: Dutton, 1997).

27. N. Scott Momaday, *The Names* (Tucson: University of Arizona Press, 1976), 55.

28. Woodard, *Ancestral Voice*, 15.

29. Gerald Vizenor, *Griever: An American Monkey King in China* (Minneapolis: University of Minnesota Press, 1987), 34

30. Gerald Vizenor, *Narrative Chance: Postmodern Discourse on Native American Indian Literatures* (Norman: University of Oklahoma Press, 1993), 13.

31. Rudolf A. Anaya, "Aztlán: A Homeland without Boundaries," in *Aztlán: Essays on the Chicano Homeland,* ed. Rudolfo A. Anaya and Francisco Lomeli (1989; rpt. Albuquerque: University of New Mexico Press, 1991), 235.

32. Anaya, "Aztlán," 236.

33. Luis Valdez and Stan Steiner, eds., *Aztlán: An Anthology of Mexican American Literature* (New York: Vintage, 1972), 403.

34. Frank Chin, "Come All Ye Asian American Writers of the Real and the Fake," in *The Big Aiiieeeee! An Anthology of Chinese American and Japanese American Literature,* ed. Jeffery Paul Chan, Frank Chin, Lawson Fusao Inada, and Shaw Wong (New York: Meridian, 1991), 27, 90.

35. Paula Gunn Allen, "Special Problems in Teaching Leslie Marmon Silko's *Ceremony,*" *The American Indian Quarterly* 14 (1990): 382.

36. Maxine Hong Kingston, "Personal Statement," in *Approaches to Teaching Kingston's The Woman Warrior*, ed. Shirley Geok-lin Lim (New York: The Modern Language Association of America, 1991), 24.

37 Silko, *Ceremony*, 126.

38. Arturo Islas with Marilyn Yalom, "Interview with Maxine Hong Kingston," in *Conversations with Maxine Hong Kingston*, ed. Paul Skenazy and Tera Martin (Jackson: University Press of Mississippi, 1998), 24, 27; Maxine Hong Kingston, "Cultural Mis-Readings by American Reviewers," in *Asian and Western Writers in Dialogue*, ed. Guy Amirthanayagam (London: Macmillan, 1982), 55.

39. Maxine Hong Kingston, "Cultural Mis-Readings by American Reviewers," 55. See also Timothy Pfaff, "Talk with Mrs. Kingston," *New York Times Book Review,* June 15, 1980, 1, 25.

40. Ramón Saldívar, *Chicano Narrative: The Dialectics of Difference* (Madison: University of Wisconsin Press, 1990), 5.

41. Michael Dorris, *Paper Trail: Selected Essays* (New York: HarperCollins, 1994), 250.

42. Kingston discusses this section of *China Men* in her interview with Donna Perry in *Backtalk: Women Writers Speak Out*, ed. Donna Perry (New Brunswick, NJ: Rutgers University Press, 1993), 183.

43. Dorris, *Paper Trail,* 135–36; Monette, *Becoming a Man,* 25. The Stonewall Rebellion, which took place in 1969, effectively began the gay rights movement in the United States (see the discussion in Chapter 4).

44. Harold Hickerson, *The Chippewa and Their Neighbors: A Study in Ethnohistory* (New York: Holt, Rinehart and Winson, 1970), 6.

45. Arnold Krupat, *Ethnocriticism: Ethnography, History, Literature* (Berkeley and Los Angeles: University of California Press, 1992), 5; Alison R. Bernstein, *American Indians and World War II: Toward a New Era in Indian Affairs* (Norman: University of Oklahoma Press, 1991), 161–62.

46. Paula Allen Gunn recalls:

    As a Roman Catholic child I was treated to bloody tales of how the savage Indians martyred the hapless priests and missionaries who went among them in an attempt to lead them to the one truth path. By the time I was through high school I had the idea that Indians were people who had benefited mightily from the advanced knowledge and superior morality of the Anglo-Europeans. At least I had, perforce, that idea to lay beside the other one that derived from my daily experience of Indian life, an idea less dehumanizing and more accurate because it came from my mother and the other Indian people who raised me. That idea was that Indians are a people who don't tell lies, who care for their children and their old people. (*The Sacred Hoop: Recovering the Feminine in American Indian Traditions* [Boston: Beacon Press, 1986], 49)

47. Fae Myenne Ng, *Bone* (New York: Hyperion, 1993). 36.

48. Autobiography, as we will see, is an important part of gay and lesbian literatures, and gay and lesbian identity often functions culturally as if it were a form of ethnic identity.

49. Carlos Bulosan, *America Is in the Heart* (1946; rpt. Seattle: University of Washington Press, 1973), 252.

50. Bulosan, *America*, 327, 310–311, 326.

51. Arnold Krupat initially describes Apess as an author whose "sense of self, if we may call it, deriv[es] entirely from Christian culture" (*The Voice in the Margin: Native American Literature and the Canon* [Berkeley: University of California Press, 1989], 145). He later revises this view to see Apess's use of the conversion narrative as a self-conscious attempt "to reconstitute and redefine his 'tribe' and its 'heritage' in Christian terms as a means of constituting and defining himself" ("Native American Autobiography," in *American Autobiography: Retrospect and Prospect*, ed. Paul John Eakin [Madison: University of Wisconsin Press, 1997], 185). Maureen Konkle reads Apess's use of Christian motifs as a mode of resisting dominant discourse in her essay on "Indian Literacy, U.S. Colonialism, and Literary Criticism," in *Postcolonial Theory and the United States: Race, Ethnicity, and Literature*, ed. Amritjit Singh and Peter Schmidt (Jackson: University Press of Mississippi, 2000), 151–75.

52. See Chin, "Come All Ye Asian American Writers of the Real and the Fake," 3; Cherríe Moraga, *Loving in the War Years: lo que nunca pasó por sus labios* (Cambridge, MA: South End Press, 1983), 111.

53. Cherríe Moraga and Gloria Anzaldúa, eds., *This Bridge Called My Back* (New York: Kitchen Table: Women of Color Press, 1983), xxiii.

54. Moraga and Anzaldúa, *Bridge*, xxvi.

55. Gloria Anzaldúa, *Borderlands/La Frontera: The New Mestiza* (1987; 4th ed. San Francisco: Aunt Lute Books, 2012), 19, 216–217.

NOTES TO CHAPTER 2

1. Okada, *No-No Boy*, 136.

2. Frank Chin, "Confessions of a Chinatown Cowboy," *Bulletin of Concerned Asian Scholars* 4.3 (1972): 66.

3. Elaine Kim, *Asian American Literature: An Introduction to the Writings and Their Social Context* (Philadelphia: Temple University Press, 1982), 177.

4. Chin, "Confessions," 74.

5. Sau-Ling Cynthia Wong, "Chinese American Literature," in *Interethnic Companion to Asian American Literature*, ed. King-Kok Cheung (Cambridge: Cambridge University Press), 48.

6. Homi Bhabha, "Signs Taken for Wonders," in *The Location of Culture* (New York: Routledge, 1994).

7. Dorris, *Paper Trail*, 137.

8. Chris Packard, *Queer Cowboys and Other Erotic Male Friendships in Nineteenth-Century American Literature* (New York: Palgrave, 2005), 9–10.

9. Badger Clark, "The Lost Pardner," in *Sun and Saddle Leather* (Boston: Gorham Press, 1922), 83–85.

10. Robert Deam Tobin notes that although Kertbeny's term would gain currency in medical circles, it actually first emerged in the context of a political

discussion about German nationalism (Tobin, "Kertbeny's 'Homosexuality' and the Language of Nationalism," *Genealogies of Identity: Interdisciplinary Readings on Sex and Sexuality*, ed. Margaret Sönser Breen and Fiona Peters [Amsterdam: Rodopi, 2005], 2); Foucault, *The Use of Pleasure*, 187.

11. Walter L. Williams, *The Spirit and the Flesh: Sexual Diversity in American Indian Culture* (Boston: Beacon Press, 1986; rev. ed. 1992), 2–3. The term *berdache* is has been replaced by the term *two-spirit* in Native American scholarship. In an author's note on the Beacon Press website (http://www.beacon.org/productde-tails.cfm?PC=1585), Williams writes:

> Shortly after the second revised edition this book was published in 1992, the term "Two-Spirit Person" became more popular among native people than the older anthropological term "berdache." When I learned of this new term, I began strongly supporting the use of this newer term. I believe that people should be able to call themselves whatever they wish, and scholars should respect and acknowledge their change of terminology. I went on record early on in convincing other anthropologists to shift away from use of the word berdache and in favor of using Two-Spirit. Nevertheless, because this book continues to be sold with the use of berdache, many people have assumed that I am resisting the newer term. Nothing could be further from the truth. Unless continued sales of this book will justify the publication of a third revised edition in the future, it is not possible to rewrite what is already printed, Therefore, I urge readers of this book, as well as activists who are working to gain more respect for gender variance, mentally to substitute the term "Two-Spirit" in the place of "berdache" when reading this text.

12. Sigmund Freud, "Letter to an American Mother," *American Journal of Psychiatry* 107 (1951): 787. The letter now resides at Indiana University's Kinsey Institute, because the woman who received the letter sent it to Arthur Kinsey with the following covering note: "Dear Dr. Kinsey: HEREWITH I enclose a letter from a Great and Good Man which you may retain. From a Grateful Mother."

13. Ludwig Lewisohn, *Up Stream: An American Chronicle* (New York: Boni and Liveright, 1922), 240.

14. Kermit Vanderbilt, *American Literature and the Academy: The Roots, Growth, and Maturity of a Profession* (Philadelphia: University of Pennsylvania Press, 1986), 367.

15. Lewisohn, *Up Stream*, 236.

16. Lewisohn, *Expression in America* (New York: Harper, 1932), 207, 213; Vanderbilt, *American Literature*, 370.

17. Roger Daniels, *Coming to America: A History of Immigration and Ethnicity in American Life*, 2d. ed. (New York: Perennial, 2002), 113.

18. Raymund A. Paredes, "The Evolution of Chicano Literature," in *Modern Chicano Literature: A Collection of Critical Essays*, ed. Joseph Sommers and Tomás Ybarra-Frausto (Englewood Cliffs, NJ: Prentice-Hall, 1979), 36; Rodolfo Acuña, *Occupied America: A History of Chicanos*, 3rd ed. (New York: Harper & Row, 1988), 19.

19. Acuña, *Occupied America*, 20.

20. Américo Paredes, *"With His Pistol in His Hand"*: *A Border Ballad and Its Hero* (Austin: University of Texas Press, 1958), 134.

21. Ronald Takaki, *A Different Mirror: A History of Multicultural America* (New York: Little, Brown, 1993; rev. ed., 2008), 165.

22. A. Paredes, *"With His Pistol,"* 149.

23. A. Paredes, *"With His Pistol,"* 234.

24. Raymund Paredes, "Mexican American Literature," in *The Columbia Literary History of the United States*, ed. Emory Elliott (New York: Columbia University Press, 1988), 802.

25. Américo Paredes, "The Folk Base of Chicano Literature," in Sommers and Ybarra-Frausto, eds. *Modern Chicano Narrative*, 11.

26. Anonymous, "El Deportado," in *Handbook of Hispanic Cultures in the United States, Volume 4*, ed. Nicolás Kanellos (Houston, TX: Arte Publico Press, 1994).

27. Theodore Roosevelt, State of the Union Message, December 3, 1901

28. Bernard Bailyn, ed., *The Great Republic: A History of the American People, Volume 2* (Boston: D. C. Heath, 1992), 107.

29. Frederick E. Hoxie, *A Final Promise: The Campaign to Assimilate the Indians, 1880–1920* (Cambridge: Cambridge University Press; Lincoln: University of Nebraska Press, 1984), 77.

30. Louise Erdrich, *Tracks* (New York: Holt, 1988), 1.

31. Allen, *The Sacred Hoop*, 152.

32. Linda Hogan, *Mean Spirit* (New York: Ivy Books, 1990), 60–61.

33. For insightful accounts of the Dawes Act and its effects, see Nancy J. Peterson, "History, Postmodernism, and Louise Erdrich's *Tracks*," *PMLA* 109 (1994), 982–94; Michael Paul Rogin, "Political Repression in the United States," in *Ronald Reagan, the Movie and Other Episodes in Political Demonology* (Berkeley and Los Angeles: University of California Press, 1987), 44–80. See also Michael T. Smith, "The Wheeler-Howard Act of 1934: The Indian New Deal," *Journal of the West*, 10.3 (1971): 524–34.

34. Daniels, *Coming to America*, 240.

35. *Daily Alta California*, San Francisco, May 12, 1852; qtd. in Don Caldwell, "The Negroization of the Chinese Stereotype in California," *Southern California Quarterly* 53 (1971): 123; John McDougal, "Address to the California Legislature" (1852), qtd. Ronald Takaki, *Strangers from a Different Shore: A History of Asian Americans* (New York: Little Brown, 1989), 81.

36. Mark Twain, *Roughing It,* in *Innocents Abroad; Roughing It,* ed. Guy Cardwell (New York: Library of America, 1984), 821.

37. Maxine Hong Kingston, *China Men* (New York: Knopf, 1980). 128; for population figures, see Takaki, *Strangers from a Different Shore*, 85

38. Kingston, *China Men*, 145.

39. Takaki, *Strangers*, 86.

40. Kingston, *China Men*, 145.

41. For dating of worker hiring, see Thomas W. Chinn, H. Mark Lai, and Philip P. Choy, *A History of Chinese in California: A Syllabus* (San Francisco, CA: Chinese Historical Society of America, 1987), 44; Kingston, *China Men*, 128.

42. See Takaki, *Strangers*, 79–131.

43. *Daily Alta California,* San Francisco, June 4, 1853; qtd. in Caldwell, "Negroization,"123.

44. Caldwell, "Negroization,"127. In the case of the Irish who came to the U.S. after the famine in the middle of the nineteenth century, of white immigrant groups as well. See Noel Ignatiev, *How the Irish Became White* (1995; rev. ed. New York: Routledge, 2008) and Matthew Frye Jacobson, *Whiteness of a Different Color: European Immigrants and the Alchemy of Race* (Cambridge: Harvard University Press, 2002).

45. Twain, *Roughing It*, 820.

46. *People v. Hall* (1854), in *"Chink!" A Documentary History of Anti-Chinese Prejudice in America*, ed. Cheng-Tsu Wu (New York: World, 1972), 37–39. See also the discussion in Takaki, *Strangers*, 102.

47. *People v. Hall*, 42.

48. Lai Chun-Chuen, "Remarks of the Chinese Merchants of San Francisco, upon Governor Bigler's Message and Some Common Objections," *Oriental*, San Francisco, February 1, 1855, 1; Norman Asing, "To His Excellency Gov. Bigler," *Daily Alta California,* San Francisco, May 5, 1852.

49. "California's Anti-Chinese Memorial to Congress" (1877), in Wu, *"Chink!"* 115.

50. Qtd. in Takaki, *Strangers*, 101.

51. Kingston, *China Men*, 152.

52. Qtd. in Amy Ling, *Between Worlds: Women Writers of Chinese Ancestry* (New York: Pergamon, 1990), 41.

53. "A New Note in Fiction: *Mrs. Spring Fragrance,*" *New York Times Book Review,* (July 7, 1912): 405.

54. Sui Sin Far, "Leaves from the Mental Portfolio of an Eurasian," in *Mrs. Spring Fragrance and Other Writings*, ed. Amy Ling and Annette White-Parks (Urbana: University of Illinois Press, 1995), 224.

55. Roger Daniels, *Prisoners without Trial: Japanese Americans in World War II* (New York: Hill and Wang, 1993), 8.

56. Sui Sin Far, "Leaves," 224–25.

57. Sui Sin Far, "Leaves," 219.

58. Sui Sin Far, "Leaves," 223.

59. Sui Sin Far, "Leaves," 228.

60. On Winnifred Eaton, see Karen E. H. Skinazi, "'As to Her Race, Its Secret Is Loudly Revealed': Winnifred Eaton's Revision of North American Identity," *MELUS* 32.2 (2007): 31–53. See also Skinazi's introduction to Eaton's *Marion* (1916; rpt. Montreal: McGill-Queens University Press, 2012).

61. Qtd. in Daniels, *Asian America*, 120.

62. James Bryce, *The American Commonwealth, Volume 2* (Philadelphia: Morris, 1889), 420.

63. Alexis de Tocqueville, *Democracy in America*, trans. Henry Reeve (New York: Schocken, 1967), 2:1.

64. Alexis de Tocqueville, *Democracy in America*, ed. J. P. Mayer, trans. George Lawrence (Garden City, NY: Anchor-Doubleday, 1969), 506.

65. Anonymous, "The Course of Civilization," *U.S. Magazine and Democratic Review* 6 (1839): 209.

66. Anonymous, "Catholicism," *Boston Quarterly Review* 4 (1841): 326, 333.

67. "Report of the Special Committee on the Condition of the Chinese Quarter, and the Chinese in San Francisco," *San Francisco Municipal Reports for the Fiscal Year 1884–85, Ending June 30, 1885* (San Francisco: W. W. Hinton, 1885), 209.

68. *Daily Alta California*, June 15, 1853.

69. "California's Anti-Chinese Memorial to Congress," in Wu, *"Chink!"* 116–18.

70. "Report of the Special Committee," 209.

71. "California's Anti-Chinese Memorial to Congress," in Wu, *"Chink!"* 120.

72. Charles J. McClain, *In Search of Equality: The Chinese Struggle against Discrimination in Nineteenth-Century America* (Berkeley and Los Angeles: University of California Press, 1996), 32–33; Daniels, *Asian America*, 34.

73. Daniels, *Coming to America*, 246–47.

74. Kingston, *China Men*, 47.

75. Ng, *Bone*, 58, 61.

76. Ng, *Bone*, 61.

77. Marlon K. Hom, *Songs of Gold Mountain: Cantonese Rhymes from San Francisco Chinatown* (Berkeley and Los Angeles, Univ. of California Press, 1987), 85, 82. For a selection of Angel Island poetry, see the anthology *Island*, ed. Him Mark Lai, Genny Lim, and Judy Yung (1980; rpt. Seattle; University of Washington Press, 1991).

78. Hamilton Holt, *The Life Stories of Undistinguished Americans, as Told by Themselves* (1906; rpt. New York: Routledge, 1990), 183–84.

79. The 1920 figures come from Harry H. Kitano and Roger Daniels, *Asian Americans: Emerging Minorities* (Englewood Cliffs, NJ: Prentice-Hall, 2001), 26.

80. Takaki, *A Different Mirror*, 210.

81. The hardship endured by Japanese women who immigrated to the United States under these circumstances is movingly dramatized in Yoshiko Uchida's novel *Picture Bride* (1987), which tells the story of the marriage between Hana Omiya and Taro Takeda, "the lonely man who had gone to America to make his fortune in Oakland, California"; the novel begins with her immigration in 1917 and ends with their internment at the Topaz Relocation Center, where Taro is mistakenly shot by a camp guard.

82. Holt, *Life Stories*, 181.

83. Chin, "Come All Ye Asian American Writers of the Real and the Fake," 12.

84. Lawrence Joseph, "Sand Nigger," in *Walk on the Wild Side: Urban American Poetry since 1975*, ed. Nicholas Christopher (New York: Simon and Schuster, 1994), 120.

85. Alia Yunis, *The Night Counter* (New York: Crown, 2009), 159.

NOTES TO CHAPTER 3

1. Kingston, *Tripmaster Monkey*, 32

2. Kingston, *Tripmaster Monkey*, 34.

3. Evan Carton and Gerald Graff, "Criticism since 1940," *Cambridge History of American Literature, Volume 8: Poetry and Criticism, 1940–1995*, ed. Sacvan Bercovitch (Cambridge: Cambridge University Press, 1996), 273.

4. Qtd. in Werner Sollors, *Ethnic Modernism* (Cambridge: Harvard University Press, 2008), 116.

5. Paul Lauter, "Melville Climbs the Canon," *American Literature* 66 (1994): 4.

6. Cain, *F. O. Matthiessen*, 136.

7. Ferner Nuhn, *American Mercury* 13 (March 1928): 328, 331. "Ferner Nuhn" was the pseudonym used by Ruth Suckow. See the discussions in Cain, *F. O. Matthiessen*, 137–38, and Vanderbilt, *American Literature*, 268–69.

8. Lauter, "Melville," 6. Lauter further notes: "In this contest a distinctively masculine, Anglo-Saxon image of Melville was deployed as a lone and powerful artistic beacon against the dangers presented by the masses; creating such an image entailed overlooking issues of race, eroticism, democracy, and the like, which have become commonplaces of contemporary Melville criticism" (6).

9. Cain, *F. O. Matthiessen*, 136. See Malcolm Cowley, *The Literary Situation* (New York, Viking, 1954), 14–15. See also David A. Hollinger, *In the American Province: Studies in the History and Historiography of Ideas* (Bloomington: Indiana University Press, 1985).

10. The term had actually been suggested to Matthiessen by his Harvard colleague Harry Levin, and Matthiessen had to argue with his publisher, Oxford University Press, about the term's suitability. See Vanderbilt, *American Literature*, 478.

11. Qtd. in Vanderbilt, *American Literature*, 414.

12. Vanderbilt, *American Literature*, 427.

13. Vanderbilt, *American Literature*, 528–29.

14. Norman Holmes Pearson, "National Education Defense Act," *Saturday Review*, November 27, 1948.

15. Vanderbilt, *American Literature*, 431.

16. Sollors, *Ethnic Modernism*, 240, 60.

17. Sollors, *Ethnic Modernism*, 64, 41.

18. William Dean Howells, *Criticism and Fiction* (New York: Harper and Brothers, 1891), 73.

19. Howells, *Criticism and Fiction*, 15–16.

20. H. H. Boyesen, *Literary and Social Silhouettes* (New York: Harper and Brothers, 1894), 73–74.

21. Boyesen, *Literary and Social Silhouettes,* 63, 78.

22. Donald Pizer, *Realism and Naturalism in Nineteenth-Century American Literature,* rev. ed. (Carbondale, IL: Southern Illinois University Press, 1984), 39.

23. Richard M. Weatherford, ed., *Stephen Crane: The Critical Heritage* (New York: Routledge, 1997), 11

24. Qtd. in Susan L. Mizruchi, *The Rise of Multicultural America: Economy and Print Culture, 1865–1915* (Chapel Hill: University of North Carolina Press, 2008), 202.

25. Walter Hines Page to Charles Chesnutt, March 30, 1898; qtd. in Helen M. Chesnutt, *Charles Waddell Chesnutt: Pioneer of the Color Line* (Chapel Hill: University of North Carolina Press, 1952), 91–92. According to Richard Brodhead, "The Chesnutt-Page correspondence makes clear that *The Conjure Woman* was partly the work of its author, but partly too of an institutional context that controlled the terms of the authors appearance." See Brodhead, Introduction to *The Conjure Woman and Other Stories* by Charles W. Chesnutt (Duke University Press, 1993), 17.

26. Qtd. in H. Chesnutt, *Charles Waddell Chesnutt,* 115.

27. C. Chesnutt, *To Be an Author: Letters of Charles W. Chesnutt, 1889–1905,* ed. Joseph R. McElrath, Jr., and Robert C. Leitz, III (Princeton: Princeton University Press, 1997), 116.

28. William Dean Howells, "Mr. Charles W. Chesnutt's Stories," *Atlantic Monthly* (1900): 699–701.

29. William Dean Howells, "A Psychological Counter-Current in Recent Fiction," *North American Review* 173 (1901): 882.

30. Rudolf Kirk and Clara M. Kirk, "Abraham Cahan and William Dean Howells," *American Jewish Historical Quarterly* 52.1 (1962): 33.

31. Abraham Cahan, *The Education of Abraham Cahan* (New York: Jewish Publication Society of America, 1969), 351.

32. William Dean Howells, "New York Low Life in Fiction," *New York World,* July 26, 1896, 18.

33. William Dean Howells, Review of *The Imported Bridegroom and Other Stories* by Abraham Cahan, *Literature 3* (December 31, 1898): 628 –29

34 Bernard G. Richards, Introduction to *Yekl and the Imported Bridegroom and Other Stories* (New York: Dover, 1969); William Dean Howells, Letter to F. A. Duneka, September 20, 1917, rpt. in *Life in Letters of William Dean Howells,* ed. Mildred Howells (New York: Doubleday, 1928), 2:375.

35. Alain Locke, Review of *Native Son, Opportunity,* January 1941, rpt. in *Richard Wright: Critical Perspectives Past and Present,* ed. Henry Louis Gates, Jr., and K. A. Appiah (New York: Amistad), 19.

36. Locke, Review of *Native Son,* 19.

37. Locke, Review of *Native Son,* 19.

38. Zora Neale Hurston, "How It Feels to Be Colored Me," *The World Tomorrow* (May 1928): 215–16.

39. Margaret Wallace, *New York Times Book Review*, May 6, 1934; rpt. in *Zora Neale Hurston: Critical Perspectives Past and Present*, ed. Henry Louis Gates and Kwame Anthony Appiah (New York: Amistad, 1993), 8.

40. Richard Wright, Review of *Their Eyes Were Watching God*, *New Masses*, October 5, 1937, 22–23.

41. Zora Neale Hurston, Review of *Uncle Tom's Children*, *Saturday Review of Literature*, April 2, 1938.

42. Alain Locke, *Opportunity*, June 1, 1983; rpt. in Gates and Appiah, *Richard Wright*, 18.

43. Irving Howe, "Black Boys and Native Sons," *Dissent* (1963): 353–68.

44. Carlos Bulosan, *America Is in the Heart* (1943, rpt. Seattle: Washington University Press, 1973), 71

45. Bulosan, "My Education," *Amerasia Journal* 6 (May 1979): 117–18.

46. Oscar V. Campomanes and Todd S. Gernes, "Two Letters from America: Carlos Bulosan and the Act of Writing," *MELUS* 15.3 (1988): 27. Campomanes and Gernes point out a number of ways in which the two books resemble one another:

    > Wright analyzes the consequences of oppression and racial fear from the perspective of a young black man trapped in an enclosed, urban environment. Bulosan, who rearticulates Wright's ideas from the perspective of a young Filipino on the road in America, extends the critique offered in Native Son by shifting the social, historical, and geographical situation. Bulosan thus links the racism, class oppression, northern migration and urban decay experienced by black Americans with the racism, class oppression, trans-Pacific migration and American colonialism experienced by Filipinos, setting his story in the mythic (but now deflated) American West. Bulosan also gives his hero the gift of figurative language, a more rapidly unfolding consciousness, and the ability to express anger-something that Wright was unwilling to do. (27)

47. Daniel Aaron, "The Hyphenate Writer and American Letters," in *American Notes: Selected Essays* (Boston: Northeastern University Press, 1994). Recalling that the adjective "hyphenate" had been used during World War I to refer "specifically to American citizens of foreign birth or descent . . . whose complete loyalty to their adopted country was suspect," Aaron notes that by the early 1960s, social scientists were using the term "descriptively rather than pejoratively": "they will speak, for example, of Italo-American or Polish-American voting blocks—less frequently of Jewish or Afro-Americans, because the hyphen is supposed to indicate national origin, not religion or race." Rather presciently, Aaron prefers to use the term "hyphenate" in what he calls its "metaphorical" rather than its "literal sense"—that is according to the older meaning, which, he suggests, still has force despite the efforts of the social scientists: "How else," he asks, "can we account for the dictionaries of ugly or contemptuous epithets that usually, if not necessarily, imply overt or concealed antipathy: mick, kike, nigger, wop, frog, spic, kraut, and the like" (69–70).

48. Aaron, "Hyphenate Writer," 72–73.

49. Aaron, "Hyphenate Writer," 83.

50. Aaron, "Hyphenate Writer," 74.

51. Aaron, "Hyphenate Writer," 74.

52. Arturo Islas with Marilyn Yalom, "Interview with Maxine Hong Kingston," *Conversations with Maxine Hong Kingston*, ed. Paul Skenazy and Tera Martin (Jackson: University Press of Mississippi, 1998), 21.

53. Toni Morrison, *The Nobel Lecture in Literature, 1993* (New York: Knopf, 1994), 1.

54. Sherman Alexie, "Defending Walt Whitman," in *The Summer of Black Widows* (Brooklyn, NY: Hanging Loose Press, 1986), 14–15.

55. Alexie, *Flight: A Novel* (New York: Black Cat, 2008), 1.

56. Thomas Bender, "New York as a Center of Difference," in *The Unfinished City: New York and the Metropolitan Idea* (New York: New Press, 2002), 185–86, 190.

57. Herman Melville, *Moby-Dick* (1851), ed. Hershel Parker and Harrison Hayford, 2nd Norton Critical Edition (New York, Norton, 2001), 98.

58. Melville, *Moby-Dick*, 4.

59. Melville, *Moby-Dick*, 427.

60. Alexie, *Flight*, 4.

61. Melville, *Moby-Dick*, 427.

62. Alexie, *Flight*, 181.

NOTES TO CHAPTER 4

1. John F. Kennedy, "Radio and Television Report to the American People on Civil Rights," June 11, 1963, available at http://www.jfklibrary.org/Historical+Resources/Archives/Reference+Desk/Speeches/JFK/003POF03CivilRights06111963.htm.

2. Coltelli, *Winged Words*, 110

3. Luis Valdez and Stan Steiner, eds., *Aztlán: An Anthology of Mexican American Literature* (New York: Vintage, 1972), xiv.

4. Louis Owens, "Interview with N. Scott Momaday," *This Is about Vision: Interviews with Southwestern Writers*, ed. William Victor Balassi, John F. Crawford, and Annie O. Esturoy (Albuquerque: University of New Mexico Press, 1990), 68.

5. Saldívar, *Chicano Narrative*, 8–9; Juan Bruce-Novoa, ed., *Chicano Authors: Inquiry by Interview* (Austin: University of Texas Press, 1980), 3.

6. Jose Antonio Villarreal, *Pocho* (New York: Doubleday, 1959), 28.

7. Villarreal, *Pocho*, 145, 108, 152.

8. R. Paredes, "Mexican American Literature," 806.

9. Bruce-Novoa, *Chicano Authors*, 38; R. Saldívar, *Chicano Narrative*, 72.

10. Qtd. in R. Saldívar, *Chicano Narrative*, 13.

11. Valdez and Steiner, *Aztlán*, 200.

12. Valdez and Steiner, *Aztlán*, 360–61.

13. Qtd. in Luís Leal and Pepe Barrón, "Chicano Literature: An Overview," in Baker, ed., *Three American Literatures*, 26.

14. Luis Valdez, "Notes on Chicano Theater," *Chicano Theatre* 1 (Spring 1973): 1; Valdez and Steiner, *Aztlán,* 361.

15. Qtd. in Bruce-Novoa, *Chicano Authors,* 160.

16. Qtd. in Bruce-Novoa, "Canonical and Noncanonical Texts," 202.

17. Villarreal, *Pocho,* xii.

18. R. Paredes, "Mexican American Literature," 806.

19. Qtd. in Bruce-Novoa, *Chicano Authors,* 148.

20. Joseph Sommers, "Interpreting Tomás Rivera," in Sommers and Ybarra-Frausto, *Modern Chicano Writers,* 94.

21. Tomás Rivera, *. . . y no se lo tragó la tierra* (Albuquerque, NM: Quinto Sol, 1971), 85.

22. Rivera, *. . . y no se lo tragó la tierra,* 160, 152.

23. *Partners in Crime* and *Ask a Policeman* are police procedurals that draw on the tradition of the detective novel. According to Ralph E. Rodriguez, *Partners in Crime* is the founding novel in a "corpus of Chicana/o detective fiction [that] has burgeoned into some twenty-odd detective novels written by five different authors (Rudolfo Anaya, Lucha Corpi, Rolando Hinojosa, Michael Nava, and Manuel Ramos)." Rodriguez argues that the detective novel, with its focus on "discerning the mysteries of identity," was an appropriate form for Chicano/a novelists who sought to move beyond Chicano/a nationalism to understand "identity not as stable, but as dynamic, not as biologically determined, but as socially constructed." Rodriguez's uses mapping of the trajectory of Chicano/a literature is consonant with my view that emergent literatures ultimately adopt a cosmopolitan stance that embraces difference and cultural boundary-crossing. See Rodriguez, *Brown Gumshoes: Detective Fiction and the Search for Chicana/o Identity* (Austin: University of Texas Press, 2005), 9, 13.

24. Rudolfo Anaya, *Bless Me, Ultima* (1973; rpt. New York: Warner Books, 1999). 2, 249.

25. Oscar Zeta Acosta, *The Autobiography of a Brown Buffalo* (1974; rpt. New York: Vintage, 1989), 11–12, 194, 195, 199.

26. Oscar Zeta Acosta, *The Revolt of the Cockroach People* (1974; rpt. New York: Vintage, 1989), 31, 153.

27. Acosta, *Revolt,* 248.

28. Acosta, *Revolt,* 230, 258.

29. R. Paredes, "Evolution," 74.

30. Kenneth Lincoln, *Native American Renaissance* (Berkeley and Los Angeles: University of California Press, 1985), 7–8.

31. Coltelli, *Winged Words,* 110.

32. Matthias Schubnell, *N. Scott Momaday: The Literary and Cultural Background* (Oxford: University of Oxford, 1983), 93; qtd. in Bonnie TuSmith, *All My Relatives: Community in Contemporary Ethnic American Literatures* (Ann Arbor: University of Michigan Press, 1994),196 n. 4.

33. Coltelli, *Winged Words,* 197.

34. "Declaration of Indian Purpose," *American Indian Conference*, University of Chicago, 1961, 5–6.

35. Russell Means and Marvin J. Wolf, *Where White Men Fear to Tread* (New York; Macmillan, 1996), 106–107.

36. "The Alcatraz Proclamation," rpt. in *American Indian History: A Documentary Reader*, ed. Camilla Townsend (Chichester: Wiley-Blackwell, 2009), 186 –87.

37. N. Scott Momaday, *House Made of Dawn* (New York: Harper & Row 1988), 11.

38. Momaday, *House Made of Dawn*, 104.

39. Allen, *Sacred Hoop*, 89.

40. Qtd. in TuSmith, *All My Relatives*, 118–19.

41. Momaday, *House Made of Dawn*, 95.

42. Qtd. in TuSmith, *All My Relatives*, 196 n. 2.

43. Qtd. in Marie Harris and Kathleen Aguero, *A Gift of Tongues: Critical Challenges in Contemporary American Poetry* (Athens: University of Georgia Press, 1987), 200; qtd. in TuSmith, *All My Relatives*, 106.

44. Silko, *Ceremony*, 29.

45. Silko, *Ceremony*, 255.

46. Silko, *Ceremony*, 125–26.

47. James Welch, *Winter in the Blood* (New York: Harper & Row, 1974), 36–37.

48. Coltelli, *Winged Words*, 186. See also William W. Thackeray, "'Crying for Pity' in *Winter in the Blood*," *MELUS* 7 (1980): 61–78.

49. Welch, *Winter in the Blood*, 2.

50. James Welch, *The Death of Jim Loney* (New York: Penguin, 1979); Kathryn W. Shanley, qtd. in *"The Death of Jim Loney* and 'Christmas Comes to Moccasin Flat' by James Welch," http://www.learner.org/workshops/hslit/session1/aw/work2.html. See also Jennifer Lemberg, "Transmitted Trauma and 'Absent Memory' in James Welch's *The Death of Jim Loney*," *Studies in American Indian Literatures* 18.3 (2006): 67–81. Using the lens of trauma studies, Lemberg reads the association of Loney with stereotypes as a sign that "Loney's death on the reservation is neither that of a victim nor of a hero. Rather, it is shown to be a culturally specific response to trauma, its meanings more readily available when viewed from a cross-cultural perspective" (77).

51. Paul Radin, *The Trickster: A Study in American Indian Mythology* (1956; rpt. New York: Schocken Books, 1972), xxiiii; Gerald Vizenor, *The Trickster of Liberty: Native Heirs to a Wild Baronage*, rev. ed. (Norman: University of Oklahoma Press, 2005), 18, x. See also Laura Coltelli's interview with Vizenor in Coltelli, *Winged Words*, 161–65.

52. Gerald Vizenor, *Bearheart: The Heirship Chronicles* (Minneapolis: University of Minnesota Press, 1990), xiii, 39, 192, 242; on "terminal creeds," see Vizenor, *The Trickster of Liberty*, x, and *Survivance: Narratives of Native Presence* (Lincoln: University of Nebraska Press, 2008), 75, 92.

53. Vizenor, *Narrative Chance*, 3; Gerald Vizenor, *Dead Voices: Natural Agonies in the New World* (Norman: University of Oklahoma Press, 1992), 9; Vizenor,

Bearheart, 1. On "wordarrows," see Vizenor, *Trickster of Liberty* and *Wordar-rows: Native States of Literary Sovereignty* (Lincoln: University of Nebraska Press, 2003).

54. Allan Richard Chavkin and Nancy Feyl Chavkin, eds., *Conversations with Louise Erdrich and Michael Dorris* (Jackson: University Press of Mississippi, 1994), 144.

55. Sherman Alexie, *Indian Killer* (New York: Grove, 1996), 220, 146.

56. Alexie, *Indian Killer*, 19.

57. Alexie, *Indian Killer*, 419–20, 314.

58. Ellen L. Arnold., ed., *Conversations with Leslie Marmon Silko* (Jackson: University Press of Mississippi, 2000), 97, 106.

59. Elaine Kim, *Asian American Literature*, 177.

60. Qtd. in Elaine Kim, *Asian American Literature*,18.

61. Qtd. in Baker, *Three American Literatures*, 201; qtd. in Elaine Kim, *Asian American Literature*, 32.

62. Monica Sone, *Nisei Daughter* (1953; rpt. Seattle: University of Washington Press, 1979), 145–46.

63. Toshio Mori, *Yokohama, California* (1949; rpt. Seattle: University of Washington Press, 1985), 128.

64. Charles Kikuchi, *The Kikuchi Diary: Chronicle from an American Concentration Camp*, ed. JohnModell (Urbana: University of Illinois Press, 1973), 42–43.

65. Okada, *No-No Boy*, 25–26, 20.

66. Okada, *No-No Boy*, 7; Hisaye Yamamoo, "Seventeen Syllables," in *Seventeen Syllables*, ed. King-Kok Cheung (Rutgers: Rutgers University Press, 1994), 22.

67. Uchida, *Desert Exile,* 5; Munson's report is quoted in Weglyn, *Years of Infamy*, 41. A copy of Munson's typescript, along with other relevant primary materials, is available at http://www.michiweglyn.com/years-of-infamy-2/michis-research.

68. Yamamoto, Interview, in *Seventeen Syllables*, 77.

69. Takaki, *Strangers from a Different Shore*, 216.

70. Toyo Suryemoto, *I Call to Remembrance: Toyo Suyemoto's Years of Internment*, ed. Susan B. Richardson (New Brunswick, NJ: Rutgers University Press, 2007), 92 –93; Susan Schweik, "The 'Pre-Poetics' of Internment: The Example of Toyo Suyemoto," *American Literary History* 1 (1989): 89–109.

71. Tuttle qtd. in *From Totems to Hip-Hop: A Multicultural Anthology of Poetry across the Americas, 1900–2002*, ed. Ishmael Reed (New York: Da Capo Press, 2002), 392; Sone, *Nisei Daughter*, 236–37.

72. Qtd. in Shawn Wong, *Asian American Literature: A Brief Introduction and Anthology* (New York: HarperCollins, 1996), 299.

73. *U. S. News and World Report*, December 26, 1966.

74. Baker, *Three American Literatures*, 228.

75. Jessica Hagedorn, *Charlie Chan Is Dead* (New York: Penguin, 1993), xxvii.

76. Chan et al., *The Big Aiiieeeee!*, 85

77. Chan et al., *The Big Aiiieeeee!*, xii.

78. Louis Chu, *Eat a Bowl of Tea* (1961; rpt. New York: Carol Publishing Group, 1995), 24.

79. Qtd. in Elaine Kim, *Asian American Literature*, 175–77.

80. Elaine Kim, *Asian American Literature*, 198.

81. In a perceptive study of narratives written by second-generation Asian American women, Erin Khuê Ninh explores the bitterness that these writers seem to feel toward their families. Simultaneously drawn to and repelled by the idea that they belong to a "model minority," writers like Jade Snow Wong, Maxine Hong Kingston, Fae Myenne Ng, and Chitra Divakaruni depict an "ingratitude" toward their immigrant families that plays a crucial role in the formation of Asian American female subjectivity. See Ninh, *Ingratitude: The Debt-Bound Daughters in Asian American Literature* (New York: New York University Press, 2011).

82. Hagedorn, *Chan*, xiii

83. Hagedorn, *Chan*, xxx.

84. Edmund White, "A Letter to Ann and Alfred Corn," in *The Violet Quill Reader: The Emergence of Gay Writing after Stonewall*, ed. David Bergman (New York: InsideOut Books, 2001), 1–4.

85. Edmund Bergler, *Homosexuality: Disease or Way of Life?* (New York: Hill & Wang, 1956), 28.

86. Alfred C. Kinsey, Wardell Pomeroy, and Clyde E. Martin, *Sexual Behavior in the Human Male* (1948; rpt. Bloomington: University of Indiana Press, 1998), 9.

87. Kinsey, *Sexual Behavior*, 627.

88. Kinsey, *Sexual Behavior*, 636–54.

89. Alfred C. Kinsey, Wardell Pomeroy, and Clyde E. Martin, and Paul Gebhard, *Sexual Behavior in the Human Female* (New York: W. B. Saunders, 1953), 469.

90. Donald Webster Cory [Edward Sagarin], *The Homosexual in America: A Subjective Approach* (New York: Greenberg, 1951), 13–14, 228.

91. "Employment of Homosexuals and Other Sex Perverts in Government," *Documenting Intimate Matters: Primary Sources for a History of Sexuality in America*, ed. Thomas A. Foster (Chicago: University of Chicago Press, 2012), 146–47.

92. Mark Blasius and Shane Phelan, eds., *We Are Everywhere: A Historical Sourcebook in Gay and Lesbian Politics* (New York: Routledge, 1997), 283.

93. John D'Emilio, *Sexual Politics, Sexual Communities: The Making of a Homosexual Minority in the United States, 1940–1970* (Chicago: University of Chicago Press, 1998), 58 n,2.

94. D'Emilio, *Sexual Politics*, 58.

95. Daughters of Bilitis, "Statement of Purpose" (1955), in Blasius and Phelan, *We Are Everywhere*, 328; Anonymous, "What about the DOB," *Ladder* (1959), in Blasius and Phelan, *We Are Everywhere*, 328–29.

96. Larry Neal, "The Black Arts Movement," *Drama Review* 12 (1968): 29; Eldriged Cleaver, *Soul on Ice* (1968; rpt. New York: Delta Books, 1992), 124; James

Baldwin, *Nobody Knows My Name: More Notes of a Native Son*, rpt. in *Collected Essays* (New York: Library of America, 1998), 137.

97. John Rechy, "Introduction," *City of Night* (1963; rpt. New York: Grove Press, 1988), xiii.

98. Rechy, *City of Night*, 368.

99. Elana Nachman/Dykewomon, *Riverfinger Women* (Tallahassee, FL: Naiad Press, 1992), 13.

100. Rita Mae Brown, *Rubyfruit Jungle* (1973; rpt. New York: Random House, 1988), 246, 203, 222, 246.

101. Patricia Nell Warren, *The Fancy Dancer* (New York: Morrow, 1976), 159.

102. Larry Kramer, *Faggots* (New York: Plume, 1987), 223.

103. Felice Picano, "Rough Cuts from a Journal," in Bergman, *The Violet Quill Reader*, 31.

104. Andrew Holleran, *Dancer from the Dance: A Novel* (New York: Perennial, 2001), 43, 18, 246.

NOTES TO CHAPTER 5

1. Richard Bernstein, "In Dispute on Bias, Stanford Is Likely to Alter Western Culture Program," *New York Times,* January 19, 1988.

2. William J. Bennett, "To Reclaim a Legacy: A Report on the Humanities in Higher Education" (Washington, DC: National Endowment for the Humanities, 1984), available at http://www.eric.ed.gov/ERICWebPortal/detail?accno=ED247880.

3. Bernstein, "Dispute on Bias."

4. Nina Baym, "Whose Great Books Are They Anyway?" *New York Times,* May 21, 1988.

5. Christopher Clausen, "It Is Not Elitist to Place Major Literature at the Center of the English Curriculum," *Chronicle of Higher Education,* January 13, 1988, A52 .

6. Dinesh D'Souza, *Illiberal Education: The Politics of Race and Sex on Campus* (New York: Free Press, 1991) 68; David Brooks, "From Western Lit to Westerns as Lit," *Wall Street Journal,* February 2, 1988, 36; Allan Bloom, *The Closing of the American Mind: How Higher Education Has Failed Democracy and Impoverished the Souls of Today's Students* (New York: Simon & Schuster, 198).

7. Reed Ueda, *Postwar Immigrant America: A Social History* (New York: Bedford, 1994), 171. The latter limits were intended to curb immigration not from Europe but from Mexico, the Carribbean, Latin America, and South America (see Leti Volpp, "The Legal Mapping of U.S. Immigrants," in *Crossing into America: The New Literature of Immigration*, ed. Louis Mendoza and S. Shankar [New York: New Press, 2003], 261). As a result of this new system, more than 20 million immigrants entered the United States legally between 1965 and 2000, with the peak occurring during the 1980s, when nearly 10 million new immigrants arrived, mostly from Asia and Latin America. From 1821 to 1995, 49 percent of legally admitted immigrants came from northern Europe, with an additional 7

percent from other parts of Europe and Canada. From 1991 to 1995, however, the number of Europeans and Canadians was far less than the historical average for the period, making up only 16 percent of the total number (Volpp, 261). More than half of the immigrants who came during the 1980s came from the following seven countries: Mexico, the Philippines, China, Vietnam, Korea, India, and the Dominican Republic (Mendoza and Shankar, "Introduction: The New Literature of Immigration," xvii). In addition, writes Ueda, the fastest-growing ethnic groups in the United States after 1965 "were Asians who had virtually no significant previous representation in the American population. Immigrants arrived from South Korea, Cambodia, Vietnam, Laos, Thailand, Indonesia, Burma, Sri Lanka, Singapore, Malaysia, Pakistan, India, and Bangladesh, while others came from areas where immigrant Asian communities had been established earlier in the century, such as the West Indies and Latin America" (65).

8. Ueda, *Postwar Immigrant America*, 139.

9. "No One Model American: A Statement on Multicultural Education," *Journal of Teacher Education* 24 (1973): 264.

10. Diane Ravitch and Maris Vinovski, eds., *Learning from the Past: What History Teaches Us about School Reform* (Baltimore: Johns Hopkins University Press, 1995), 121.

11. Michi Weglyn, *Years of Infamy: The Untold Story of America's Concentration Camps* (New York: Morrow Quill Paperbacks, 1976); Uchida, *Desert Exile*, 42; Sone, *Nisei Daughter*, xvi.

12. *Personal Justice Denied: Report of the Commission on Wartime Relocation and Internment of Civilians* (1982–83; rpt. Seattle: University of Washington Press, 1997), 459, 18.

13. Carolyn Porter, "What We Know That We Don't Know: Remapping American Literary Studies," *American Literary History* 6 (1994): 467–68, 506.

14. Sacvan Bercovitch and Myra Jehlen, eds., *Ideology and Classic American Literature* (Cambridge: Cambridge University Press, 1986), 1, 423.

15. Frederick Crews, "Whose American Renaissance?" in *The Critics Bear It Away* (New York: Random House 1992), 16-47. The essay was originally published in the *New York Review of Books*, October 27, 1988, 68–81. The other books reviewed were Walter Benn Michaels and Donald E. Pease, *The American Renaissance Reconsidered* (1985); Russell Reising, *The Unusable Past: Theory and Study of American Literature* (1986); Donald Pease, *Visionary Compacts* (1987); David S. Reynolds, *Beneath the American Renaissance: The Subversive Imagination in the Age of Emerson and Melville* (1988); and Philip Fisher, *Hard Facts: Setting and Form in the American Novel* (1985). Crews described Reynolds's study as "an ambitious and at least partially successful new book that professes cultural pluralism while departing sharply from New Americanist premises" (40).

16. Crews, "Whose American Renaissance?"19.

17. Gregory S. Jay, *American Literature and the Culture Wars* (Ithaca, NY: Cornell University Press, 1997), 172.

18. Jay, *American Literature and the Culture Wars*, 15.

19. Amy Kaplan and Donald Pease, eds., *Cultures of United States Imperialism* (Durham, NC: Duke University Press, 1993), 16–17.

20. Frederick Jackson Turner, "The Significance of the Frontier in American History," *The Frontier in American History* (New York: Henry Holt and Company, 1947), 1–2, 37.

21. Harold Bloom, "Mr. America," *New York Review of Books*, November 22, 1984, 23.

22. Lester D. Langley, *The Americas in the Age of Revolution, 1750–1850* (New Haven, CT: Yale University Press, 1996), 261–63.

23. Bainard Cowan and Jefferson Humphries, eds., *Poetics of the Americas: Race, Founding, and Textuality* (Baton Rouge: Louisiana State University Press, 1997), 106.

24. Homi Bhabha, "The Commitment to Theory," in Bhabha, *The Location of Culture*, 37; Bhabha, Introduction, *The Location of Culture*, 1. For a useful account of the critical genealogy of "hybridity," see Robert J. C. Young, *Colonial Desire: Hybridity in Theory, Culture and Race* (London: Routledge, 1995), 129.

25. Bakhtin, *The Dialogic Imagination*, 358.

26. Frank Chin, *The Chickencoop Chinaman; And, The Year of the Dragon: Two Plays* (Seattle: University of Washington Press, 1981), 51; Chin, "Confessions," 58.

27. Appiah, "The Case for Contamination," 52.

28. See Arturo Morales Carrion, *Puerto Rico: A Political and Cultural History* (New York: Norton, 1983); José Cabranes, *Citizenship and the American Empire* (New Haven, CT: Yale University Press, 1979).

29. Jose Lorenzo-Hernandez, "The Nuyorican's Dilemma: Categorization of Returning Migrants in Puerto Rico," *International Migration Review* 33 (1999): 989.

30. Lorenzo-Hernandez, "The Nuyorican's Dilemma," 991.

31. Taino Inter-Tribal Council, "Dictionary of the Spoken Taino Language," available at members.dandy.net/~orocobix/tedict.html.

32. According to Lorenzo-Hernandez, "Returning migrants, labeled as Nuyoricans, may be wrongly perceived as hybrids who may 'contaminate' the culture with influences from the North" ("The Nuyorican's Dilemma," 991).

33. Esmeralda Santiago, "A Note to the Reader from Esmeraldo Santiago," *When I Was Puerto Rican: A Memoir* (1993; rpt. New York: Da Capo, 2006), 278.

34. Christopher Lehmann-Haupt, "A Talk with Piri Thomas," *New York Times Book Review*, May 21, 1967, 47.

35. Daniel Stern, "One Who Got Away," *New York Times Book Review*, May 21, 1967, 44.

36. Piri Thomas, *Down These Mean Streets* (New York: Knopf, 1967), ix–x; Lehmann-Haupt, "A Talk with Piri Thomas," 45.

37. Leonard Buder, "School Ban Ends on Piri Thomas Book," *New York Times*, December 27, 1975, 21.

38. Stern, "One Who Got Away," 1.

39. Lehmann-Haupt, "A Talk with Piri Thomas," 47.

40. Miguel Algarín and Bob Holman, eds., *Aloud: Voices from the Nuyorican Poets Cafe* (New York: Henry Holt, 1994), p. 5.

41. Algarín and Holman, *Aloud,* 8.

42. Evelyn Nieves, "Again, Clubs for Poets to Read and Rage," *New York Times,* November 19, 1990, B1.

43. Eve M. Kahn, "The Word's Turn: Urban Poets Re-Emerge," *New York Times,* January 31, 1992, C1.

44. The film was directed by Paul Devlin (see www. slamnation.com); Cristin O'Keefe Aptowicz, *Words in Your Face: A Guided Tour through Twenty Years of the New York City Poetry Slam* (New York: Soft Skull Press, 2007), 288.

45. Lin-Manuel Miranda, *"In the Heights," Gothamist,* February 22, 2008, http://gothamist.com/2008/02/22/linmanuel_miran.php.

46. Mendoza and Shankar, Introduction, xxi.

47. Alpana Sharma Knippling, *New Immigrant Literatures in the United States: A Sourcebook to Our Multicultural Literary Heritage* (Santa Barbara, CA: Greenwood, Publishing Group, 1996), xv.

48. Mendoza and Shankar, Introduction, xxii.

49. Lisa Lowe, *Immigrant Acts,* 68. For scholarship that builds on the foundations that Lowe sets out, see, for example: Kandice Chuh, *Imagine Otherwise: On Asian American Critique* (Durham, NC: Duke University Press, 2003); Inderpal Grewal, *Transnational America: Feminisms, Diasporas, Neoliberalisms* (Durham, NC: Duke University Press, 2006); and Crystal Parikh, *An Ethics of Betrayal: The Politics of Otherness in Emergent U.S. Literatures and Culture* (New York: Fordham University Press, 2009).

50. Susan Koshy, *Sexual Naturalization: Asian Americans and Miscegenation* (Stanford: Stanford University Press, 2004), 158.

51. Grewal describes *Jasmine* as a novel that constructs a postcolonial cosmopolitanism that easily fits into U.S. multicultural liberalism: "Mukherjee's cosmopolitanism coexisted easily with her belief in the nation-state as the guarantor of rights and privileges as well as with a stable ethnic identity" (*Transnational America,* 39).

52. Qtd. in Mendoza and Shankar, Introduction, xxii.

53. Rodriguez, *Hunger,* 26–28.

54. For Divakaruni's biographical account, see www.chitradivakaruni.com/about/bio/; Grewal argues that Divakaruni's *Mistress of Spices* produces a "postcolonial cosmopolitanism," by participating in a "transnational circulation of knowledges of Asian women, but it did so to romanticize and exoticize the notion of 'tradition,' incorporating it within a belief in a liberal multicultural state in the United States as well as in India." Divakaruni's strategy of "respress[ing] the inequalities and the violence of the spice trade" enables her to "produce a narrative of racial solidarity among Indian immigrants, Mexican immigrants, Native Americans, and African Americans." See *Transnational America,* 39–40, 78.

55. Seung Hye Suh and Robert J-Song Ku, "The New Immigration and the Literature of Asian America," in Mendoza and Shankar, eds., *Crossing into America*, 322.

56. Kingston, *Tripmaster Monkey*, 5.

57. Maria Elena Fernandez, "Two Sides of an American Identity: Authors: Julia Alvarez's Novels Shed Light on the Immigrant Experience," *Los Angeles Times*, March 23, 1997, http://articles.latimes.com/1997-03-23/news/ ls-41128_1_american-identity/.

58. Ricardo Ortiz, "Cuban American Liteature," in Knippling, *New Immigrant Literatures*, 188; Perez Firmat, *The Cuban Condition*, 14; R. Ortiz, "Cuban American Literature," 188.

59. Qtd. in Elaine Kim, "Korean American Literature," in Cheung, ed., *Interethnic*, 176.

60. King-Kok Cheung, ed., *Words Matter: Conversations with Asian American Writers* (Honolulu: University of of Hawai'i Press, 2000), 94–95. The question of whether Korean immigrants should produce literature written in Korean or English is debated among Korean American writers. The poet Ch'oe Yun-hong has suggested that Koreans' lack of interest in the problems of Korean Americans has discouraged the production of American poetry written in Korean, and scholars of Korean literature have suggested that Korean American literature should distinguish itself by turning to English and focusing on immigrant life rather than memories of Korea. Ch'oe suggests that the harshness of life for many Korean Americans has fueled a "desire for poetry," but at the end of the twentieth century, Korean American poetry remained an underdeveloped corner in the field of Asian American poetry.

61. See, for example, Scott Veale, "Beyond 'Call It Sleep': New Immigrant Classics," *New York Times*, November 21, 2004.

62. Cristina García, *Dreaming in Cuban* (New York: Ballantine Books, 1993), 3.

63. García, *Dreaming in Cuban*, 7, 236.

64. Bridget A. Kevane and Juanita Heredia, *Latina Self-Portraits: Interviews with Contemporary Women Writers* (Albuquerque: University of New Mexico Press, 2000), 71, 75.

65. Ricardo L. Ortíz, "Cuban-American Literature," *New Immigrant Literatures in the United States: A Sourcebook to Our Multicultural Literary Heritage*, ed. Alpana Shanna Knippling (Westport, CT: Greenwood, 1996), 187–206

66. Monique Truong, "Vietnamese American Literature," in Cheung, ed., *Interethnic*, 219.

67. Alice B. Toklas, *The Alice B. Toklas Cookbook* (1954; rpt. New York: Harper Perennial, 2004), 186–93.

68. Monique Truong, *The Book of Salt* (New York: Houghton Mifflin, 2003), 9.

69. Junot Díaz, *The Brief Wondrous Life of Oscar Wao* (New York: Riverhead, 2007), 83, 1. Other novels that dramatize the terrors of the Trujillo regime are Enrique Laguerre's *The Labyrinth* (1959), which was inspired by the murders of two

journalists who had published exposes about corruption of the Trunillo government; Viriato Sencion's *They Forged the Signature of God* (1992), which tells the interlinked stories of three young seminary students who become involved in the political world of the Dominican Republic.

70. Amy Tachiki, ed., *Roots: An Asian American Reader* (Los Angeles: Continental-Graphics, 1971), 114–15.

71. See Jodi Kim's analysis of the relationship between the Cold War and Asian American cultural production in *Ends of Empire: Asian American Critique and the Cold War* (Minneapolis: University of Minnesota Press, 2010). Kim argues that "the Cold War as an entrenched production of knowledge has shaped how Americans narrate this history of military intervention and how Korean and Asian Americans have come to know their very selves" (3).

72. Ueda, *Postwar Immigrant America*, 170.

73. In contrast to Chinese, Japanese, and Filipino Americans, "Korean Americans," writes Roger Daniels, "had no substantial community in the United States until after the Korean War" (*Guarding the Golden Door: American Immigration Policy and Immigrants since 1882* [New York: Hill & Wang, 2004], 167). About 7,000 Koreans had emigrated to Hawai'i between 1903 and 1905 under the auspices of the Hawaiian Sugar Planters Association, though once Japan declared Korea a protectorate in 1905, the flow of migrants stopped. The Japanese occupation of Korea ended with the surrender of Japan to the Allies in 1945, and Korea was divided at the 38th parallel, with troops from the Soviet Union occupying the northern part of the country and troops from the United States occupying the south. After the Korean War ended in 1953, Korean immigration began with the arrival of "military brides," who had married American soldiers stationed in Korea. From 1961 to 1990, nearly 800,000 Koreans immigrated to the United States.

74. Ronyoung Kim, *Clay Walls* (Sag Harbor, NY: The Permanent Press, 1987), 105.

75. Gary Pak, *A Ricepaper Airplane* (Honolulu: University of Hawai'I Press, 1998), 25.

76. Younghill Kang, *East Goes West* (1937; rpt. Houston, TX: Kaya Production, 1997), 369. See also E. Kim, "Korean American Literature," 159.

77. Walt Whitman, "The Sleepers," in *Complete Poetry and Collected Prose*, ed. Justin Kaplan (New York: Library of America, 1982), 545–46. Lee quotes from the final revised version of the poem (1881); an earlier version was published in the first edition of *Leaves of Grass* (1855). See Whitman, *Complete Poetry*, 107.

78. Chang-rae Lee, *Native Speaker* (1995; rpt. New York: Riverhead Books, 1996), 83, 346; Whitman, "Salut au monde!" in *Complete Poetry*, 294–96; Lee, *Native Speaker*, 83.

79. Jonathan Arac, "Violence and the Human Voice: Critique and Hope in *Native Speaker*," *boundary 2* 36 (2009): 58, 56.

80. Roger Daniels, *Guarding the Golden Door: American Immigration Policy and Immigrants since 1882* (New York: Hill & Wang, 2004), 149.

81. http://www.fas.harvard.edu/~lowinus/

82. Ronald Bayer, *Homosexuality and American Psychiatry: The Politics of Diagnosis.* (Princeton, NJ: Princeton University Press, 1987), 193–94.

83. Blasius and Phelan, *We Are Everywhere*, 563–64.

84. Edmund White, "The Joy of Gay Lit," *Out* (September 1997): 110; Edmund White, *The Farewell Symphony* (New York: Knopf, 1997), 247.

85. Bergman, *The Violet Quill Reader*, 170.

86. White, "Out of the Closet, Onto the Bookshelf," *New York Times Magazine*, June 16, 1991): 22.

.87 Felice Picano, "Rough Cuts from a Journal," in Bergman, *The Violet Quill Reader*, 53.

88. Edmund White, *The Burning Library: Essays*, ed. David Bergman (New York Vintage, 1995), 277.

89. Jill Johnston, *Lesbian Nation: The Feminist Solution* (New York: Simon and Schuster, 1973), 97.

90. Edmund White, "The New Gay Fiction: After Years of Neglect from the Mainstream, Queer Lit Undergoes a Renaissance," *Village Voice*, June 13, 2006.

91. Jasbir K. Puar, *Terrorist Assemblages: Homonationalism in Queer Times* (Durham, NC: Duke University Press, 2007), 5–6; Lisa Duggan, "The New Homonormativity: The Sexual Politics of Neoliberalism," in *Materializing Democracy: Toward a Revitalized Cultural Politics*, ed. Russ Castronovo and Dana Nelson (Durham, NC: Duke University Press, 2002), 179.

92. Tony Kushner, *Angels in America: A Gay Fantasia on National Life* (New York: Theatre Communications, 1995), 234, 52

93. Appiah, "The Case for Contamination," 37.

94. Kushner, *Angels in America*, 277–80.

NOTES TO THE CONCLUSION

1. Appiah, *Cosmopolitanism*, 144.

2. Appiah, *Cosmopolitanism*, 143.

3. Appiah, *Cosmopolitanism*, 140.

4. JanMohammed and Lloyd, *The Nature and Context of Minority Discourse*, 68.

5. Warren's book *What Was African American Literature* (2011) had its origins in a lecture entitled "W. E. B. Du Bois's *Dusk of Dawn*: The End of a Beginning in African Americanist Inquiry," given during the 2002–2003 lecture series "Public Intellectuals / Public Issues" at the Hart Institute at Pomona College.

ABOUT THE AUTHOR

Cyrus R. K. Patell is Associate Professor of Literature at NYU Abu Dhabi and Associate Professor of English at NYU in New York. He is coeditor, with Deborah Lindsay Williams, of *The Oxford History of the Novel in English* (general editor, Patrick Parrinder), volume 8: *American Fiction after 1940.*

Made in the USA
Columbia, SC
08 January 2018